Bad Language

Edwin L. Battistella

Bad Language

Are Some Words Better than Others?

OXFORD
UNIVERSITY PRESS

OXFORD
UNIVERSITY PRESS

Oxford University Press, Inc., publishes works that further
Oxford University's objective of excellence
in research, scholarship, and education.

Oxford   New York
Auckland   Cape Town   Dar es Salaam   Hong Kong   Karachi
Kuala Lumpur   Madrid   Melbourne   Mexico City   Nairobi
New Delhi   Shanghai   Taipei   Toronto

With offices in
Argentina   Austria   Brazil   Chile   Czech Republic   France   Greece
Guatemala   Hungary   Italy   Japan   Poland   Portugal   Singapore
South Korea   Switzerland   Thailand   Turkey   Ukraine   Vietnam

Published by Oxford University Press, Inc.
198 Madison Avenue, New York, New York 10016

www.oup.com

First issued as an Oxford University Press paperback, 2007

Oxford is a registered trademark of Oxford University Press

Library of Congress Cataloging-in-Publication Data
Battistella, Edwin L.
Bad language : are some words better than others? /
Edwin L. Battistella.
p. cm.
Includes bibliographical references and index.
ISBN 978-0-19-517248-5; 978-0-19-533745-7 (pbk.)
1. Slang.   2. Swearing.   3. Sociolinguistics.   4. English language—Slang.
5. English language—Social aspects.   I. Title.
P409.B38 2005
417'.2—dc22   2005040880

Printed in the United States of America
on acid-free paper

Preface

I don't want to talk no grammar. I want to talk like a lady.
                                                   —Eliza Doolittle

Like many linguists, I have wrestled for years with the issue of Standard English. How do I reconcile the fact that language change is natural and inevitable with the more visceral feeling that some usage bothers me personally? Certain changes I resist. Others I embrace. As an occasional teacher of writing, I have a more difficult problem. I recognize that many traditional rules of grammar and exposition are essentially arbitrary. Yet I often continue to teach them because they are expected. This is perhaps socially justified, but the contradiction undermines the teaching enterprise.

For those who reflect on language, other troubling contradictions arise as well. Offensive or vulgar speech is one such language problem.

Supporters of the abstraction of free expression may still be troubled by language that is derogatory, uncivil, or crude. Should we regulate the civility of speech or trust that the free exchange of ideas will separate the good from the bad?

Language diversity is another issue that provides apparent contradictions. Those who embrace diversity and multiculturalism in society may still feel that a common public language is necessary for efficiency, national unity, and economic success. What sort of encouragement, support, coercion, or policy should be aimed at language standardization, if any?

When it comes to language, our opinions and reactions about what is good may sometimes be at odds with our other beliefs.

This work arises from the tensions that such language issues as grammatical change, stylistic variety, incivility, and diversity create. Language problems like these seem to have some things in common. This book is thus motivated by another question as well: to what extent is bad language a created and evolving concept as opposed to a natural, fixed one? If it is the former, we should explore how the various characterizations of bad language (and, by contrast, of good language) serve parallel functions, how they employ similar arguments, and how they evolve.

Examining various kinds of bad language together can also illuminate and situate language among some broader cultural issues and it can engage us in a more meaningful discussion of grammar, coarse speech, and variation. That is what this work is about.

Acknowledgments

The idea for this book emerged from an after-dinner discussion at Lawrence Rosen's 1992 National Endowment for the Humanities Seminar on the Anthropology of Law. I didn't actually begin work on the project until eight years later, in 2000, and the ideas presented here have undergone several incarnations since then. I am grateful to Anne Lobeck, Terry Langendoen, and Sharon Klein for comments on a very early draft of this work. All agreed that the first draft was too boring. I am also indebted to various referees for Oxford University Press for their excellent help and to Maureen Flanagan for extensive comments on the penultimate version. Special thanks also to Peter Ohlin of Oxford University Press for his valuable assistance. And a tip of the hat to Anna Beauchamp and the interlibrary loan staff at Southern Oregon University's Lenn and Dixie Hannon Library for their help in obtaining many of the materials needed for this project.

Contents

Bad Language

One Bad Language: Realism versus Relativism

What does the phrase "bad language" mean to you? Perhaps you think of swearing or slang. Is it bad language to curse if you hit your thumb with a hammer? Is it bad language for a novelist to use the f-word in dialogue? What about the speech of a sitcom character, newscaster, or presidential candidate? Is it bad for young people to use slang like *dude, chill, my bad, hook up,* or *bling-bling?*

Some people think of regional or ethnic dialects as bad English. Texas writer Molly Ivins, for example, once suggested that to Northerners "a Southern accent is both ignorant and racist." She cited the World War II genre of movies, whose stock characters included "a Midwestern hero, a wise-cracking New Yorker, and a dumb Southerner" as one source of dialect stereotypes.[1] Is it really bad English to pronounce *ten* and *pen* as "tin" and "pin" or to use the pronoun *y'all?* Another stigmatized dialect form is the New York City dialect. Are pronunciations like "cawfee" and "chawklit" bad English? And what about Ebonics? Are pronunciations like "aks" or grammatical usages like "He been married" bad?

People also identify bad English with a foreign accent or with English mixed with another language. In a 1952 episode of the program *I Love Lucy*, Lucy Ricardo hires an English tutor to polish her speech so her son won't learn her bad habits. Commenting on her husband Ricky's Cuban accent, she says "Please, promise me you won't speak to our child until he's nineteen or twenty."[2] Is it bad English to speak with a Cuban accent and mix Spanish with English, as in "Okay, gracias" (or "Yo quiero Taco Bell")? More than fifty years after "Lucy Hires an English Tutor," accent modification is big business in the United States and internationally.

Even if you don't have a definite opinion on swearing, slang, and accents, it is likely that you equate bad English with certain forms of grammar or word use. I once heard someone talk about his office being made the *escape goat* for problems. Even though the phrase was a natural reinterpretation of the word *scapegoat*, it suggested to me that the speaker hadn't read much. When I teach writing, I try to model standard usage and I correct nonstandard forms such as "I seen the Cascade Mountains," "We should of found another route," and "There had to be a way in which to do that." But there are many so-called errors that I do not correct. Consider, for example, these items, from practice tests in an early twentieth-century grammar correspondence course:[3]

What do you think of (me—my) going to town?
I was frightened at (that examination's length—the length of that examination).
You must act (quicker—more quickly).
The order was (only intended—intended only) for the major.
You must report to me (more often—oftener).

In each case, the test maker intended the first choice to be marked out as incorrect. But none of these seem to me to be errors worth correcting, and the last example actually seems smoother with *more often* rather than *oftener*.

Bad English is hard to define. One way is simply to say that it is English that doesn't follow the rules. That of course raises a new question. What do we mean by the rules of a language? Broadly speaking there are two ways of thinking about rules. One view is that rules describe the regularities that speakers follow in using their language. For example, consider how English speakers form simple questions. We invert the helping verb (also known as the auxiliary verb) and the subject. In order to make a question from the simple statement *Mary has left*, we shift the auxiliary verb *has* to the front yielding *Has Mary left?* Similarly, the sentence *Is John busy?* is the question form of *John is busy*; *Will you close the door?* is the question form of *You will close the door*; and so forth.

What if there is no auxiliary verb in the statement form? In that case we add the special auxiliary verb *do* and put that in front of the subject. So *Do you see that?* is the question form of *You see that*. A rule of English is that questions are formed from statements by moving the auxiliary to the left of the subject or by adding a form of *do* when no other auxiliary is present. Such rules document how the English language works. They also provide building blocks for deeper investigation into the patterns of language. From very simple questions such as these, we could go on to investigate questions with interrogative pronouns, such as *What are you reading?* or we could study the use of *do* in negative sentences, as in *I didn't see that movie*.

The study of language that focuses on patterns of use and rules like this is known as descriptive grammar. Descriptive grammar is the basis for dictionaries, which record changes in vocabulary and usage, and for the field of linguistics, which aims at describing languages and investigating the nature of language. Taking the description of language seriously means paying attention to such details as how questions are formed and similar patterns of language. It also means recognizing that these patterns are subject to variation and change. Dictionaries provide the most obvious illustration of the way that language changes. As new editions of dictionaries are published, they document new words that arise like *Botox, identity theft, phat*, and *bioterrorism*. They document new meanings of existing words such as the use of the word *nuke* as a verb meaning to heat by microwaving, or the change in the meaning of the verb *print* from mechanical to electronic reproduction of text and images.

Rules of grammar change as well. A moment ago I discussed the pattern of question formation in present-day English. But Shakespeare's characters ask questions that reflect a different pattern of question formation. They ask such questions as *What said he?* and *Came he not home to night?* These questions are formed by inverting the main verb rather than by adding *do*, which was the common pattern in earlier English. In Shakespeare's time, questions could be formed by inversion of the main verb or by adding *do*, as in *And did you not leave him in this contemplation?*[4] The different options were used in different styles and situations, but eventually the forms with *do* became the only pattern for questions not having an auxiliary. In other words, the rules for forming questions have changed over the centuries.

The idea of following a rule is so deeply associated with correct behavior that it is tempting to think of rules as applying only to formal language and to view informal language as being without rules or being lax about them. But informal speech obeys rules as well. Take contraction, for example, a process that occurs in much informal language. Contraction of the verb *is* takes place in sentences such as *Where's my pen? Who do you think's going to be there?* and *What's going on?* But contraction does not typically occur at the end of a sentence. We can say *I wonder who that is* but not *I wonder who that's.*[5] Other informal language is systematic as well. Even apparent conversational filler words have a system and meaning to them.[6] *Like*, for example, is used to indicate approximation or exaggeration, as in *He has, like, six sisters* and *He's, like, 150 years old.* It may also serve as an informal synonym for *says*, as in the sentence, *I tried to play some music and he was all like "Quit making so much noise."*

It is also tempting to think of regional dialects as breaking the rules of good English. The grammar of regional speech varies from that of

Standard English, but the variation is systematic and patterned. It is more accurate, then, to view dialects as having different rules from the standard. In Appalachian English, for example, speakers sometimes put an *a*-sound before words that end in *–ing*. This results in familiar expressions like *a-hunting we will go*. But speakers who use this dialect feature do not simply put the *a-* before any word that ends in *–ing*. Appalachian speakers who use the *a-* prefix might say *Everyone went a-hunting* but not *Everyone likes a-hunting* or *I bought a new a-hunting dog*. The *a-* is possible when the *–ing* word is a verb, but not when the *-ing* word is a noun or adjective.[7] So the grammar of Appalachian English has a fairly sophisticated rule of *a*-prefixing that is missing in Standard English.

Dialect variation also occurs in the usage of individual words as well. An example involves the use of the adverb *anymore*. In Standard English, its primary use is in negative sentences (such as Yogi Berra's famous statement that "*Nobody goes there anymore. It's too crowded*") and in questions (such as *Do you go there anymore?*).[8] In some parts of the county, however, speakers also use *anymore* in sentences such as *Everyone is cool anymore* or *Anymore you're working too much*. The extension of *anymore* to positive statements does not mean breaking a rule. Rather, different speakers have different rules for using this adverb, and dictionaries recognize such variation in usage notes. The eleventh edition of *Merriam-Webster's Collegiate Dictionary*, for example, notes that positive *anymore* "is now reported to be widespread in all speech areas of the U.S. except New England."

The idea that dialect and informal speech are organized systems with rules is an important one. Suppose you try to write a novel with an Appalachian or Midwestern character. It is possible to use the rules of the dialect to draw a convincing portrait of that character's speech or to bungle the rules of the dialect to create an ineffective portrayal. Or suppose you are an advertiser or politician wishing to appeal to an audience of young people, blue- and pink-collar workers, or senior citizens. You are likely to want to tailor the level and formality of your speech to them, and to follow the rules for the speech variety you believe is most effective for your audience.

The variability of language is significant in another way. It means that good and bad language cannot be defined in absolute terms. The standard language of one era, generation, medium, or region might well differ from the standard of another. The editorials of the *New York Times* or *Wall Street Journal* differ from the arts and culture reporting in *Time* magazine. Educated speech in Atlanta or Austin differs from educated speech in Seattle or Boston. Speakers shift their styles depending on their audience, using vocabulary, pronunciation, and grammar that fit well. And vocabulary, grammar, and pronunciation norms all change. If they did not change, we might still be using dictionaries from one hundred years ago and Chaucer and Beowulf would be much more popular with students.

Language change does not mean that any novelty automatically becomes the norm and achieves widespread educated usage. Some innovations become widely used while others fail. Television is an excellent source of newly coined vocabulary but some new vocabulary takes hold and some does not. A coinage like *regift*, from the series *Seinfeld*, seems to me to be a likely candidate to become standardized. Other novelties, such as *low-talker*, *hand-sandwich*, and *shushee* (also from *Seinfeld*) or *kitteny*, *frowny*, *girl-powery*, *knifey*, and *huntery* (from *Buffy the Vampire Slayer*) are unlikely to become widely used.[9]

Innovation and variation in pronunciation and grammar evokes similar strong feelings. Some variation is unremarkable while other variation is contentious and stigmatized. Consider the pronunciation of the words *economic, Uranus, Oregon,* and *nuclear,* for example. The variable pronunciation of the first two words is typically treated as a matter of alternate standard pronunciations: *EEKonomic* versus *ECKonomic* or *YOURunus* versus *youRAYnus.* The pronunciation of *Oregon* as *or-uh-GUN* or *or-uh-GAWN* varies according to whether one is native or an outsider.[10] The pronunciation of *nuclear* is different. For many it is a marker of education and refinement whether one says *NU-clee-ur* or *NU-cu-lar.*

For an example from the realm of grammar, consider the choice between relative pronouns in the following pair of sentences:

You will work in an office (that—which) you will see later.
You will work with a colleague (who—whom) you will meet later.

In each example, the two choices represent usage variation. In the first example, the choice between *that* and *which* is stylistic. Writers, speakers, and editors may have preferences but either choice is good usage. In the second example, however, some speakers, writers, and editors see the choice between *who* and *whom* as one of correctness. For them, the use of *who* in this example is bad grammar because the pronoun is the logical object of the verb *meet*. We will return to this particular example in more detail in chapter 3.

Language variation presents us with choices, and as a result we may often be unsure what is best in any particular situation. There is a natural tendency for speakers and especially writers to look for a fixed standard of language, and this desire for fixed standards leads to a second notion of rule. This second kind of rule is one that judges usage as correct or incorrect, and that prescribes the use of one form over another. In fact, we call such an approach prescriptive grammar. In the case of medicine, prescriptions have a clear function—to cure a condition or alleviate a symptom. The medical metaphor is revealing in that some people see the standard language as representing linguistic health and see variation as a metaphorical infection. The prescriptive approach sees certain fixed rules as defining the standards of clarity, logic, precision, and discipline, and as respecting authority and tradition. For prescriptivists, disobeying the rules or changing them indicates a disregard for these qualities.

The descriptive and prescriptive viewpoints come into particular opposition around the question of standard language. Prescriptivists tend to view standards as following from rules largely independent of usage, rules that reflect the tastes of the most refined and most discriminating among us. Prescriptivists believe that usage ought to conform to this authority, and nonstandard language is a source of inaccuracy and anarchy—it is a language problem. Because prescriptivism aims at conserving traditional distinctions, usages, and forms, changes to the standard are generally resisted rather than embraced, even when the changes are widespread among the educated. Descriptivists, on the other hand, tend to see standards as following from the norms of widespread mainstream usage. These norms are subject to change and may be influenced by such things as fashion, the media, casual speech, and nonstandard usage. Descriptivists also emphasize that nonstandard usage is regular, even though it may be ineffective for many purposes. They thus tend to be relativists who see norms as following the usage of the educated mainstream, while prescriptivists tend to view norms less flexibly and to see them as informing, correcting, and judging the tastes of the people. For prescriptivists, good language is central to character and should be widely evident in all one's language. For descriptivists, language is made up of alternative forms of order that might be adopted by speakers depending on their purpose.

The contest between descriptivism and prescriptivism has been at the center of discussions of grammar and good English through much of the last century. Concerns about the moral consequences of relativism in language were a topic of considerable attention in the middle of the twentieth century, for example. In a 1961 review of *Webster's Third New International Dictionary*, newspaper columnist Sydney J. Harris complained about its descriptivist approach:

> Relativism is the reigning philosophy of our day, in all fields.
> Not merely in language, but in ethics, in politics, in every field
> of human behavior. There is no right and wrong—it is all
> merely custom and superstition to believe so.[11]

Harris's worry was that failure to uphold standards of language—grammatical right and wrong—would lead us down the slippery slope to nihilism and anarchy. We can contrast Harris's view with the positive view of relativism presented just a decade earlier by the National Council of Teachers of English in its 1952 report *The English Language Arts*:

All usage is relative. The contemporary linguist does not employ the terms "good English" and "bad English" except in a purely relative sense. He recognizes the fact that language is governed by the situation in which it occurs.[12]

The two quotes reflect the opposite views of good English held by prescriptivists and descriptivists. The first quote implies an approach in which there is an abiding right and wrong to usage and the second an approach in which standards are determined by situation and context. Since language is a product of culture, these views reflect opposite pictures of cultural standards as well. As a consequence, questions of good and bad language are part of a much broader debate between those who advocate recognizing and promoting just a single cultural tradition (traditionalists) and those who advocate the value of competing traditions in language, the arts, history, and literature (relativists).

This book examines how language is characterized as "good" and "bad," focusing on grammar, vocabulary, and accent. For the mainstream of speakers, good language is seen as grammatically correct, rhetorically simple, free of regionalisms and foreign influences, and neither too coarse nor too avant-garde. The picture that emerges is one in which the notion of "good language" often reflects social desires for uniformity, conformity, and perceived tradition. The concepts of good and bad language also reflect relationships among different groups, especially between a perceived mainstream and various others. Examining the social interpretation of language yields such distinctions as polite versus coarse, correct versus incorrect, native versus foreign, pedantic versus colloquial.

What other ideas underlie notions of good and bad language? One is social mobility. The United States has a strong egalitarian tradition, and the doctrine of mobility through education links mainstream language with success. Grammar and language are part of the cultural capital that individuals pursue in order to improve their social and economic situation. Whether economic status can be changed through language betterment remains to be demonstrated of course, but the idea that speaking and writing a certain way is a ticket to a better life seems to be ingrained in the public consciousness. The wide number of newspaper and magazine features dealing with language suggests that consumers of the print media have a great interest in language as cultural capital. The many courses on English as a second language and programs on accent reduction also suggest that nonnative and dialect speakers worry about language as well. This interest is not at all new. At the beginning of the twentieth century, writer Sherwin Cody began advertising a series of books on *The Art of Writing and Speaking the English Language*. The books offered a guide to self-correction of grammar and pronunciation. Early versions of Cody's advertisements headlined the claim that "Good English and Good Fortune Go Hand in Hand." Later versions led even more directly with the simple question "Do you make these mistakes in English?" In various forms the ad ran continuously in magazines for forty years.[13]

A second set of ingrained ideas connects language with intelligence and character. Some believe that nonstandard language reflects unclear and incorrect thinking or that it arises from a lack of initiative. For example, members of the usage panel of the 1975 *Harper Dictionary of Contemporary Usage* describe usage they disapprove of as "Slack-jaw, common, [and] sleazy," "sloppy," "an abomination," and a "barbarism."[14] Of course, all norms are moralized to some extent. From yard care to table manners, communities judge their members in part based on conformity to certain behaviors. Norms of language in particular emerge from a tradition that has often linked grammar with intellectual discipline and social graces and that has viewed nonstandard language as potentially debasing polite society.

We also find much politicization of language norms. Attention to the ideological and political consequences of language is part of a long tradition made popular by writer George Orwell. However, the focus on "political correctness" in the last decade of the twentieth century has placed word choice squarely in the public consciousness. Today, for example, the choice among the words *queer, gay,* and *homosexual,* between the expressions *Merry Christmas* and *Happy Holidays,* or between *Founding*

Fathers and *Founders* is as much a sign to others as one's grammar and pronunciation. While grammar and pronunciation are viewed as signals of education, word choice is often seen as a signal of political beliefs. Some speakers see traditional usages as reinforcing existing privilege and view new inclusive usage as necessary language change. Others see the older norms as perfectly serviceable and new usages as radical attempts to enforce sensitivity or to impose political agendas.

Politicization of languages issues is also very evident in broader beliefs about the civic value of English. Many of us agree that fluency with the standard language aids civic participation—that knowing a certain type of English helps in having one's voice heard. And people of diverse backgrounds also believe that it is useful for immigrants to adopt English. Many in fact believe that language assimilation is crucial because it creates shared national values. By contrast, supporting and maintaining languages other than English is seen by some as dividing society and encouraging separatism. These attitudes are especially evident in controversies over English-only laws and bilingual education, but we will also find similar attitudes focused on the nonstandard speech of some African-Americans.

The treatment of language norms as cultural commodity, as intellectual ability, as moral virtue, and as political ideology provides a strong motivation for speakers to conform to a standard that is associated with perceived refinement, intelligence, education, character, and commitment to national unity or mainstream political values. Of course, if none of these qualities is inherently connected to language, such judgments of people's language are really characterizations of their willingness, their need, or their ability to adjust to the language practices of others. This will be part of the explorations that follow.

Anything Goes

The field of linguistics is concerned with the serious study of language. It asks questions aimed at discovering how languages work, how particular languages developed historically, how language functions socially and psychologically, and even how language is organized in the brain. Many linguists see themselves as scientists as well as humanists, and as a profession linguistics takes a descriptive approach to issues of usage. Because of this, the terms "descriptive grammar" and "descriptive linguistics" are often used interchangeably. What connects linguistics to broader debates over cultural values is the idea of relativism. Descriptive linguistics acknowledges the possibility of multiple and shifting standards and emphasizes that good usage is relative to the audience and purpose of communication. This aspect of linguistics is often mischaracterized by prescriptive traditionalists as the automatic denial of standards. The argument seems to be that recognizing multiple standards entails that there is no standard, and some traditionalists remain convinced that relativism in language is a moral, social, and intellectual danger and a model of permissiveness.

Since a broader debate about relativism plays such a key role in language controversies, we should consider in more detail the nature of some objections to it.[15] One version of antirelativist sentiment appears in critic William A. Henry III's book *In Defense of Elitism*.[16] Henry focuses on the contrast between elitism and egalitarianism, seeing the latter as committed to the idea (paraphrasing humorist Roger Price) that everyone not only begins the race equal but finishes equal. Elitism, conversely, maintains the possibility of some culture and cultures being superior. For Henry, superior cultures are ones that preserve liberty, provide a comfortable life, promote science, medicine, and hygiene, and produce permanent art of some complexity.[17] In his view, relativist egalitarianism results in anti-intellectualist populism that scorns

> intellectual distinction-making . . . respect and deference
> toward leadership and position, esteem for accomplishment,
> especially when achieved through long labor and rigorous
> education; reverence for heritage, particularly in history,
> philosophy and culture; commitment to rationalism and

scientific investigation; upholding of objective standards; most important, the willingness to assert unyieldingly that one idea, contribution or attainment is *better than* another.[18]

There are several problems with such attacks on relativism. First, the equation of relativism with anti-intellectualism is faulty. The conclusion that tradition is constructed and arbitrary does not imply that it is impossible to make distinctions and evaluate alternatives. Nor does the fact that a cultural form is popular make value judgments impossible. Those versed in contemporary music, folk art, and animation can often make fine distinctions and critical assessments about works in those domains. The elite may be unfamiliar with these subjects, but the same intellectual distinction-making and appreciation is possible in popular culture as in high culture.

Equating relativism with nihilism is also faulty. The flawed reasoning goes something like this: since different cultures treat ethical, social, linguistic, and cultural issues in different ways, it must be impossible to find absolute values or standards or even to evaluate competing ideas. If everything is relative, there is no canon, no standard, no right. However, an understanding of the constructed nature of traditions ought to encourage the evaluation of competing ideas by opening both tradition and innovation to rigorous study. Relativism can thus best be understood as the view that received wisdom is not beyond challenge.

The romanticized view of culture set forth by William Henry parallels the romanticized view of prescriptive grammar. The reasonable idea that there ought to be a common standard is transformed into the belief that such a standard reflects an inherent good. When tradition is romanticized in this way, departures from it, whether grammatical or cultural, are apt to be represented as corruption and decay rather than innovation or progress. But romanticism of tradition is not merely a characteristic of criticism by nostalgic grammatical and cultural conservatives. The political center and left also sometimes see nonstandard language and mass culture as a danger to civic norms and shared democratic values. Progressivist romanticism manifests itself in the idea of self-improvement and public cooperation through common language and, more generally, through a common culture. The progressive case for standard language as an aspect of modern education is notably summarized by E. D. Hirsch in his book *Cultural Literacy.* Hirsch writes that after the industrial revolution:

> The worker had constantly to adapt to new, more efficient, methods. Because of the continually changing occupations that were increasingly demanded by large industrial societies, people had to communicate with a wider economic and social community. Achieving wider communication required literacy and a common language. At the same time, the political system had to become correspondingly bigger, requiring wider circles of communication to carry out laws and provide centralized authority.[19]

Hirsch cites Ernest Gellner's *Nations and Nationalism,* which stresses that members of an industrial society "must be able to communicate by means of impersonal, written, context-free, to-whom-it-may-concern type messages."[20] The implication is that such communications must be in a shared, common language. For such writers as Hirsch and Gellner, standardization is not so much a moral issue as a functional one—an issue of an individual's practical economic needs and of a society's administrative and political ones. Hirsch holds a similar position with respect to the content of cultural literacy, seeing cultural literacy as "the basic information needed to thrive in the modern world."[21]

There are, then, different sources for romanticization of grammar and culture. On the one hand, there is nostalgic traditionalism, which is partly grounded in the belief in the superiority of elite forms, the corruption of mass culture, and the nihilism of relativism. On the other hand, there is progressivism, which sees access to standards of language and culture as a prerequisite for meaningful social participation and which sees the influence of nonstandard language and mass culture as potential impediments to participation.

A Culture of Engagement

In this book, I ask how language attitudes are represented and constructed. How do certain language varieties come to be characterized as uneducated, vulgar, immoral, foreign, ethnic, provincial, ephemeral, convoluted, or politicized? How is other language, by contrast, characterized as respectful, accessible, clear, direct, authoritative, and democratic? In exploring language attitudes, I hope not just to show that simple notions of good and bad language fail but also to suggest how we might think more productively about language.

It is possible, I think, to be discriminating about language in the middle space between moralism and nihilism. The correct approach to questions of language involves something like the model of law or philosophical ethics. Judges recognize that there are a variety of ways that the meaning of a statute can be interpreted. In fact the so-called canons of legal interpretation in some ways parallel traditional grammar. These canons are rules available to judges for interpreting the meaning of laws. But as legal theorist Karl Llewellyn demonstrated more than half a century ago, it is possible to find competing and contradictory rules for interpreting laws.[22] As a result, judges have considerable latitude in interpretation—a judge can, for example, follow the original intent of a law or its plain language. Any judge will develop a judicial practice that guides his or her interpretation of laws. No grammatical rulebook can automatically determine the meaning of a law. If it could, Supreme Court decisions on matters of statutory interpretation would always be unanimous and immediate. Reasoning in philosophical ethics is similar. Philosophers recognize that one cannot always follow principles like the Golden Rule (do unto others as you would have them do unto you), Immanuel Kant's Categorical Imperative (treat humanity as an end rather than a means), or Utility (maximize the greatest good for the greatest number) to determine ethical behavior. Sometimes these principles conflict, and sometimes the application and consequences of a principle are not obvious. Getting ethics or law right requires analysis that dissects and balances the different ways in which a decision might be valid.

Language use (and ultimately language policy) is likewise a matter of asking questions and solving problems. Just as judges must balance different interpretive rules and ethicists must balance different concepts of right, so speakers and writers must balance language conventions. Speakers must do this balancing pragmatically, continually reassessing usage. The reason for this continual reassessment is that language questions are really questions about appropriateness, and what is appropriate for the classroom versus the living room, or for diplomacy versus politics, will vary. The art of using language, like that of any other complex decision making, lies in deciding which of various principles applies and why. And authority, whether in law, ethics, or language, comes from the method in which decisions are made, not from mere adherence to tradition or popular opinion.

The same need for engagement and continual reassessment exists in other fields as well. Consider literature, art, and music, fields in which there have long been tensions between mass culture and elite culture and between the contemporary and the classical. Education has as one of its goals to encourage people to think about literature, art, and music, not just to become familiar with a set of great authors, artists, and composers. We expect students to develop the ability to explain aesthetic choices and we want them to demonstrate habits of mind that will allow them to make informed cultural choices as citizens.

Some commentators link the development of these abilities and habits with a canon of traditional works determined by objective standards of aesthetic superiority. William Henry, for example, suggests that Americans have always felt more comfortable with contemporary and folk culture than with classical, but he views folk art forms such as weaving, the blues, and square dancing as "lesser forms of art than oil painting, ballet, and opera because the techniques are less arduous and less demanding of long learning, the underlying symbolic language is less complicated, the range of expression is less profound, and the worship of beauty is muddled by the lower aims of community fellowship."[23] Henry suggests that more highly valued forms of art can be identified by arduousness of technique, length of learning, the complexity of symbolic language, and the profundity of range of expression. Suppose this is true. It is still an open question whether such rigor, complexity, and profundity can be found in popular works, in contemporary works, or only in works passing a test of time. And in fact, many scholars and teachers of literature, art, and music recognize that the canon changes. We teach Saul Bellow, Toni Morrison, Sylvia Plath, and Ralph Ellison in literature classes along with Chaucer, Milton, and Dickens. We teach Andy Warhol, Jasper Johns, and Richard Serra along with da Vinci, Rembrandt, and Titian. And we teach Thelonius Monk, Aaron Copland, and the Beatles along with Bach, Mozart, and Beethoven.

The point of studying cultural change is to engage the canons of the past with the culture of the present, not to subordinate one to the other. This is a point that such critics as Henry seem to resist. The goal ought to be intellectual engagement, and that means viewing canons, rules, and conventions as objects of inquiry, not mere cultural currency. It does not mean denying the usefulness of canons, rules, and conventions. Richard Keller Simon provides some examples of the engagement of tradition and popular culture in his book *Trash Culture*. In his teaching, Simon analyzes canonical literature—*The Faerie Queene, Much Ado About Nothing*, and *The Iliad*, among others—and demonstrates how its structure and themes are paralleled in popular culture. Simon typically begins by having his students study the complexity of canonical texts and moves on to show how such texts interweave with popular narratives and how contemporary popular culture often recycles themes of canonical works. So for example, he discusses how the early episodes of the television comedy *Friends* parallel the play *Much Ado About Nothing*, how *Star Wars* mines *The Faerie Queene*, and how *Rambo* draws on *The Iliad*. Simon's approach does not mean that he is teaching courses about *Stars Wars*, *Friends*, and *Rambo* (though one could certainly imagine commentators making that assertion). Rather, what Simon is doing is using the canon to help students understand and analyze the cultural discourses that they most frequently encounter, while at the same time fostering appreciation for the canon. Such an approach does not entail claiming that *Rambo* is as good as *The Iliad* or that there are no distinctions of quality. It instead attempts a constructive engagement between the traditional canon and contemporary works.

At a different level, there can also be a constructive engagement between tradition and theory in literature. Traditional approaches focus on the character of the literature—its literariness, influences, or universal value. Theoretical approaches, including the postmodern, ask how reading, interpreting, and canon formation reflect competing and contested discourses and how the process of reading affects interpretation. Often, however, the tension between the traditional and the theoretical is exaggerated as a contrast between defenders and destroyers of culture or between theoretical sophistication and cultural fundamentalism. What is needed instead is some constructive engagement of traditionalist and theorist. In his book *Loose Canons: Notes on the Culture Wars*, Henry Louis Gates, Jr., suggests one approach. Gates suggests that a canon is important not because it represents the reading material of the power elite but because it is "the commonplace book of our shared culture, in which we have written down the texts and the titles that we want to remember."[24] In attempting to articulate a canon of African-American literature, Gates finds himself searching for a position between those "who claim that black people can have no canon, no masterpieces," and those "who wonder why we want to establish the existence of a canon, any canon, in the first place."[25]

This position between is the space that I think it is productive to occupy in language as well: a space that engages tradition and innovation by accepting that canons, standards, and hierarchies are socially constructed objects but that still maintains the possibility of making distinctions and choices. We seek a space that recognizes that outsider literature, mass culture, and nonstandard language have a structure and a context that can be productively studied. In many cases such study illuminates the traditional forms of literature, culture, and language as well.

Linguists are sometimes pessimistic about public understanding of their field. But I think they have less cause for pessimism than many other fields. The general public is not always interested in art, poetry, or classical music. The public is interested in language, so a sustained and coherent articulation of a realistic message has a wide potential audience. And while descriptive linguistics has detractors, it faces nothing like the organized opposition that biology has or the academic marginalization of education or critical theory. Linguistics is well positioned to establish a culture of engagement between the canonization of Standard English and the denial of the possibility of a common language. The engagement of these two perspectives means understanding that canons and traditions are constructed but also inevitable. And it means understanding that the real object of study ought to be how standards emerge and change, not merely what they consist of.

My goal in what follows is to focus on "bad language" as a cultural construct and to show how badness is a much more complex phenomenon than it first appears to be. In developing this position, it is necessary to consider (and reject) alternatives. The chief alternative is the notion that good language is a simple matter of following the logical patterns established by tradition and that bad language is simply due to laziness, stupidity, social decay, bad influences, and the decline of standards. In rejecting this, I adopt what I call the realist position. The realist view is that standard language is important not because it represents the language of the best-educated speakers but because it is a cultural touchstone of the social history of the English language. It is crucial for educated people to understand that social history and the many factors that influence and modify the standard. These include competition among dialects and styles and relationships between native and nonnative speakers. A realistic view of language also means understanding the inevitability of grammatical norms, of etiquette, and of a tradition of pubic writing. None of these can be ignored or dismissed by those seeking full participation in commerce, culture, and civic life. But variation and innovation cannot be ignored either. Realism thus lies in understanding the constructed nature of the standard and the role of linguistic variation.

This introduction has aimed at raising some broad issues of tradition versus innovation in culture in order to place the discussion of realism in perspective. The remainder of this work is organized as follows. Chapter 2 further introduces the realist position by looking at prose style, with the aim of showing that good writing is a relativistic concept. Chapter 3 then examines traditional grammar, attitudes toward grammar, and the correctionist approach to usage. Chapter 4 discusses contested vocabulary—coarse words, slang, and politicized language (so-called political correctness)—to illustrate how the comfort level of a perceived mainstream helps to define good language. Chapters 5 and 6 shift the focus slightly to consider how language varieties other than mainstream English have been viewed as targets of assimilation. Together chapters 3–6 examine social forces that determine what is good and bad language—correctionism, conventionalism, and assimilationalism. Chapter 7 concludes, summarizing prevailing misconceptions about language and usage and the images of language that underlie such misconceptions. The conclusion also gives some final suggestions for ways to foster a culture of engagement with language rather than a standoff between tradition and nihilism.

Two Bad Writing

It is nothing new for authorities to complain about students' writing skills. In 1871 Harvard president Charles Eliot complained that the young men entering Harvard, while otherwise well prepared, often suffered from "Bad spelling, incorrectness as well as inelegance of expression in writing, [and] ignorance of the simplest rules of punctuation." Over one hundred years later, a 1975 *Newsweek* cover story explored the theme "Why Johnny Can't Write."[1] *Newsweek* writer Merrill Sheils wrote that "if your children are attending college, the chances are that when they graduate they will be unable to write ordinary, expository English with any real degree of structure and lucidity." In 2003, we still find Johnny in trouble. An article in the *Chronicle of Higher Education* is headlined "Why Johnny Can't Write, Even Though He Went to Princeton." The writer of the piece notes that "professors cite a host of writing-related shortcomings among students" and reports on a new wave of writing reform.[2]

In part the enduring perception that writing skills in America are in decline may come from our experience with universal education.[3] The United States has continually moved in the direction of mass education, adding new groups that had previously had little experience with academics. In the 1860s free high schools began to produce a new group of college-bound students; at the beginning of the twentieth century increasing numbers of immigrants entered schools; in the post–World War II period, veterans received new educational benefits; in the 1960s, the expansion of university systems recruited more new populations into higher education. Each time the base of higher education expands, concerns arise about literacy and decline of standards. These concerns are reflected in comments like those of Eliot and Sheils. They are also manifest in periodic reform initiatives having to do with the teaching of writing.[4] The fact that reform initiatives are a regular part of the teaching of writing also suggests that writing instruction is difficult to institutionalize. There are many reasons for this, but one is simply that it is difficult to define good writing in an absolute sense. What counts as good writing is tied to context and purpose. Good writing is a relative matter, and that relativity is the focus of this chapter.

The Craft of Writing

Writing is often viewed in two largely opposite ways—as a skill, which can be mastered by understanding certain rhetorical models, grammatical basics, and critical thinking techniques, or as a natural talent of expression that defies systematic instruction. In actuality, writing is neither so mysterious that it requires one to be touched by a muse nor so simple that all it requires is a foundation in grammar and logic. Writing is a craft, like carpentry, medicine, or being able to tell a joke. Natural talent and early experience with discourse of certain kinds no doubt play a role, but principles of organization, clarity, and coherence can be taught, fostered, and improved through exposure, analysis, modeling, and practice.

How do we tell if someone can write adequately? Higher education has traditionally viewed college-level literacy as the ability to read and understand certain kinds of texts and to emulate that style in exams and term papers. However, beginning in the 1970s, many institutions of higher education shifted from seeing academic literacy as an entrance requirement for college to seeing it as an end goal. This shift involved a reassessment of the role of English composition courses and the development of remedial courses for skill building. It also involved the creation of writing-across-the-curriculum programs to encourage writing in the major discipline after the first year of college.

The transition from general writing courses to disciplinary ones creates some problems. Historically, academic literacy had been a relatively homogeneous notion, assuming a common language across different fields. But fields as diverse as biology, philosophy, business, literature, sociology, and education no longer have disciplinary conventions in common. Just compare the opening paragraphs of professional articles in the journal *Science* and in *PMLA*, the journal of the Modern Language Association. Different disciplines are often separate discourse communities, like the dialects of a common language. Nevertheless, some features are shared in most academic discourse and are the foundation for education about writing. Successful academic writers articulate reasons and evidence as opposed to mere feelings, opinions, and reminiscences. They are clear about assertions, claims, and organization. They provide support and critical research, and they analyze premises and consider other points of view. Academic writing also involves a process that includes research, drafting, revising, and editing. The implementation of these broad rhetorical objectives, however, varies in different intellectual traditions and fields.

How is writing taught to novices? Handbooks for college students always provide models of good writing. They also describe a process that involves critical thinking, research, composition, and revision. Beyond that, writing instruction tries to identify features of effective prose. Often these features are presented as general advice about organization of material, development of ideas, and unity, coherence, and clarity of exposition. These categories are explicit in works like the *Harbrace Handbook*.[5] They are also implicit in William Strunk and E. B. White's *The Elements of Style*, which provides eleven principles of composition. Some of Strunk and White's principles focus on organization, giving such advice as "choose a suitable design and stick to it" and "make the paragraph the unit of composition." Others are prescriptions for coherence and clarity like "use the active voice," "put statements in a positive form," "use definite, specific, concrete language," and "place the emphatic words at the end of a sentence."[6]

Abstractions of organization, development, unity, coherence, and clarity are only part of writing instruction. There is also the issue of content. What should students write about? What should a writing class be about? Some professors argue that colleges should do away with composition courses because they have no academic content—that in many instances students merely write about themselves rather than writing about literature or history. In part this objection reflects the fact that many writing instructors begin with the personal essay before moving on to a research paper. But the reason for starting with the personal essay is to begin with familiar content. In this way students practice skills of development, organization, unity, coherence, and clarity before moving on to types of writing in which they must develop, organize, unify, and clarify ideas about unfamiliar subject matter. As Peter Elbow has noted, nonacademic discourse—particularly the personal essay—has a place in writing instruction because people will do far more nonacademic writing in their lives than academic writing (unless, of course, they become college professors).[7] Personal writing also helps students to learn to reflect on life's experiences, which may be as helpful a life skill as knowing how to write a research paper.[8] In addition, much of the writing that people do once they are out of school will involve a variety of contexts and purposes that go beyond the research paper—job applications, accident reports, letters of complaint, holiday newsletters, diaries, journals, and blogs.

Personal writing is something that people use to do things in their jobs, professions, and lives.

In colleges and universities, much of the writing that students do after they have completed a required writing class or two—usually English composition—is writing in their major field or a general education discipline such as history, political science, literature, or philosophy. Such writing involves new texts and new information in largely unfamiliar subjects. The connection to context and purpose again suggests that writing is more than a generalized skill certified by graduation from high school or by passing one or two basic courses in composition. And just as personal writing has a variety of functions, academic writing should also be viewed as a set of language practices that people use to solve problems in their academic majors.

The rhetorical transition between writing personal essays and writing about a field of study is sometimes difficult. Those who teach writing are familiar with the criticism that some students still do not write particularly well after their English composition sequence. And those who teach in other disciplines have probably encountered students who, upon having their writing critiqued, complain that they didn't know they had to worry about *how* it was written. The first observation reflects the difficulty some students may have in applying skills of organization, development, unity, coherence, and clarity while at the same time attempting to understand new and difficult content. A gap may remain between the ability to write competent personal essays and the ability to fluently use the discourse of an academic field to solve problems.

The observation about student attitudes reflects a complementary issue also. This is the attitude that once one has been certified as a passable writer by completing a composition class, only content is really important. In part, this attitude may reflect the false dichotomy of content and mechanics—the deep-rooted assumption that writing is just a matter of grammatically expressing one's ideas rather than organizing and supporting them. The artificial association of adequate composition with mere adherence to traditional grammar was noted by writer Rudolph Flesch in his 1949 book *The Art of Readable Writing*. Flesch summarized the mismatch between the teaching of grammar and the world of work this way: "Unless you are different from most people, your knowledge of rhetoric probably consists of a handful of half-forgotten rules, overlaid by the vague notion that they apply to the writing of themes but hardly to anything a grownup person does between nine and five on a weekday."[9] Flesch recommended that writers focus on information, organization, and development in colloquial English rather than fixating on traditional rules of grammar. Over thirty years later, researcher Lester Faigley underscored that distinction with the results of a study of language attitudes of students and working professionals. His survey found that freshmen college students tended to see good writing as the absence of error. On the other hand, college-trained members of the workforce saw good writing as attending to the needs of the reader as well, with correctness viewed more broadly than conformity to handbook rules. Faigley remarks that "notions of good writing held by people on the job are often very pragmatic," since writing affects employees in terms of time, accountability to supervisors, client perceptions, and legal liability.[10] Flesch and Faigley identify a key problem—that composition instruction is sometimes understood in terms of correctness while professional writing is understood in terms of effectiveness.[11] In other words, writing instruction needs to embrace a relativistic approach that goes beyond viewing goodness as the absence of error.

Clear and Direct

There is more to good writing than mere correctness, but what? One important line of thought about good writing is that it involves language that is clear and direct. Since 1974, the National Council of Teachers of English has awarded an annual Doublespeak Award, a satirical honor given to speakers and institutions whose public language is deceptive and euphemistic. The award has gone to presidents, government officials and agencies, corporations, and media figures, many of whom are well known. The National Council of Teachers of English has also given an annual Orwell Award since 1975. This award recognizes writers who have made contributions to the critical analysis of public discourse. With the exceptions of the creators of *Dilbert* and *Doonesbury*, these winners are less well-known figures.

The idea behind both awards is that in a democratic society, clarity and directness are necessary in order to prevent our being manipulated by language. The most well-known proponent of this idea was writer George Orwell. In his novel *Nineteen Eighty-four*, Orwell described a fictional state-sanctioned language called Newspeak. Its purpose was to limit people's ways of thinking about their world and their lives and to train them to think the way the state wanted them to think. The Ministry of Truth (Minitrue, in Newspeak) was established "not only to provide a medium of expression for the world view and mental habits proper to the devotees of IngSoc [English Socialism] but to make all other modes of thought impossible."[12] The name Minitrue and the names of the other fictional government ministries illustrate how Newspeak is supposed to work: "the Ministry of Peace . . . concerned itself with war; the Ministry of Love . . . maintained law and order; and the Ministry of Plenty . . . was responsible for economic affairs."

Orwell saw certain language practices of the literary elite as impediments to clear and honest communication. His views are developed in his 1944 essay "Propaganda and Demotic Speech" and in his 1946 essay "Politics and the English Language." In the former, Orwell argued that the vocabulary and accent (in the case of broadcasting) of much news reporting was ineffective in communicating with the mass of the public.[13] In "Politics and the English Language," he gave recommendations for clear writing and discussed the political consequences of unclear language:

[P]olitical language has to consist largely of euphemism, question-begging and sheer cloudy vagueness. Defenseless villages are bombarded from the air, the inhabitants driven out into the countryside, the cattle machine-gunned, the huts set on fire with incendiary bullets: this is called *pacification.* Millions of peasants are robbed of their farms and sent trudging along the roads with no more than they can carry: this is called *transfer of population or rectification of frontiers.* People are imprisoned for years without trial, or shot in the back of the neck or sent to die of scurvy in Arctic lumber camps: this is called *elimination of unreliable elements.* Such phraseology is needed if one wants to name things without calling up mental pictures of them.[14]

Euphemism and academic language, Orwell argued, blur the meaning of facts and cover up details.

There are two complementary aspects to Orwell's thinking on language—alarm at the ability of language to manipulate thought and a call for stylistic simplicity and sincerity. Taken together, these two aspects reflect the widespread view that clarity and simplicity enhance critical thinking and frank exchange of ideas, while needless complexity in language is a tool of self-deception or manipulation. Such books as Flesch's *The Art of Readable Writing* and Richard Lutz's *Doublespeak* have also developed this theme further. Flesch, for example, produced a famous readability index and served as a consultant for simplifying federal regulations. Lutz has critiqued the language of corporations, institutions, and governments, arguing that they use ambiguity, vagueness, and inflated language to misdirect us. He has also argued that, for both individuals and institutions, wordiness, jargon, and euphemisms replace frankness in dealing with people and complicate what might otherwise be simple and direct.

Denseness of language often plays a role in satires of intellectualism. It was also an issue in the so-called Sokal hoax of 1996. New York University physicist Alan Sokal had a bogus essay on the social construction of scientific truth accepted and published by the journal *Social Text.* Commenting on his hoax article "Transgressing the Boundaries: Toward a Transformative Hermeneutics of Quantum Gravity," Sokal wrote that theoretical sophistication seemed to substitute for reasoning and that "incomprehensibility becomes a virtue; allusions, metaphors and puns substitute for evidence and logic."[15] What is shared by Orwell, Flesch, Lutz, Sokal, and others is the belief that an idealized simplicity both embodies and enhances clear critical thinking. Even *Roget's Thesaurus,* the staple of high school vocabulary building, comes under criticism from popular author Simon Winchester. Winchester suggests that the thesaurus "should be roundly condemned as a crucial part of the engine work that has transported us to our current state of linguistic and intellectual mediocrity."[16] By providing synonyms without definition, the thesaurus, in Winchester's view, promotes bad writing and linguistic laziness.

Language is an issue in literary aesthetics as well, as was evident in B. R. Myers's critique of writers Cormac McCarthy, Annie Proulx, Don DeLillo, Paul Auster, and David Guterson. In a 2001 essay in the *Atlantic Monthly,* Myers condemned these writers for engaging in "hit-and-miss verbiage" (McCarthy), "exploit[ing] the license of poetry while claiming exemption from poetry's rigorous standards of precision" (Proulx), "spurious profundity" (DeLillo), the "flat, laborious wordiness" that signals avant-garde prose (Auster), and "repetitive sluggishness" (Guterson). Myers recommended older work such as Saul Bellow's 1947 *The Victim* as exemplifying unaffected writing.[17] While his focus is on aesthetics, the thrust of Myers's argument that "clumsy writing begets clumsy thought, which begets even clumsier writing" echoes Orwell's position that language can corrupt thought.[18]

Is Orwell's critique of dense and complex language convincing? It is and it isn't. Certainly, writers seeking clarity want to avoid needless length, complexity, and confusion. But not all topics are the same. Some require more complex exposition to fully articulate a point. Some require technical language for precision. And sometimes experimentation with language is the point of a work (as with some literary fiction and much poetry). If we assume that effective writing should always be minimal in syntax and vocabulary, we do a disservice to the range of topics and expression.

It is also a mistake to equate all vocabulary change with thought control or manipulation. Sometimes attitudes toward concepts change (as with the change from *crippled* to *handicapped* to *disabled*). Sometimes groups or organizations reexamine and reorganize themselves. What, after all, are we to make of the 1947 government reorganization that eliminated the U.S. Department of War and created the Department of Defense? To some, the renaming may imply the correction of a previous misnomer or the clarification of peaceful intent in a new nuclear age; to others it might seem to be an obfuscation of militaristic tendencies as deceptive as Orwell's Ministry of Peace. More recently, the Department of Homeland Security was created in 2002 combining the Coast Guard, the Customs Service, the Federal Emergency Management Agency, and the Immigration and Naturalization Service. On what grounds would we decide whether the name Homeland Security is a step toward clarity or obfuscation? This is the stumbling block to Orwell's position—deciding what is clear and what is misleading.

Concerns about style such as those raised by Orwell are not novel, and similar language issues have dominated in other times. The Renaissance, for example, was characterized in part by attempts to improve English by borrowing and coining new terms, many of them of classical origin and many others borrowed from French, Italian, and Spanish. This activity, coupled with the emergence of English as a language of educated discourse, caused a tremendous expansion of the vocabulary. Borrowing was not universally welcomed, however. In 1549, Thomas Caloner criticized the use of such terms to make a writer appear more clever and literate, and he compared the practice to putting "a gold ring in a sow's nose." Thomas Wilson, author of the 1553 *Art of Rhetoric*, wrote that writers should "speake as is commonly received: neither seeking to be over fine, nor yet living over-carelesse." And John Cheke, in a preface to Thomas Hoby's 1561 translation of *The Courtier*, wrote that English should be written "cleane and pure, unmixt and unmangled with borrowing of other tunges," invoking an economic metaphor of bankruptcy by borrowing.[19] Yet many writers, among them Thomas Elyot, John Dryden, and Richard Mulcaster, found innovation unobjectionable, citing the need to improve the language. Edmund

Spenser and Sir Thomas More were great coiners of new words, Spenser's often drawing on earlier English.

Among other things, the recurring debate over ornament and artifice in prose indicates that style is a relative matter. Harvard's Charles Eliot and *Newsweek*'s Merrill Sheils worry about language that is bad because it is grammatically incorrect. But there is also a complementary tradition of complaint about rhetorical excess. In one instance, language is bad because it is seen as insufficiently rich; in the other, language is perceived as bad because it is too complex.

The Relativity of Style

Notable literary prose in English has exhibited a range of styles and devices, shifting with the mood of the times much as music or art does. The foundation of English prose is the *Anglo-Saxon Chronicle*, a historical record that began in the eighth century and continued until the twelfth. Early influences on prose included the conversion to Christianity and the Norman Conquest. The conversion of England to Christianity, spearheaded in 597 by St. Augustine, led to the expansion of vocabulary and to the adoption of Latin forms of expression to convey new religious philosophy. After the Norman Conquest of 1066, English entered a period in which French and Latin discourse models predominated. From about the middle of the fifteenth century, the spread of printing affected style by slowing the rate of change in spelling and grammar.

The spread of printing also increased the availability of foreign language literature, which, in turn, facilitated borrowing. As I have already noted, scholars increasingly coined words in the arts, literature, and philosophy. Latin and Greek provided a source for much new vocabulary during the Renaissance, and those languages provided grammatical and prose models as well. Some writers viewed Latin as a means of supplementing English and looked to the established grammar and vocabulary of Latin as models. Others saw a danger in a Latin influence that might limit understanding by the common person. The stylistic difference is apparent in the contrast between Renaissance writing that is more plain and succinct (such as that of Roger Ascham) and writing that is more heavy with classical allusion, syntactic and rhetorical ornamentation, and phonological devices such as alliteration and rhyme (such as that of John Lyly).[20]

The type of literature that dominated in a particular period also influenced prose style. Seventeenth-century English was heavily influenced by drama, which often demanded a style providing the illusion of natural conversation. The prose of Shakespeare, for example, was ornate yet colloquial, occupying a middle ground between the pedantic and the common. Another influence on English prose style during this time was the King James Bible, intended to bring the Bible to the common person without excessive ornament or idiosyncrasy of style. When it was completed in 1611, the King James version brought to English writing a style that emphasized such features of Hebrew poetry as parallelism, allegory, imagery, and analogy. Another influence evident during the Restoration was the royal court, which took the French language as a model of elegance rather than more ornate Latin or Italian. Arbiters of taste increasingly were court wits rather than scholars, and writing continued to move in the direction of spoken language, with less figurative and shorter, clearer exposition such as is found in the writing of John Dryden, for example.

Political and commercial influences have also helped to define good writing. The growth of English newspapers after the end of censorship in 1693 provides one illustration. Daniel Defoe began the *Review* in 1704, Richard Steele began the *Tatler* in 1709, and together with Joseph Addison started the *Spectator* in 1711. Political parties also rose in this period, and soon pamphleteering and journalism developed as techniques to influence public opinion. Jonathan Swift, for example, was an influential contributor to the Tory Party's *Examiner*, and Steele and Addison created an early style of literary journalism that helped to give the essay its modern form. In the eighteenth century, as politicians needed opinion makers less, writing became somewhat independent of politics. Style also showed the influence of Romanticism in poetry, as essays took on a more personal focus and came to reflect more of the writer's personality. The wide range of prose style in the Romantic period is exemplified by writers like William Hazlitt, who wrote about topics like prizefighting in straightforward, colloquial prose; Lord Macaulay, whose histories and essays relied on antithesis, contrast, and topic-sentence style; and Thomas De Quincey, whose style was characterized by archaism, imagery, poetic rhythms, and inversions. The following three samples hint at the different styles of the early to mid-nineteenth century:[21]

In the first round, everyone thought it was all over. After making play a short time, the Gas-man flew at this adversary like a tiger, struck five blows in as many seconds, three first, and then following him as he staggered back, two more, right and left, and down he fell, a mighty ruin. (from Hazlitt's 1821 essay "The Fight")

Few things have ever appeared to us more inexplicable than the cry which has pleased those who arrogate to themselves the exclusive praise of loyalty and orthodoxy, to raise against the projected University of London. (from Macaulay's 1826 essay "The London University")

The romance has perished that the young man adored; the legend has gone that deluded the boy; but the deep, deep tragedies of infancy, as when the child's hands were unlinked for ever from his mother's neck, or his lips for ever from his sister's kisses, these remain lurking below all, and these lurk to the last. (from De Quincey's 1845 "The Palimpsest of the Human Brain")

Variation can also be found in essay and journalistic practice in America. The first colonial newspaper publishers were essentially printers who published information brought to them, a tradition that continues today in some small town weeklies. Newspapers like James Franklin's *New England Courant,* begun in 1721 and modeled on the essay papers of Addison and Steele, tended to be the exception. The political press of colonial times, which saw the publication of many of the *Federalist Papers* in New York, gave way in the first half of the nineteenth century to the sensationalist penny press and eventually to Horace Greeley's *New York Tribune* (founded in 1841) and the *New York Times* (founded in 1851). Both the *Tribune,* whose weekly edition became known as the "Bible of the Midwest," and the *Times,* the country's "newspaper of record," helped to define a style of impersonal and less literary reporting. In 1896 Adolph Ochs took over the ownership of the *Times* promising to give the news in a plainer civic style rather than an oratorical one.[22] In the twentieth century, the *Times* saw competition from news magazines and other media and its style adapted so that today it incorporates features of the "new journalism" or creative nonfiction style pioneered by Truman Capote, Jimmy Breslin, and others. And as former editorial page editor Jack Rosenthal noted in the paper's 150th anniversary issue in 2001, the style of the *Times* has become increasingly casual to fit with a perceived ascendance of spoken English, but the paper still aims at "taste" and "credibility."[23]

Magazine publishing in America shows a similar evolution. Its roots may be traced to James Franklin's younger brother Benjamin, who in 1741 published his *American Magazine,* which along with *Pennsylvania Magazine,* the *Farmer's Weekly Museum,* and the *American Museum,* were some of the earliest in the colonies. Magazines founded in the nineteenth century include the *North American Review* (1815), *Harper's Monthly* (1850), the *Literary Digest* (1890), and the *Nation* (1865). Today literary and public affairs magazines such as the *Atlantic Monthly* and *Harper's* serve as opinion-leaders for the educated, bringing certain complex issues to the public consciousness outside of the regular news cycles. Perhaps the most celebrated of current literary magazines is the *New Yorker,* which provides commentaries, profiles, fiction, and reviews for opinion makers. While the *Atlantic Monthly, Harper's,* and the *New Yorker* are heirs to the tradition of literary commentary, the expansion of the publishing world and the rise of general news magazines also affected journalistic writing by promoting a more vigorous popular style. *Time* magazine, founded in 1923, adopted a style developed by its cofounder Britton Hadden, which emphasized terseness, forceful verbs, compound adjectives, and a preference for inverted sentence structures. This style, which gave the news both a novelistic tone and an urgency, came to be satirized as early as 1936 by the *New Yorker*, in which a commentator wrote: "Prosey was the first issue of *Time* on March 3, 1923. Yet to suggest itself as a rational method of communication, of infuriating readers into buying the magazine, was strangely inverted Timestyle."[24] *Time* and other news magazines have come to serve a different niche from the literary magazines, focusing on current news and cultural review. Journalistic prose thus involves different strata—newspapers, weekly news magazines, and literary/public affairs magazines. Each type—and competitors within a type (for example, the *New York Post* versus the *New York Times*)—may adopt a different style to more easily be differentiated from the competition and to match their perception of readers' tastes and abilities. For publishers, style is a matter of appropriateness to audience.

Two final examples illustrate the way in which style varies. Consider scientific writing, which we think of as typifying the impersonal and objective. But writing about science has not always involved the approach many of us are familiar with from high school and college lab reports. Scientific writing began in the form of letters between scientists and in reports to monarchs and patrons, with scientists like Sir Isaac Newton reporting their results in the first person. The scientific article emerged in the seventeenth century, developed by Henry Oldenburg of the London Royal Society in the Society's *Philosophical Transactions*. The genre of professional scientific writing that has emerged today supposes to model the process of empirical discovery by recording experimental procedures, results, and findings. In addition, today's professional scientific writing is primarily geared toward an audience that is already interested in and very familiar with the topic at hand, and so the contemporary scientific writing of scholarly journals generally reflects the professionalization of scientific writing as communication among peers. A parallel tradition remains of scientists writing for the lay public, exemplified by such writers as Thomas Edison, Michael Faraday, Bertrand Russell, George Gamow, Richard Feynman, Stephen Jay Gould, Carl Sagan, Stephen Hawking, and Steven Pinker. But for some scientists the differentiation of styles reflects a difference between "real scientific work" and "popularization." Within science, and other fields as well, some worry that simplification of the results of scientific research by over-reduction (as when one tries to explain evolution in terms of "survival of the fittest") and analogies (as when one tries to explain Newtonian mechanics by making reference to baseball) does a disservice to the nature of scientific inquiry and invites misinterpretations.

Legal writing provides another example of stylistic variety. Many people consider legal writing to be wordy, dense, convoluted, unnecessarily abstract, and archaic. As Peter Tiersma notes in his book *Legal Language*, the written language of the law developed from the legal profession's use of three languages—English, Latin, and French—as a way of managing the society in place after the Norman Conquest. This is why we find doublets like *last will and testament*, which combine Anglo-Saxon and Latinate synonyms.[25] The legal language of the courts and court opinions creates its own style in a way that makes its proceedings and pronouncements more identifiable and authoritative. Legal language also reflects the quest for statutory precision: the language of laws often seeks to specify the relevant instances rather than leaving a statement vague. So for example, a law might refer to *automobiles, motorcycles, trucks, buses, and vans*, rather than just *vehicles*. This makes it clear that bicycles, skateboards, and golf carts do not fall under its scope. Legal writing also often reflects the process by which laws are drafted. Laws are the work of committees with various perspectives and interests—some drafters may want to leave a point vague while others may want to have its meaning more fixed. The resulting compromise is cumbersome, as anyone who has ever written by committee can attest. But once again writing is function based. The creation of laws demands a balance of precision and flexibility while the gravity of the court system requires language that reinforces seriousness with attention to precedent and tradition in language.

What Is Good Writing?

In this chapter I have argued that good writing is a relative notion. This argument is based in part on the observation that different types of writing are recognized as "good" in different ways. Writing in the schools often places a premium on identifying errors and on qualities of organization, development, and unity. Journalistic writing emphasizes simplicity, information, and traditional standards of correctness. Serious fiction often values evocativeness and craft, with the avant-garde emphasizing experimentation and innovation. Legal writing focuses on precision of definition and on precedent. Scientific writing, somewhat similarly, favors objectivity, impersonality, and precedent. And bureaucratic writing strives for a neutrality of voice that evokes invisible authority.

Within categories of writing, form often matches function, creating further variation. Columnists on deadline aim for convincing hooks, facts, and argumentation. Longer, more literary essays and reviews such as those found in the *New Yorker* and the *Atlantic Monthly* employ style as a complement to content. Emphasis, balance, parallelism, pacing, and freshness are used to focus, hold, and direct the reader's attention. Narrative fiction may seek realism and authenticity of voice or may try to emphasize a thematic direction. And effective personal letters approximate both conversation and storytelling. Despite such variation, all good writing requires a discernable logic and a degree of organization, cohesion, unity, and clarity appropriate to the subject and audience. What good writing shares—whether it is personal, impersonal, entertaining, or bureaucratic—is a control that creates audience confidence and authorial credibility.

So the short answer is that good writing is writing that is effective—writing that is convincing to a particular audience. Whether they are students or working professionals, writers learn to be credible by becoming engaged with content and acquiring the discursive practices associated with it. Thus, when writers try to engage a particular audience—a particular discourse community—they often will accede personal idiosyncrasy to the group norm, at least initially. Like speakers switching among speech communities or registers, good writers are pragmatists who try to find the most appropriate language for their purpose and audience.

Three Bad Grammar

In the last chapter, we saw how written style is judged according to its effectiveness for its audience and function. The same is true for grammar. We modify our grammatical style to match our audience. We speak informally with friends and family, more formally in school and at work, and excruciatingly correctly on some occasions. In most situations, however, formality is tempered by the need for effective communication. This often means putting aside prescriptions about correctness in favor of current usage. Writer William Zinsser begins a chapter of his book *On Writing Well* by pointing out to would-be writers that "Soon after you confront this matter of preserving your identity, another question will occur to you: *Who am I writing for?*"[1] Zinsser could have chosen to write *For whom are you writing?* But that would have been a less effective way of making his point that writers must allow their personalities to come through. While some contemporary writers like Zinsser recognize the need for flexibility in grammar, others are part of a tradition that still considers *Who are you writing for?* a serious error.

As we will see in this chapter, there is a long-standing tradition of such complaints about English usage. Probably the most often cited example of the complaint tradition is Jonathan Swift's "Proposal for Correcting, Improving, and Ascertaining the English Tongue." Like many other writers in the 1700s, Swift was concerned that change would make literary works incomprehensible to posterity. Swift noted that with the exception of the Bible and prayer books, the English of earlier periods was already difficult to read and understand, and he suggested finding appropriate models that would permit English to be codified and comprehensibility to be preserved. Swift and others also hoped that the creation of a fixed standard of correct English would facilitate efficient communication, elegance, development of character, and the acquisition of social graces. Many saw standard grammar as encapsulating logic, and as reflecting tradition, fine points, and presumed subtleties of usage such as the distinction between *shall* and *will*, the use of *whom* for objects, and the avoidance of split infinitives and contractions. The method of error correction in schools developed from the complaint tradition, as did the public attitude of grammar being simply right or wrong.

In the eighteenth century, another grammatical tradition developed that emphasized changing usage as a basis of standards. Writers like George Campbell and Joseph Priestly saw standards as determined less by logic and tradition than by current usage and good taste. Standards were determined by the practices of educated speakers and writers. The same two views persist today: some, like Swift, see standard grammar as a correctness reflecting logic and propriety and others, like Campbell and Priestly, see standard grammar as reflecting the changing practices of the educated. This chapter considers these two views of good and bad grammar and argues that linguistically informed usage is the soundest basis for determining standards.

Prescriptive Grammar

Prescriptive grammar is what is found in many K–12 English textbooks, college rhetoric manuals, and practical English handbooks. Prescriptive grammar involves a minimal definition of sentence structure and a limited purpose for grammar. The sentence and its parts of speech are identified with categories of thought (such as "complete idea," "thing," and "action"). The purpose of grammatical analysis, in turn, is to foster correctness in writing and speech and a precise, logical rendering of thought into words.

The problem is that as a description of English, traditional terminology is hopelessly imprecise. Even basic definitions, such as the treatment of a subject as "the person, object, or idea being spoken of" fail if they are applied with any seriousness. Sentences as simple as *It was raining* or *There was a book on the table* illustrate the weakness of the definition. In the first example, we are talking about the weather, but the subject is the placeholder *it,* which doesn't refer to the weather or to the sky. In the second example, we are talking about the book, but the grammatical subject is again a placeholder (*there*), not a person, object, or idea. Problems aren't just restricted to sentences with *it* and *there.* Even in a sentence as simple as *Jane saw Dick,* one can ask why it isn't as much a description of Dick as of Jane. So the definition of subject as "the person, place, or thing that is spoken of" does not uniquely identify the noun *Jane* in the example.[2]

In addition, many prescriptive rules are ignored. The prohibition against sentence fragments, for example, is widely ignored in speech and by writers of fiction. Dialogue and narrative often include fragments to capture the rhythm of normal speech. Advertising and popular music draw on nonstandard grammar as in such examples as "Think Different" and "Got Milk" or "The times, they are a-changin'" and "I can't get no satisfaction."[3] Prescriptive authorities also disagree about the rules. Take the rule forming the possessive of singular words ending in *s,* for example. When a singular noun ends in an *s,* is it correct to add the apostrophe only or should you add the apostrophe plus a second *s*? Is it *Keats's poetry* or *Keats' poetry*? The 1984 Modern Language Association handbook says that "All singular proper nouns, including the names of persons and places, form their possessive in the same manner," by adding *'s*.[4] The United Press International stylebook gives a different rule: "If the singular ends in an *s* or *z* sound, add the apostrophe and *s* for words of one syllable. Add only the apostrophe for words of more than one syllable unless you expect the pronunciation of the second *s* or *z* sound." Strunk and White's *The Elements of Style* agrees with the Modern Language Association and suggests forming the possessive singular by adding *'s* regardless of the final consonant. But they follow with a long list of exceptions, which include: "the possessives of ancient proper names in *-es* and *-is*, the possessive *Jesus'* and such forms as *for conscience' sake, for righteousness' sake*." This is merely a sample of the variation in the treatment of the apostrophe. But the lack of consistency among sources suggests that prescriptive grammar is neither authoritative nor uniform.

As a final example of the looseness of prescriptive grammar, consider the definition of the sentence. Traditionally, we are taught that a sentence consists of a subject and predicate and expresses a complete thought. But what happens when we apply this definition to the following:

> In circulation, the *News* often ran dead last. But by 1970 it had
> worked its way into the black, and it achieved a goal that
> eluded many of its rivals: it survived.

Is the sequence beginning with *But by 1970* and ending with *it survived* a single complete thought? It seems to be, since its parts are grammatically connected by the conjunction *and* and by the colon following *rivals*. However, the sequence consists of three smaller parts, each of which also seems complete: *by 1970 it had worked its way into the black, it achieved a goal that eluded many of its rivals*, and *it survived*. So perhaps we should say that the sentence consists of three complete thoughts, not just one.

The conjunction *but* introduces a further grammatical complication. The prescriptive rule says that commas separate independent clauses connected by a coordinating conjunction. Does that mean that the second sentence is somehow incomplete—and thus incorrect—because it begins with *but*? Depending on how we choose to analyze things, the whole passage might be considered a single complete thought with the word *but* linking the second sentence to the first. Or the passage might be considered three or even four complete thoughts. The notion "complete thought" is vague enough to permit a wide range of possibilities.

Our look at these grammatical definitions and prescriptive rules is of course not a complete discussion of traditional grammar. Rather, it is a sample intended to suggest that traditional grammar is interesting precisely to those who need it the least. If one understands how to use commas, then the misleading nature of the comma rule discussed in the last example is a curious fact about that rule: ideas that are coordinated by a conjunction can be connected by a comma but don't have to be. If one doesn't understand how to use commas, then the rule that a comma separates independent clauses joined by a conjunction is both useless and confusing.

Does it make sense, then, to teach such grammar as a means of improving students' understanding of language? Parents and policy makers sometimes assume that this is so—that getting back to the basics of traditional grammar will improve speaking and writing. But teaching oversimplified rules of grammatical structure and correctness is like teaching oversimplified biology or history. Oversimplifications and social fictions are perhaps necessary at an early age but they are not appropriate for the curriculum at the secondary or college level, when students are making the transition to a more complex social and professional setting. Inquisitive students will spot the inconsistencies of traditional grammar and may come to see grammar as arbitrary and irrelevant, particularly if their teachers cannot provide a good explanation for the inconsistencies. In addition, students who are struggling with grammar may find the vagueness and inconsistency of traditional grammar a source of confusion and frustration in learning the conventions of writing. And teachers themselves are apt to be frustrated when trying to teach traditional grammar because of its vagueness and inconsistency.

The Emergence of Prescriptivism

English prescriptive grammar has its roots in the classical education model that relied heavily on the study of Greek and Latin, and hence on grammar, translation, and parsing. A key assumption was that education should exercise reason and memory and that this exercise was provided by the study of classical languages. The earliest grammars of English appeared in the late sixteenth century, based on William Lyly's Latin grammar. The study of English grammar often aimed at introducing the grammatical terms that would facilitate the later study of Latin. Presumably it was easier for students to learn Latin grammar if they were comfortable with the grammar of their native language, which was thought by many to be based on Latin and on grammatical universals reflected in that language. As scholars compared English with Latin, they came to see it both as irregular and as inferior to that long-codified language, and many grammars of the eighteenth century had the aim of teaching speakers of English to use their native language correctly. As was evident from Jonathan Swift's sentiments noted earlier, grammar was seen as a way of establishing proper use so that further decline might be prevented. The prevailing sentiment of decay is also illustrated by Thomas Sheridan's comments in his 1780 *General Dictionary of the English Language*. Sheridan writes that "out of our most numerous array of authors, very few can be selected who write with any accuracy . . . [S]ome of our most celebrated writers, and such as hitherto passed for our English classics, have been guilty of great solecisms, inaccuracies, and even grammatical improprieties."[5] For Sheridan, the usage of the best writers was less important than the rules laid out by grammarians.

There were other factors as well in the emergence of prescriptive grammar and correctionist teaching. Eighteenth-century England saw the beginning of the industrial revolution, which resulted in an upwardly mobile urban middle class. Social mobility reinforced the role of grammar as a means of marking class distinctions and increased attention to class distinctions. That attention to class distinctions, in turn, furthered the attitude that language and society were in a period of decay. The growth of English as an imperial language also spurred efforts to standardize the language, in parallel with movements toward standardization taking place in Italy and France. Together these factors provided both an impetus for correctionist English grammar and a market for it—a group of speakers with social aspirations who wished to learn to write and who wanted to improve their English.

The intelligentsia of the eighteenth century was concerned with the health of the language, and the central idea of the prescriptive tradition of the eighteenth century was adherence to usage determined by experts. Key among the experts was Bishop Robert Lowth, whose 1762 *A Short Introduction to English Grammar* was the most well known and influential of the eighteenth-century prescriptive grammars. Lowth's grammar was imitated and adapted in school grammars by Lindley Murray and others, and Murray's grammar, in turn, became widely used in America. His approach employed the method of providing examples of false syntax, or bad grammar, which learners were expected to correct.[6] Murray's approach also combined elements of the correctionist teaching method with aspects of moral education, helping to establish a tradition of promoting virtue, patriotism, and religion through grammar study. Following Murray, such American grammarians as Goold Brown and Samuel Kirkham set the pattern and tone of education with mass-produced grammars that also adopted a correctionist stance and treated the grammatical prescriptions of Lowth and others as already a matter of established tradition. By 1810 English grammar was offered in most schools and by the mid 1800s acquaintance with English grammar was required for entrance at a number of American colleges.[7] Prescriptive grammar had become the pedagogical norm.

The Doctrines of Usage and Utility

Prescriptive grammar has two main features. One is the conviction that traditional grammatical rules are based on logic, reason, and truth independent of usage. The second is the sense that language and society will suffer unless grammatical inaccuracies and errors are corrected. A contrasting position, held by eighteenth-century rhetoricians such as George Campbell and Joseph Priestly in England and by Thomas Jefferson in the United States, was that usage determines what is correct. Priestly's 1761 *Rudiments of English Grammar* suggested that grammarians were hasty in standardizing the language and that "the custom of speaking is the only original and only just standard of any language." It should, he argued, "be allowed to have some weight, in favour of those forms of speech, to which our best writers and speakers seem evidently prone."[8]

Campbell's position, developed in his 1776 *Philosophy of Rhetoric*, was similar. He wrote that "It is not the business of grammar, as some critics seem preposterously to imagine, to give law to the fashions that regulate our speech. On the contrary, from its conformity to these, and from that alone, it derives its authority and value."[9] However, Campbell argued that it was not just any usage that should be considered authoritative, only usage that was "reputable, national, and present." But how does one decide whose usage is reputable, national, and present? These categories often involved subjective judgments by Campbell and others, replacing the categories of logic, reason, and truth with those of reputable, national, and present. What was needed to make these notions more precise was an original and independent analysis of English. But to grammarians of the eighteenth century this was a new problem.

In the latter part of the nineteenth century and in the first half of the twentieth century, a new group of scholars took up this challenge, refining and championing the doctrine of usage. Reacting at times to late nineteenth-century critics of bad English,[10] writers like Thomas Lounsbury and William Dwight Whitney pointed out the role of educated usage in determining correctness. They also pointed out the tenuous nature of older, fixed standards of correctness. Especially noteworthy was George Philip Krapp, whose 1909 book *Modern English* systematically explored the relativity of correctness by noting that good usage was tied to the audience of a speaker or writer.[11] Krapp was also concerned with the problem of settling on a standard—of deciding who the best speakers and writers are. And he encouraged an approach in which individuals observed language in action and made informed choices. In his 1927 book *The Knowledge of English*, Krapp suggested that the desire to control and regulate language through rules of correctness arose from fear of linguistic decay and he argued that utility (as opposed to usage) is a governing force for linguistic order. Utility is the ability of language to do the work of communication. "Utility," he wrote, "has to do with the effective applications of language, especially with the bond of union between the speaker or writer and the rest of the world."[12] The inner ethic of a speaker is the other governing force in linguistic order. Krapp wrote that this personal aspect must also be considered in defining good English: "English is good English when it meets these two requirements, when it adequately performs its work as far as the world is concerned, and when at the same time it begets in the heart of the speaker or writer the assurance that he has honorably exercised his privileges and his obligations as a free citizen in the commonwealth of the English language."[13] However, Krapp's approach was not one of *anything goes*. He wrote that "If correctness and conformity to appointed rules are discarded as final tests of good English, anarchy is not the only remaining alternative. . . . Whatever is is not necessarily good in the English language."[14]

What does it mean for one to exercise such privileges and obligations? To do so entails an engagement with language. Good English and a sound personal ethic of language involve not just reacting to standards of correctness but being interested enough in language to try to use it effectively, to feel that there is some value in using it effectively, and to inquire into the nature of effectiveness. Linguistics provides a vocabulary and methodology to help people make personal grammatical judgments. As Krapp emphasizes, good grammar requires a principled engagement with usage, not slavish adherence to authority. Linguistic study provides a way to reflect on one's usage and the usage of others rather than merely reacting. For example, I maintain the distinction between *infer* and *imply* because this seems like a distinction worth making. I use *ain't* only for effect (and very rarely). And I never use perfectives like *had went*. Not using *ain't* and *had went* is a social matter of avoiding stigmatized usages. However, I freely and happily split infinitives (as in *to boldly go*). I say *who* rather than *whom* and I end sentences with prepositions (as in *Who did you give it to?*). And I often use *hopefully* to modify an entire sentence (as in *Hopefully, the game will be over soon*). All of this usage is second nature to me, but I can reflect on it, explain it, and defend it, drawing on social and linguistic considerations.

Linguistics has an important role in the analytic toolbox of anyone who needs to make grammatical choices or wishes to understand language. To illustrate, let's look at some examples of how knowledge of linguistics can help to clarify usage issues. First, consider the word *hopefully*, a usage that has exercised traditionalists for about half a century. Many prescriptivists object to using this adverb to modify a sentence. Often the objections are simply ad hominem attacks on those who employ the usage. Responding to a 1971 survey, members of the *American Heritage Dictionary* usage panel referred to *hopefully* as a "bastard adverb," "slack-jawed, common, sleazy," and "popular jargon at its most illiterate level."[15] Putting the ad hominem aside, what are the grammatical or social issues? The problem is not one of avoiding usage that the majority of the educated public finds to be stigmatized. *Hopefully* is widely accepted by educated speakers and grammarians (unlike, for example, *had went* or *ain't*). The problem is also not a matter of clarity. *Hopefully, the game will be over soon* is just as clear as *I hope that the game will be over soon* and equally succinct in terms of syllables. An issue of clarity does arise in sentences with animate subjects when the adverb occurs between the subject and predicate, as in *The children hopefully will apply to college one day*. But this is a stylistic issue that applies to adverbs like *frankly* and *happily* as well. There is no ambiguity when the adverb begins a sentence with an inanimate subject.

If social stigma and clarity are not issues, what remain are possible arguments from tradition and logic. The argument from tradition is commonly reflected in concerns about meaning and etymology. Objections to *hopefully* sometimes have to do with the apparent meaning of *hopefully* as "full of hope." However, this argument is unconvincing because it is so selectively applied. Should we object to the use of *print* to refer to the action of a computer printer rather than a printing press? Or should we object to the use of *awful* in its contemporary meaning, insisting instead that we treat it as meaning "full of awe"? Meanings change, so the objection to *hopefully* cannot just be that it doesn't reflect its etymology.

The other common objection to *hopefully* concerns the logic of the construction. Does the use of *hopefully* as a sentence modifier create a problem of logic for the language as a whole?[16] Prescriptivists may suggest that sentence-initial *hopefully* destroys the parallelism with *hopelessly*. But this argument fails once we recognize that *hopelessly* is not restricted to meaning that subjects of sentences are without hope. Consider examples like *The game was hopelessly tied* or *The negotiations were hopelessly deadlocked*. A look at the adjectival uses of *hopeful* and *hopeless* reinforces the point that their meanings are not restricted to animate nouns. We talk about *a hopeful suitor* or *a hopeful applicant*, but we can also talk about *a hopeful look, a hopeful inquiry,* or *a hopeful letter*. Similarly we also talk about *a hopeless suitor, a hopeless cause,* or *a hopeless attempt*. And *a hopeless writer* is not one who is without hope, but rather one who is hopelessly bad. So on balance, there is little to object to in the use of *hopefully*. The perspective of linguistics—an understanding of change together with analysis of the uses of a word—provides a basis for individual judgments about usage.

A second, briefer, example comes from the testing industry. In 2003, the Educational Testing Service adjusted the scores of 450,000 students who took the October 2002 PSAT. Students had been asked to identify the grammatical error, if any, in the sentence: "Toni Morrison's genius enables her to create novels that arise from and express the injustices African Americans have endured." The testing service initially scored the item as having no error. However a Maryland teacher, Kevin Keegan, challenged that answer. He argued that the pronoun *her* had no antecedent because the possessive was an adjective rather than a noun phrase. Keegan noted that some grammar books assert the incorrectness of such constructions and, after much correspondence, persuaded ETS that the question was ambiguous enough that more than one answer should be accepted.[17]

From a testing (and a public relations) perspective, this is perhaps a fair result since, as Keegan noted, some handbooks assert a rule.[18] Grammatically, however, this is the wrong result and an analysis better informed linguistically could have clarified this point. As the testing service's experts and many commentators observed, the construction is completely clear and widely used. It parallels sentences like *Mother's experience enables her to create fine works of art* or *John's children admire him*. In addition, however, the basis of the supposed rule—that *Toni Morrison's* is an adjective—is flawed. Possessives are historically nouns (or noun phrases) and pattern much differently from true adjectives. For example, possessives may be modified by articles, adjectives, and prepositional phrases themselves, as in *the former director's proposal* or *the queen of England's crown*. That possessives are nominal is particularly evident if we look at the situation in which pronouns attempt to refer to real adjectives. So consider the contrast between *Lincoln's descendants often look like him* and *Lincolnesque people often look like him*. In the first example, with a possessive noun, reference is obvious and clear; the second example, with a real adjective, is ungrammatical. In terms of grammar, ETS was right all along. The handbooks that assert this nonrule are simply wrong. A more linguistically informed approach by handbook writers, or by teachers using handbooks, might have made this nonerror a nonissue.

As third example, let's return to the choice between pronouns *who* and *whom* mentioned in chapter 1. There we looked at the pronoun use in the sentence *You will work with a colleague (who—whom) you will meet later.* Traditional grammar says that *who* is the nominative pronoun and *whom* is an objective pronoun. For traditionalists, this means that *who* should be used for subjects (and complements of linking verbs like *be*) while *whom* should be used for objects of verbs and prepositions. Traditional grammar often treats only *whom* as correct in the example above, since the relative pronoun functions as the logical object of the verb *meet.* The sentence *You will work with a colleague who you will meet later* would be bad grammar.

Prescriptivists sometimes characterize such examples as errors by otherwise educated speakers, inappropriately tolerated by a lax society. Theater critic and prescriptive grammarian John Simon, for example, sees the potential loss of *whom* as resulting in potential "[a]mbiguity and confusion." He asks "why should we lose this useful distinction? Just because a million or ten million or a billion people less educated than we are cannot master the difference?"[19] For Simon, usage is beside the point. William Zinsser's question *Who am I writing for?* is bad grammar, as are the sentences *Who have we here? Who do we have to thank for this? Who are you looking for? Who do you trust? Who do you love? It's not what you know but who,* and *No one knows who to trust anymore,* all of which are typical of the usage of the educated. "Who Do You Love?" was the title of a 1970 song by Bo Diddley and the lyric appears in many other songs as well. And a television quiz show called *Who Do You Trust?* aired from 1956 to 1963.[20] Such examples suggest that the use of objective case *who* is quite natural.

In fact, the use of *whom* is rather limited. For many speakers and writers, it is natural only after prepositions (as in *Who did what to whom?*) and in set phrases (such as *To whom it may concern*). Reference books recognize this. Robert Burchfield's 1996 *The New Fowler's Modern English Usage* lists such forms as *Who are you writing for?* under "legitimate uses" in modern English. The editors of the 2001 *New Oxford American Dictionary* write in that volume that the use of *whom* "has retreated steadily and is now restricted to formal contexts." And the 2003 edition of *Merriam-Webster's Collegiate Dictionary* notes that *whom* is often considered "stilted."[21] While dictionaries and usage guides vary in the way they state it, they tend to recognize the objective *who* as normal practice in educated English. Another indication of the status of *whom* is its use in humorous dialogue such comedian Lily Tomlin's tag line "Is this the party to whom I am speaking?" The silliness of the question is reinforced by the formality of the speech.[22]

Linguists have also documented the usage of *who* and *whom* in various ways. It was a topic of Sterling Leonard's 1932 *Current English Usage*, which surveyed over 200 individuals on disputed usage. A majority of Leonard's judges found the objective case *who* acceptable. Leonard wrote that "Apparently this is acceptable in informal spoken English, but most authorities do not approve it for written English."[23] Charles Fries, in his 1940 *American English Grammar*, confirmed the use of *who* in a different way. Fries compiled and analyzed a corpus of 3,000 letters or portions of letters written to the federal government in the 1920s and independently cataloged social status and grammatical usage. Looking at the actual use in three social levels, Fries showed that *Who did you apply to?* was typical usage for all social levels while *Whom did you apply to?* was not.

Descriptivists thus see the widespread use of *who* by educated speakers as evidence of grammar change. But this is unlikely to sway the most entrenched prescriptivists. For them, the fact that educated speakers and writers use objective *who* is merely evidence of the widespread nature of the error. It may not be possible to convince a prescriptivist who has this view, but linguistic analysis can at least advance the discussion beyond a dispute between the assertions that "change is inevitable" and "change confuses important distinctions." Linguistics advances the discussion by pointing out that there are two rules underlying the majority usage of *who* and *whom*. The first rule is a simple structural one: *whom* is used for the object of prepositions; *who* is used elsewhere. This rule is simpler than the traditional one in that it relies on the structural notion "object of a preposition" rather than "nominative case versus objective case." The second rule is the stylistic rule that in more formal language *whom* is often used when the pronoun functions as an object. This rule requires an understanding of the distinction between formal contexts and informal ones and it also draws on the nominative versus objective case distinction. The two rules underlying actual usage are more complex than the traditional characterization of *who* and *whom*, but they make it clear that examples such as *Who have we here?* and *Who do you trust?* are not errors but rather are the product of rules of colloquial English.[24]

These three examples demonstrate ways that descriptive grammar tries to make sense of the facts of language use. Descriptivism makes it clear that the choice between prescribed forms and other variants is social and rhetorical. Descriptive grammar also challenges the idea that the prescriptive rules are the *only* source of linguistic regularity and logic. But pointing out that Standard English is based on usage rather than tradition does not signal an intention to subvert Standard English.

The English Language Arts and Beyond

In the twentieth century, the study of usage became increasingly established as a scholarly discipline. The period from 1880 to 1925 saw the emergence of such societies as the Modern Language Association, the National Council of Teachers of English, the American Dialect Society, and the Linguistic Society of America. As disciplines developed, scholars found venues for the examination of issues of usage and correctness. As linguist Albert Marckwardt has noted, English usage was sometimes the subject of Modern Language Association presidential addresses that attempted to reconcile the new perspectives with traditional value judgments and with practical teaching concerns. The first half of the twentieth century also saw a great deal of work by scholars critical of traditional grammar. Such work, of course, engendered responses both from scholarly quarters and from the literary public.[25]

Within the education community, issues of grammar were a focus of the 1952 report *The English Language Arts*, published by the National Council of Teachers of English. This report included a chapter titled "The Modern View of Grammar and Linguistics," which explained that language change was both ongoing and expected. It also endorsed the ideas that correctness is based on spoken usage and that usage is relative to context. Traditionalists saw these ideas as advocating a society in which all usage was equally appropriate in any context and as damaging to standards both in language and in culture more generally. Columbia University historian Jacques Barzun, perhaps the most influential humanist of the 1950s, condemned *The English Language Arts* as "one long demonstration of the authors' unfitness to tell anybody anything about English."[26] Barzun went on to characterize the "one great maxim" of the report as the assertion that change is not corruption but improvement. However, Barzun's critique misread the council's report. The report advocated that "the teaching of correctness in school and college courses must shift from the laying down of negative rules to the development of positive insights."[27] In actuality, more than half of the chapter on linguistics was devoted to the value of and teaching of grammar.

The misreading of the intent of *The English Language Arts* report points to a broader misconstrual of the doctrine of usage as anything-goes relativism. What the council's report emphasized was the need to modernize the teaching of English usage. The goal was a program in which students might become aware that effective language was a matter of appropriateness, rather than assuming that the good language resulted from following a single, fixed set of rules. The report's point was that standards should be derived from the facts of usage rather than from a romanticized notion of correctness based on traditional rules and vague definitions. It was not that Standard English should be swept away under the motto that one usage is as good as another.

The commitment to Standard English was certainly apparent in the textbooks of the descriptive linguists. For example, Charles Fries, in his 1940 book *American English Grammar*, distinguished between Vulgar and Standard English, adding that "the obligation resting upon the schools is to teach the knowledge of and the ability to use the 'standard' English of the United States."[28] And Robert Pooley, in his *Teaching English Usage*, identified "errors to be attacked for elimination" in the elementary grades and junior and senior high schools. For senior high school, he cited such forms as *I am as tall as him, He has drank all the water, It don't matter when we go, Did you see John and I?* and *Where is the party at?* among others. Pooley also provided a list of "forms to receive no class instruction," suggesting that students who inquire be told that they are colloquial but not formal. These included *They invited my guests and myself, Athletics are stressed in most schools, He said that New York was a large city, I only have fifty cents, He tried to thoroughly understand the problem, What was the reason for Henry objecting?* and *Who is it for?*[29] Such recommendations as Pooley's acknowledged changing usage as acceptable but certainly did not claim that all usage is equal or that anything goes.

Contrast this approach with that of a traditionalist like Barzun. Barzun treated language prescriptions as a means of encouraging high standards and clear thinking. He saw usage "*as a whole* more bad than good, . . . signs that the spirit and sense of the language is at a low ebb."[30] While Barzun acknowledged that language must change, he saw change as something to be resisted, since uncertainty of expression was an inevitable result. Barzun's linguistic conservatism was both symbolic (representing a commitment to standards) and functional (preserving distinctions and precision). For linguists like Fries, however, prescriptivism was a lowering of standards because it separated the standards from the behavior of educated speakers and relegated the teaching of language to dogmatism and prejudice. Change, being inevitable, was something to be studied, and language variation was a tool to broaden speakers' stylistic repertoires and guide them toward a standard. It was inevitable that these two perspectives would clash.[31]

Conflicts over grammar ideology in the 1950s also reflected a broader gulf between the humanities and the sciences that arose as science challenged the humanities as a means of discovering truth.[32] Many traditionalists objected to the application of the scientific method to language as irrelevant or misguided. This view was elaborated most forcefully by Barzun, who saw the humanities disciplines, and especially linguistics, as going astray in pursuit of the prestige of science and in mimicking the method of science. In a 1957 essay, he wrote that "'scientific' opponents of grammar and usage . . . in their crusade were using the fallacious arguments of natural growth, irresistible change, and democratic freedom" and that their aim "was to encourage rather than restrain the anarchy which is the unavoidable first fact in the use of language."[33] The humanistic tradition represented by Barzun saw bad faith, bad sense, and an impulse to emulate science as resulting in a crusade against important linguistic distinctions.

Barzun portrayed Fries as "the theorist who engineered the demise of grammar in American schools." Fries, Barzun claimed, wanted a "classless speech corresponding to the usage of the most numerous" and promoted approaches to language arts in which ten-year-olds were asked to follow the same method as linguistics researchers.[34] However, the claim that descriptive linguistics encouraged anarchy does not mesh with what linguists like Krapp, Pooley, Fries, and others were actually saying. Fries acknowledged the responsibility of schools to teach Standard English at the same time advocating that the definition of the standard be flexible and recognize actual usage. And Barzun's assertion that linguists wanted schoolroom language arts instruction to parallel linguistics research was also a rhetorical exaggeration. The suggestions in Fries's *American English Grammar* aimed at a "workable program in English" for the schools that would be based on agreement about the kind of English the schools must teach, accurate information about Standard English usage, and ways of encouraging students to observe actual usage.[35] Nevertheless, Barzun's positioning of linguistics, recycled by many other commentators, has become received wisdom for many.[36]

At the same time that linguists and English educators were attempting to elaborate the role of usage in grammar, a key debate over usage occurred with the publication of *Webster's New Third International*

Dictionary in 1961. Under the leadership of Philip Gove, who had become editor in 1951, *Webster's Third* continued the tradition of the *Oxford English Dictionary* (1889–1928) and of the 1934 *Webster's Second*—it relied on citations of usage to establish current meaning. Gove, however, made several significant changes in the way that the doctrine of usage was implemented in the dictionary. He placed less reliance on usage labels to illustrate the status of words and relied instead on usage notes and illustrative quotations to imply appropriate use. Herbert Morton, in *The Story of Webster's Third*, reports that Gove reserved the label *nonstandard* for clear deviations from educated usage (rather than disputed ones), he eliminated the label *colloquial* (which dictionary users had sometimes taken to signal strictly regional or local usages), and he used the label *slang* only sparingly.[37]

The result was a dictionary that embroiled the Merriam Company in the ongoing traditionalist versus relativist debate. Reaction to the dictionary was intense, with news stories of the time focused on the inclusion of *ain't*, on the use of illustrative quotes from popular writers like Mickey Spillane and speakers like Bob Hope, and on the elimination of 150,000 entries from *Webster's Second*. The controversy was exacerbated by media inaccuracies and by weak public relations on the part of the Merriam Company, but to a large extent the issues raised were those that had been developing throughout the century—the fictive nature of grammatical correctness, on the one hand, and the fear of linguistic anarchy, on the other.

The dictionary became a cause célèbre for the traditionalists of the time—Barzun, Garry Wills, Dwight Macdonald, Wilson Follett, and Sheridan Baker. News stories and editorials talked about "Permissiveness Gone Mad," "Madness in their Method," and "Sabotage in Springfield," and asserted "New Dictionary Cheap, Corrupt." Playing on the words *third international*, one reviewer criticized a "bolshevik spirit" that was willing to abandon standards. Gove himself was vilified and, like Fries before him, was compared with Alfred Kinsey as an advocate of social permissiveness.[38]

Conservatives and Progressives

In the period after the furor surrounding *Webster's Third*, the 1960s received special attention as a locus of grammatical decay in books like Edwin Newman's *Strictly Speaking* (1974) and *A Civil Tongue* (1975), and John Simon's *Paradigms Lost* (1980). Newman, for example, saw a "decline in language" stemming from the influence of television together with "the great and rapid change this country went through in the 1960s" in such areas as civil rights, environmental activism, and youth culture.[39] John Simon, in *Paradigms Lost*, singled out four groups to blame for the decline of language—feminists, "Black Power" advocates, academics, and the media. He saw the decline of language as reflected in egalitarianism and permissiveness about usage change, asserting that "nearly every change in language" begins with some form of "illiteracy that is seldom, if ever, inventive." Slowing change, he says, would "presuppose a group of speakers who (a) knew better and (b) were not afraid of correcting an ignoramus." But he sees this as unlikely in an egalitarian and permissive society.[40]

At times, Simon treats his conservatism in terms of a supposed ethical obligation to preserve grammatical tradition and distinctions, echoing Barzun.[41] Elsewhere, however, he portrays standard versus nonstandard English as a matter of language versus nonlanguage. Discussing Black English, Simon writes that patterns of invariant *be* (such as *He be late*) "may indeed be comprehensible but they go against all accepted classical and modern grammars and are the product not of a language with roots in history but of ignorance of how language works."[42] Again discussing Black English, Simon asks, "Why should we consider some, usually poorly educated, subculture's notion of the relationship between sound and meaning? And how could a grammar—any grammar—possibly describe that relationship? Grammar exists mainly to clarify meaning."[43]

The answer to Simon's first question is that we should consider dialect variation because it is part of the heritage of English (like East Midlands and Northumbrian) and because a better understanding of variation is likely to aid education in the language arts. The answer to his second question is that grammar describes any regular and systematic sound-meaning relation. Simon's key themes—his dividing usage into language versus nonlanguage and his equating good grammar with good morals and high standards—form the basis for the most divisive version of prescriptivism, which sets language users against one another.[44]

Arguments like Simon's are typically characterized as politically conservative because of their appeal to tradition, but there is also a version of the argument for traditional grammar based in the rhetoric of social mobility. As Geoffrey Nunberg has noted, "For most of its history the English grammatical tradition has been associated with classical liberalism" and eighteenth-century intellectuals like Johnson, Swift, and others saw in grammar a cultural authority independent of aristocracy.[45] Today's progressive argument is that fluency in a standard language is a necessary skill in a modern industrial society—for career entry and later advancement. This is the view articulated in E. D. Hirsch's book *Cultural Literacy*, and mentioned earlier in chapter 1. For Hirsch, traditional grammar and standard language are a social tool rather than a cultural virtue. Standardization of language is not a matter of individual morality. Rather, it is a matter of an individual's practical needs and of a society's administrative and political ones. The assumption is that efficient, widespread communication requires a common standard language. Employers, teachers, and others in authority expect this type of language, the argument goes, and those who fail to learn it will do worse in the job market. The idea that facility with standard language is economically empowering is also apparent in articles like Joseph Williams's 1977 "Linguistic Responsibility." Williams calls for university English departments to pay more attention to the types of writing used in the business world, noting that "we know almost nothing about the way individuals judge the quality of writing in places like Sears and General Motors and Quaker Oats."[46]

Progressives who take this view may be just as opposed to innovation as conservatives, feeling that a fixed common standard is necessary to put everyone on an even playing field. This view of correct language as a social skill has some inconsistencies, however. Language is certainly used to sort and evaluate individuals in the marketplace, but language skills are not an obvious predictor of economic success or social mobility: many people with good language skills remain economically or socially marginal, and many people are economically successful despite nonstandard language. Nevertheless, the idea that traditional grammar is a tool for self-improvement remains as robust today as it was when writer Sherwin Cody asked the American public "Do you make these mistakes in English?"

The Necessity for Grammar

Traditional grammar is advocated by both conservatives (arguing from social correctness) and progressives (arguing from social necessity). It is not surprising, then, that proponents of the doctrine of usage have sometimes been viewed as permissive. Popular writer Robert Claiborne, for example, attributes bad writing by students in part to "muddled-headed experts on linguistics" who lay the foundation for an educational philosophy of permissiveness by asserting that "there is no such thing as good and bad in language."[47] The opinion-leader media seems to find permissive linguists a comfortable symbol of the causes of the decline of language. John Updike, in a 1996 review of Robert Burchfield's *The New Fowler's Modern English Usage*, talked about linguistics as "a slippery field for the exercise of moral indignation" and characterized Burchfield as "lenient." Discussing *ain't*, Updike saw Burchfield as "pleading the outcast's case like a left-wing lawyer."[48] Updike concluded by saying that "some discipline should be maintained and some syntactic civility should bind us together." Moral indignation, discipline, and civility come together in Updike's characterization of tradition. Lenience, liberalism, and slipperiness prevail in his characterization of linguistics.

Updike's comments highlight an interesting contrast between traditionalist critics of the nineteenth century and those of the twentieth century. Nineteenth-century writers often saw correctness as a question of the character of speakers, with the supposed barbarisms of the lower classes and immigrants reflecting their morals. As Edward Finegan has noted, in the twentieth century, the narrative about grammar shifted from focusing on the supposed low morals of nonstandard speakers to focusing on the social and economic disadvantage of incorrect speech.[49] The focus of moralizing has shifted as well, to a scorn for the permissiveness of those blamed for allowing bad grammar to persist—linguists, dictionary makers, and educators.

Novelist David Foster Wallace, writing in 2001, provides a recent example of the traditionalist concern. Wallace sees descriptive linguistics as reflecting an outdated faith in observation. He remarks that "Structural linguists like Gove and Fries are not, finally, scientists but census-takers who happen to misconstrue the importance of 'observed facts.'"[50] In his view, the value-free descriptivism attributed to Gove and Fries undercuts semantically useful distinctions that facilitate communication (such as the distinction between *infer* and *imply*).

Wallace argues that since all interpretation is biased, it is naive to believe that accurate description of usage is possible.[51] But he misses the point in his critique of observation. The fact that all observations have some bias does not mean we should accept idiosyncratic prescriptions that are at odds with widespread educated usage. Aside from his dismissal of the idea of neutral and unbiased observation, Wallace presents a discussion of usage that in some ways converges with that developed by Krapp in the early part of the twentieth century. Norms, Wallace argues, are important because they "help us evaluate our actions (including utterances) according to what we as a community have decided our real interests and purposes are." Wallace concedes that many prescriptive rules are arbitrary and illogical. But he argues that many prescriptive rules are consequential for the same reason that dexterity in colloquial English is important—to be accepted by one's peers.

As Wallace puts it: "'Correct' English usage is, as a practical matter, a function of whom you're talking to, and how you want that person to respond—not just to your utterance but to *you*. In other words, a large part of the agenda of any communication is rhetorical and depends on what some rhet-scholars call 'audience' or 'Discourse Community.'" Here, of course, Wallace acknowledges the main point of descriptivism—that usage is relative—and finds himself recognizing that grammar is simultaneously socially important, relative, and arbitrary.

More broadly, however, Wallace views grammar ideology as involving a political opposition between "tradition and egalitarianism." Mediating this opposition requires what he calls a democratic spirit, combining rigor and humility. Wallace sees the middle ground between tradition and egalitarianism as found in a helpful technocratic approach, similar to good judicial decision making. Such approaches he sees as achieving credibility not from "irony or scorn or caustic wit," but from being knowledgeable, passionate, fair, and reasonable. In this way, the technocrat becomes "a thoroughly modern and palpable image of Authority, . . . immune to the charges of elitism/classism that have hobbled traditional Prescriptivism." Though his criticism of linguistics is off the mark, this aspect of Wallace's position is not unreasonable and differs markedly from the views of many conservative traditionalists. Grammar serves rhetoric, not culture, and is thus technical and not moral.

Wallace's essay highlights an important point. While critics like Barzun and others see language as a civic issue too important to be left to scientific experts like linguists, Wallace emphasizes instead that grammar is a technical subject requiring a practical judicial temperament rather than a fundamentalist one. What is crucial is that any discussion of civic values requires technical expertise. If usage is too important to be left to scientific experts, it is also too important to be left to the idiosyncrasies of self-appointed experts. And if usage requires independent judgment, that judgment requires a certain amount of informed technical knowledge. Is there a role for linguistics in all of this?

Certainly. Linguistics defines analytic tools and methods that check the vagueness and inaccuracy of traditional grammar and the idiosyncrasies of literary and journalistic authorities. And it emphasizes the actual facts of usage, language history, and dialect diversity, rather than myths and misconceptions.

Does this mean that traditional grammatical notions should be removed from the curriculum or replaced by methods in structural linguistics or by the most cutting-edge version of linguistic theory? No. It is necessary for educated persons to be familiar with the canon of traditional grammar, just as it is important for them to be familiar with mythology, manifest destiny, or isolationism. But it is even more important for educated persons to understand the limits of traditional grammar and the social function of Standard English. Linguistic study should ground students in the history of English, from which it is evident that dialects are regular and rule-governed. And linguistic study should make it apparent—as more sophisticated prescriptivists like Wallace concede—that correctness is a convention placed on dialects by society and history. Understanding all of this allows us to recognize the ways in which standards develop and the fact that they grow and change. So teaching linguistics in order to understand grammar is like teaching government, economics, and history as a way of helping students to understand current events and public policy. It is part of the realism and intellectual content we expect in education.

David Foster Wallace, like George Phillip Krapp, sees good grammar as an informed engagement with usage rather than mere acceptance of authority. He demonstrates this, for example, when he talks about a favorite colloquial phrase of his: "Where's it at?" Wallace notes that the preposition *at* serves the useful function of permitting the contraction ("Where's it?" does not conform to the rules of English contraction). His point draws implicitly on the analytic tools of linguistics to help him reflect on usage and negotiate choices. The preposition *at* is helpful because something is required at the end of the sentence by the rules of contraction. But no one would call David Foster Wallace permissive.

The position developed in this chapter is not so different from that developed by Krapp at the turn of the last century—and reiterated by linguists like Pooley, Fries, and others. We need to know Standard English, but we need to know it critically, analytically, and in the context of language history. We also need to understand the regularity of nonstandard variants. If we approach good and bad grammar in this way, the study of language will be a liberating factor—not merely freeing learners from socially stigmatized usage by replacing that usage with new linguistic manners, but educating people in what language and linguistic manners are all about.

Four Bad Words

In Walter Mosley's novel *Always Outnumbered, Always Outgunned*, ex-convict Socrates Fortlow has the following exchange with Darryl, a boy he has befriended:

> "Bet you didn't know you could cook, huh?" Socrates asked.
> "Shit no!" the boy said.
> "Keep your mouth clean, lil brother. You keep it clean an'
> then they know you mean business when you say sumpin'
> strong."[1]

What is noteworthy about the exchange is that it attempts to provide a rationale for why one would sometimes keep a clean mouth and sometimes curse. Contrast this with the view presented in an advertisement for Turner Classic Movies in which comedian Bill Cosby remarks that there is "too much cursing" by today's movie tough guys but "no cursing" in Turner Classic Movies. These two views encapsulate one of the key issues in the long history of cursing—the relativity of so-called four-letter words. For Socrates Fortlow, cursing is a matter of situation and context; for Turner Classic Movies, it is an absolute—a matter of too much cursing versus none.

In this chapter we explore the relativity of vocabulary choice. The words one uses—proper or improper, coarse or polite—establish the tone of one's language. Attitudes toward cursing also demonstrate the evolving social nature of propriety. Cursing is, however, only one type of contested usage, and the question of relativity applies equally to slang usage and to so-called politically correct usage. The three categories—offensive language, slang, and political correctness—turn out to have some commonality, most notably in the way they create usage problems for conventional speakers by making vocabulary choice an issue of group identity. The broader goal of this chapter is thus to both explore how some words are bad and to reinforce the view that effective usage is less a matter of permanent fixed traditions than it is a matter of flexible and contextual conventions.

Cursing in the Media and the Arts

Worries about cursing in popular entertainment are not particularly new and have arisen in theater, radio, comedy, publishing, film, and television. George Bernard Shaw's *Pygmalion*, for example, sparked a controversy during the 1914 theater season, when the actress playing Eliza Doolittle used the expression "Not bloody likely!" Almost fifty years later, the language of Edward Albee's 1962 play *Who's Afraid of Virginia Woolf?* was considered so shocking that the Trustees of Columbia University rejected the vote of its Pulitzer Prize committee. And today, network television dramas receive attention for their linguistic frankness: writers and network standards departments contest scripts, citizens groups organize protests, and entrepreneurs even market 'profanity filters' for televisions and DVDs.

One of the concerns consistently raised about graphic language on television and in the movies is the influence that such language will have on youth. Again, this is nothing new. Under the British Hicklin doctrine of 1868, for example, the test for obscenity was whether material had a tendency to "deprave and corrupt those whose minds are open to such immoral influences." The Hicklin test left the freedom of expression of writers to the real or imagined effects that a work might have on the most impressionable. In the 1933 case *The US v. one book called 'Ulysses,'* American judge John Woolsey argued instead that obscenity was the capacity to arouse the average person (in that case the judge and some consulting readers) and that under this definition *Ulysses* was not obscene. Woolsey wrote that "the words which are criticized as dirty ... are known to almost all men and, I venture, to many women."[2] While the publishing business has often been in the forefront of efforts to promote realism in language and verisimilitude in the portrayal of life, it is nevertheless still possible today to evoke a literary reaction on the basis of language alone. Thus when James Kelman's *How Late It Was, How Late* received the 1994 Booker Prize, some critics objected to giving the award to a novel that used the word *fuck* over 4,000 times.[3] Others, however, including Kelman himself, argued that the novel represented the language of working-class Scots whose true voices had often been assimilated to middle-class norms of language.

Because of their broader audience, the motion picture and television industries had long maintained standards somewhat more restrictive than those of the theater or the publishing industry. The 1934 Hollywood Production Code drawn up by Will Hays and administered by Joseph Breen excluded references to drug trafficking, miscegenation, perversion, and revenge (reference to biblical vengeance, however, was permitted). Films such as *Gone With the Wind* (1939), *The Naked and the Dead* (1948), and *From Here to Eternity* (1951) were once considered provocative for their language, though the word *shit* was not used in an American film until 1961 (in the film *The Connection*). In his *Cursing in America*, Timothy Jay finds a tripling of the average amount of cursing in films from the 1960s to the 1970s; Jay's sample included seventy-seven films ranging from *A Raisin in the Sun* (1961, with 7 instances) to *Lethal Weapon* (1987, with 149).[4]

Network television, of course, competes for audiences with the film industry and now with the video, cable, and Internet industries. The appearance of Stephen Bochco's ABC series *NYPD Blue*, whose 1993 premiere carried the disclaimer "This police drama contains adult language," renewed discussion of broadcast standards. Journalist Tad Friend noted the tension between competing for an audience and respecting advertisers' sensitivities in his recounting of a discussion between writer-producer Steven Bochco and ABC executive Alan Braverman over the use of the word *bullshit*. Responding to Braverman's concerns about regulators' and advertisers' reactions, Bochco said that "the audience that watched my 'N.Y.P.D. Blue' and hears 'scumbag,' 'douche bag' and 'prick' isn't going to reach for the remote if it hears 'bullshit.' When you are surrounded by junkies and whores in a jailhouse bullpen, the word just goes by naturally."[5]

Another example concerns the scene in the 2001 season finale of the NBC drama *The West Wing* in which the president's secretary refers to the president's father as a *prick*. NBC executive Alan Wurtzel permitted the expression because the character was making a serious statement. Wurtzel explained, "I know who this character is, and the very fact that you would never think she would say that is significant—all of a sudden there is a resonance with respect to that dialogue."[6] While television drama employs coarse language for verisimilitude and dramatic emphasis, it also occurs in less serious programming. It is not uncommon to hear such expressions as "You backstabbing son-of-a-bitch" in situation comedies that are not otherwise noted for realism, and even cartoons employ coarse language for comedy rather than realism.[7] As the line between network television, cable, and feature film blurs, we can expect that networks will continue to move in the direction of cable and film standards. The *New York Times* reports that "Broadcast television is under siege by smaller cable competitors that are winning audiences while pushing adult content. In that climate, broadcast is fighting the perception that its tastes are lagging behind those of a media-saturated culture whose mores have grown more permissive."[8]

The public airwaves are regulated by the Federal Communications Commission (FCC) and that group sometimes makes its influence felt. In 2004, after singer Janet Jackson's breast was exposed during the Super Bowl halftime performance, the FCC received a new wave of complaints about indecency in the broadcast media. The commission toughened its rules on what can be considered indecent on the public airwaves and increased its fines. While the FCC changes were seen as an overreaction by many broadcasters, they changed some practices. Radio personality Howard Stern, for example, was fired by Clear Channel Communications after violating its zero-tolerance policy with interview questions about anal sex and penis size. Clear Channel had been assessed a $495,000 fine for the broadcast by the FCC.

The American press also, for the most part, eschews vulgar language. In March of 1998, CNN reporter Bernard Shaw, quoting from Howard Kurtz's book *Spin Cycle*, said the word *fuck* on the air, and he later apologized to any viewers who were offended. And during the 1998 Clinton-Lewinsky media coverage, many newspapers steered clear of most explicit language in quotes from the Starr Report. The public language of politicians is similarly elevated. Presidents Jimmy Carter, George H. Bush, and George W. Bush all received media attention in campaigns when they used the word "ass": "I'll whip his ass" (Carter, referring to Edward Kennedy), "I kicked a little ass last night" (George H. Bush, referring to his debate with Geraldine Ferraro), and "major-league asshole" (George W. Bush referring to reporter Adam Clymer). Of course, while the public standard is for propriety, the private tapes of Presidents Lyndon Johnson and Richard Nixon suggest that the use of expletives is not uncommon for presidents.

What is apparent is that different media and different types of communication have different levels of tolerance for offensive language. While some may believe that offensive language is at an all-time high and rising, concerns about offensive language are not new, as we will see below. First, however, we should explore just what is meant by offensive language, why some people object to it, and why some see it as important to defend.

Offensive Language

Offensive language falls into several categories: epithets, profanity, vulgarity, and obscenity. Epithets are various types of slurs, such as *wop, raghead, bitch,* or *fag.* Usually these refer to race, ethnicity, gender, or sexuality, but they may also refer to appearance, disabilities, or other characteristics (as for example with the epithets *midget, gimp,* and *retard*). Profanity is religious cursing. This ranges from a mild *hell* or *damn* to a more emphatic *goddamn,* and it involves the coarse use of what is taken to be sacred. Vulgarity and obscenity refer to words or expressions which characterize sex-differentiating anatomy or sexual and excretory functions in a crude way, such as *shit* and *fuck,* with the distinction between vulgarity and obscenity being primarily a matter of degree and prurience. The categories of epithet, profanity, and vulgarity/obscenity are not exclusive and compound expressions may belong to more than one category, as in the exclamation *God fucking dammit.*

The labeling of various types of offensive language only takes us so far. We need to ask what is bad about bad language. What makes language offensive? As noted earlier, objections to obscenity and vulgarity in public language often focus on the idea of protecting some listeners from bad language. Stereotypically it is women and children who are assumed to need such protection. This stereotype was evident in the 1999 conviction of the so-called cursing canoeist, a man fined $100 for violating an 1897 Michigan law that banned swearing in front of women and children.[9] The rationale for men not cursing in the presence of women is apparently a nineteenth-century version of decorum.[10] The rationale for not swearing when children are present is the impressionable minds argument noted earlier in the discussion of *Ulysses.* This argument, in its essentials, is that hearing offensive language will lead children to repeat it in the wrong situations and expose them to ideas that they shouldn't be exposed to. Paul Boyer notes that the antivice societies of the nineteenth century arose in part from a concern that the young people migrating to urban areas were separated from community influences, such as family and church, that fostered a common moral code. Among the bad urban influences cited was coarse language.[11]

Even today language objections are a basis for many book censorship efforts in schools. The American Library Association Office for Intellectual Freedom reports that between 1990 and 2000, there were 6,364 challenges to books recorded by their office: of these, 1,427 were for material considered to use offensive language.[12] Protecting children from offensive language also played a role in the FCC's filing a complaint against the Pacifica Foundation in 1978 for broadcasting George Carlin's monologue "Filthy Words." The FCC found that since the monologue depicted sexual and excretory activities in an offensive manner and that since it was broadcast in the early afternoon when children were likely to be in the listening audience, the broadcast was prohibited by legislation which forbids the use of "any obscene, indecent, or profane language by means of radio communications."[13]

A related objection has to do with the idea that offensive language fosters disrespect for authority. This is most apparent in the case of religious authority, where profanity is sometimes thought to subvert religion fairly directly. The objection also applies to disruption of civic process (classroom activity, court arguments, public meetings) or interpersonal communication. The concern is that the angry tone of vulgarity adds to whatever other civic or interpersonal problems need to be addressed. In their 1975 article "Four-Letter Threats to Authority," David Paletz and William Harris note that obscenity is sometimes considered a departure from rational discourse. Examining the use of four-letter words in college newspapers, they see opposition to offensive language as involving three factors: subversiveness, cultural-linguistic "poverty," and shock-value. Paletz and Harris add that "On the most elementary level the public use of four-letter words disrupts the aura in which authority is maintained. It makes for public insecurity in that it challenges the solemnity and respectability associated with authority or its symbols."[14]

Another objection is that some vulgar language can lead to an atmosphere in which sexuality is inappropriately emphasized. Some recent sexual harassment law has evolved along these lines, and the Equal Employment Opportunity Commission guidelines include as sexual harassment "verbal or physical contact of a sexual nature [having] the purpose or effect of unreasonably interfering with an individual's work performance or creating an intimidating, hostile, or offensive work environment."[15] However, the boundary between language that is vulgar and language that is inappropriately sexual is not always obvious, and as a precaution some employers have adopted rules prohibiting a wide range of offensive language in the workplace.

Epithets are often objectionable on the theory that words injure— that offensive language is more likely than polite language to cause breaches of the peace and thus ought to be restricted. This objection is in part related to the doctrine of fighting words developed in the Supreme Court's 1942 *Chaplinsky v. New Hampshire* decision. Chaplinsky was a religious pamphleteer arrested for calling a police officer "a God-damned racketeer" and "a damn fascist." Upholding Chaplinsky's conviction, the Court denied constitutional protection for words that "by their very utterance inflict injury or tend to incite an immediate breach of the peace." There have been attempts to extend the notion of injurious speech to racial and ethnic epithets on the grounds that they create a broader atmosphere of tolerance for bigotry. The St. Paul Bias-Motivated Crime Ordinance of 1990, for example, made it a misdemeanor to display or place symbols "which one knows or has reasonable grounds to know arouses anger, alarm, or resentment in others on the basis of race, color, creed, religion, or gender." However, that law was struck down by the Supreme Court in 1992 on the basis that it proscribed more than fighting words.[16]

There have also been grassroots efforts focused on the impact of racial epithets in dictionary contexts. In 1997 two Michigan women, Kathryn

Williams and Delphine Abraham, began to organize a boycott over the definition of the word *nigger* in the *Merriam-Webster Collegiate Dictionary*. The primary definition, based on Merriam's policy of listing the oldest definition first, read: "1. A black person, usu. taken to be offensive." Critics of the definition argued that a better phrasing would be "derogatory term used to describe a black person" since the original definition focused on reference (a black person) rather than connotation (a derogatory term). Merriam-Webster reviewed its definitions for a wide variety of terms and the 1999 edition of the *Collegiate Dictionary* placed a usage warning at the start of the entry so that it read "1. usually offensive; see usage paragraph below: a black person." The dictionary similarly revised entries for more than 200 offensive words.[17] Another example of reactions to epithets concerns a book by Harvard law professor Randall Kennedy analyzing the use of the word *nigger* in a wide variety of instances. Though Kennedy believes that the use of the word as a term of affection by some young African-Americans and some whites will gradually reduce its power, many others disagree. Columbia Law School professor Patricia Williams, for example, commented that "That word is a bit like fire—you can warm your hands with the kind of upside-down camaraderie that it gives, or you can burn a cross with it. But in any case it depends on the context and the users' intention, and seeing it floating abstractly on a book shelf in a world that is still as polarized as ours makes me cringe."[18]

What is evident from the various objections to coarse language and epithets is the idea that certain words are not used in polite speech—that public language should be suitable for all possible groups of listeners, from one's children and grandparents to worldly adults and working folks. Language falling outside this range is often characterized as impolite, inappropriate, disruptive, disrespectful, immoral, injurious, or dangerous, and as such is constrained by etiquette, workplace rules, and law.

Why does offensive language persist? There are several arguments for tolerance of coarse language. One is the idea that bad words are "only words" and that offensiveness lies in listeners' attitudes toward topics rather than in the words themselves. The argument about listeners' sensibilities is most straightforwardly applied to certain types of language such as references to excrement and some body parts and physical acts. In other instances—as with racial and sexual epithets—the expression of objectionable attitudes *is* thought to injure. But even in these situations the argument may focus on how a word can force people to confront the ideas underlying it. This is in part Randall Kennedy's argument (and was also the view of 1950s comedian Lenny Bruce). Erroll McDonald, Randall Kennedy's editor, explains that "It is just such a curious word that provokes atavistic passions in people, and I thought it was time for a proper reckoning with it. I for one am appalled by that euphemism 'the N word.' It seems an elision of something that would be better off talked about."[19]

A number of Supreme Court decisions have also focused on reasons that vulgar language is used and tolerated. In the 1971 case *Cohen v. California*, the Court noted the importance of the emotive force of words and the difficulty of prohibiting offensive words without also prohibiting unpopular ideas. The Court wrote that "Surely the State has no right to cleanse public debate to the point where it is grammatically palatable to the most squeamish among us."[20] And in its 1975 decision permitting the performance of the Broadway musical *Hair* in Chattanooga, Tennessee, the Court emphasized the rights of those who "for a variety of reasons, including a conscious desire to flout majoritarian conventions, express themselves using words that may be regarded as offensive by those from different socio-economic backgrounds."

Another argument for tolerating coarse language focuses on realist aesthetics and maintains that certain types of verbal art (fiction, poetry, film noir) require language that reflects the way that people actually talk. This is the position of James Kelman and Steven Bochco, mentioned earlier. In a review of *How Late It Was, How Late*, critic James Ledbetter notes that "Kelman has mounted a sustained assault on social and literary politeness. Sammy [Kelman's protagonist] has no patience for correct language, and little patience for most people."

Ledbetter sees the novel's language as authentic both for its setting and for its theme of the class and culture struggle, and he compares it to American hip-hop in its "insistent vulgarity."[21] And Steven Bochco's observation that the language of the criminal justice system has a higher tolerance for offensive language received confirmation in a Texas court case in 1994 in which a Texas attorney was acquitted of disorderly conduct charges. Mary E. Conn was charged with disorderly conduct for vulgar language she used when passing through a metal detector at a courthouse. In part her successful defense was based on the contention that similar emphatic vulgarity was commonly used in criminal courthouses.[22]

Because offensive language is both improper and daring, it takes on a role as a status marker in ordinary speech. Renatus Hartogs and Hans Fantel, in their 1967 book *Four-Letter Word Games: The Psychology of Obscenity*, suggest that "the quasi-decorous use of profanity in a fashionable context becomes a handy instrument for having one's world both ways. With a judiciously dropped four-letter bon mot we can, in sophisticated circles, be at the same time rebellious and respectable, prim and prurient."[23] Hartogs and Fantel see middle-class ambivalence about taboo speech as reflecting a cultural split between propriety and conventionalism, on the one hand, and sophistication and libertinism, on the other. In the context of this cultural split, the use of vulgar language can provide covert prestige to otherwise conventional speakers. During the 2004 election campaign, for example, both candidate John Kerry and Vice President Dick Cheney used forms of the word *fuck*, Kerry in an interview with the *Village Voice* and Cheney in an aside on the Senate floor. Both received some mild criticism for their language but each man also positioned himself as a speaker who puts directness over convention.

What we see is that the use or nonuse of offensive language is not a simple matter of propriety or impropriety but rather involves effects, intentions, rights, and identity. Arguments for the tolerance of offensive language may focus on any of several themes: the importance of coming to grips with the ideas underlying offensive language; the rights of those who wish to be vulgar; the way in which people actually speak; the potential for realistic language in the arts to create authenticity; and the social value of flouting convention. Arguments against offensive language, in turn, emphasize the desire for public language to be suitable to all listeners, and the possibility of some language being impolite, immoral, injurious, disruptive, or dangerous.

Bad Words as a Social Construction

Objections to and defenses of coarse language reveal ways in which members of society view such language. The history of swearing also provides insight into how the notion of bad language changes. Practices of swearing have often shifted during the history of the language. As Geoffrey Hughes notes in his 1991 history of English swearing, the swearing in *Beowulf* took the form of warrior oaths reflecting serious assertions (recall Socrates Fortlow's advice to his friend Darryl). Profanity was rare in the Old English period: Hughes notes that God is mentioned 30 times in *Beowulf* "but never invoked as a prop and never named in vain."[24] In Middle English, however, Hughes sees strong language as increasingly characterized by religious swearing and by vilification of competing religious groups (as "pagans," "heathens," "infidels," etc.). He also emphasizes the robust profanity of the *Canterbury Tales*, in which Chaucer used cursing to differentiate characters, including "those who take religious language seriously; those who exploit it cynically, and those who use it with a casual looseness."[25] The Reformation brought about changes in the types of religious epithets used. Hughes suggests that whereas earlier religious abuse had been directed at so-called infidels and heathens, it now focused increasingly on "papists" and "Rome-runners," with such terms as "devil" and "antichrist" pressed into service. In addition, sexual language (such as "harlotry," "fornication," and "whore") was also adapted to religious vilification.[26]

Hughes sees the Renaissance as showing a shift from religious themes to secular ones and as reflecting tension between license and repression. License was reflected in the work of writers like Shakespeare and Ben Jonson. Shakespeare's usage encompassed both traditional and minced oaths as well as bawdy wordplay.[27] Jonson's works, such as his 1598 "Every Man in His Humour," simultaneously satirized swearing and employed it, though Jonson seems to have engaged in self-censorship as his career progressed.[28] Repression is reflected in censorship by secular authorities and in the influence of fundamentalist groups such as Puritans and Quakers. The position of Master of the Revels had been established in England in 1574, with the power to censor plays for political or doctrinal offenses. After the reign of Elizabeth, these strictures were extended to linguistic offenses, and the 1606 Act to Restrain the Abuses of Players established a fine of 10 pounds for players who spoke profanely.[29] An even more general prohibition on swearing was passed in 1623, establishing a fine of a shilling for all profane swearing or cursing. The language of the 1623 act reflects the concerns of Puritans that "all profane Swearing and Cursing is forbidden by the word of GOD."[30] Ashley Montagu emphasizes that Puritans viewed profanity as a threat to religion and notes that the seventeenth-century Puritan literature against swearing numbered hundreds of books and pamphlets.[31] In the seventeenth century the theater continued to be a special target of anti-swearing efforts, and in September of 1642 public theater was banned in England. The ban lasted until the return of the monarchy in 1661, though a tradition of underground theater developed in the interim. The English Restoration, in turn, yielded a period of vigorous licentiousness in drama, reflected in the work of John Wilmot, the Earl of Rochester. In large part, the language of the Restoration reflected the mores and tastes of the court of Charles II. But there was also continued commentary on swearing, such as Jeremy Collier's 1698 *A Short View of the Profaneness and Immorality of the English Stage*.

The Augustan and Victorian periods provide a transition to present-day attitudes toward cursing. Hughes observes that Augustan writers such as Alexander Pope "rigorously maintained a strict separation of registers, upholding the principle of decorum even in the most virulent satires."[32] Jonathan Swift was a notable exception to decorum provided by Pope, Addison, and Steele, with his 1730 "The Lady's Dressing Room" containing the line "O, Celia, Celia, Celia shits!" During this period the inclusion of coarse language in dictionaries became an issue for the early lexicographers as well. Nathaniel Bailey included the word *fuck* in his 1721 *Universal Etymological Dictionary*, but Samuel Johnson avoided it in his 1755 *A Dictionary of the English Language*.[33]

During the nineteenth and twentieth centuries, as public decorum became a social concern in both Victorian England and frontier America, it was natural that strictures on language would become prominent. Reactions to such strictures developed as well. As John Burnham notes, swearing in America conveyed rebelliousness and defiance of conventional authority.[34] Burnham sees swearing as a social leveler that allowed speakers to fit in with the lower social classes. He writes that many nineteenth-century Americans

> believed that swearing embodied tendencies to overturn good
> order and level propriety, to substitute roughneck standards
> for civilized and restrained behavior. In the cities, members of
> the lower orders often shocked visitors from abroad with
> rough language that they used to defy authority and consoli-
> date comradeship among themselves.[35]

Conversely, avoiding offensive language became more clearly a matter of class symbolism, signaling those who observed public versus private standards and those who failed to make such distinctions. Thus Edwin Whipple in his 1885 essay "The Swearing Habit" wrote that "The conventional gentleman, though fifty or eighty years ago he might consider an oath as an occasional or frequent adornment to his conversation in all societies, now reserves it for 'gentlemen' only, and is inclined to deem it slightly improper in the society of ladies."[36]

At the beginning of the twentieth century, however, middle-class American attitudes about profanity began to shift. Burnham notes that articles began to appear upholding swearing and concludes that "By the late 1930s journalists portrayed formal opponents of swearing as merely quaint eccentrics."[37] There were also a number of scholarly studies by linguists and folklorists aimed at documenting actual usage and explaining the function of swearing. In 1931, L. W. Merryweather wrote in *American Speech* that "*Hell* fills so large a part of the American vocabulary that it will probably be worn out in a few years."[38] And in 1934, Allen Walker Read published an essay in the same journal titled "An Obscenity Symbol," which concluded that "obscenity is an artificially created product" whose function is symbolic. Read's article identified but did not mention the obscenity symbol in question. Nevertheless, he argued that the tacit "conspiracy to maintain the sacredness of these symbols" has the opposite effect from that intended by moralists. Read suggested that rather than protecting children, taboos merely reinforced the titillating appeal of the word.[39]

Burnham notes other factors in the increased tolerance of cursing in the twentieth century, such as an increasing frankness in literature and, with the emergence of the movie industry, a sympathetic representation of antiheroes in film. War was also a significant factor. World War I helped to relax the constraints on swearing among the civilian population, with slogans like "To hell with the Kaiser" commonly used. Among the military, swearing was an integral part of bonding. In *Songs and Slang of the British Soldier, 1914–1918*, John Brophy and Eric Partridge indicate that *fuck* had become so common among soldiers as to lose its force:

> From being an intensive to express strong emotion it became a merely conventional excrescence. By adding –*ing* and –*ingwell* an adjective and an adverb were formed and thrown into every sentence. It became so common that an effective way for the soldier to express emotion was to omit this word. Thus, if a sergeant said, "Get your—ing rifles!" it was understood as a matter of routine. But if he said, "Get your rifles!" there was an immediate implication of urgency and danger.[40]

Burnham suggests that men's use of aggressive language was similarly affected by World War II and that after that war women's attitudes changed as well, with acceptance of strong language coming to be seen as a mark of sophistication (recall the observation of Hartogs and Fantel noted earlier). The depression and war years show continued commentary and concerns. For example, Montagu notes that in November of 1942, Norman Vincent Peale observed in a sermon, "It seems that we are developing quite an aggregation of 'tough boys' in American public life today. I refer to the fact that it is scarcely possible to read a newspaper any more that does not contain the explosive 'damns' of public figures."[41] And Burges Johnson, in his 1948 book *The Lost Art of Profanity*, remarks that he omits some words in a citation from *Tristam Shandy* in part due to his "realization that a majority of my readers still maintain certain reticences—or obey certain taboos—and I owe them some degree of courtesy."[42] He adds that the taboos will fade of their own accord as society progresses.

Like World Wars I and II, the Vietnam War engendered a soldier's language of the 1960s. The antiwar movement and some of the social and political movements of that time also occasionally used offensive language to shock and challenge authority. The Berkeley Free Speech Movement, begun in 1964, was labeled the Filthy Speech Movement by some after a 1965 incident in which a small group of protestors chanted and displayed coarse expressions. And the Cohen v. California court case mentioned earlier originated with the 1968 arrest of war protestor Paul Robert Cohen for wearing a jacket inscribed with the phrases "Stop war" and "Fuck the draft."

What is the status of coarse language today? As I noted at the beginning of the chapter, the publishing and entertainment industries have long provided an impetus for linguistic frankness. Corporate, religious, and civil authorities—and audiences themselves—continue to provide a counterbalancing influence. But while linguistic etiquette constrains coarse language in the public sphere, tolerance for certain types of coarse language is evident. The de-moralization of profanity, sexual and scatological expression seems to reflect both the cachet of coarse language in American society and the twentieth-century trend for the mainstreaming of popular culture. One aspect of language where taboos remain strong, and in fact have probably strengthened over the last fifty years, is ethnic and racial epithets. The targets of epithets shift over time, and the groups targeted reflect racism arising from social competition and nationalism arising from commercial and military competition. Relatively unassimilated groups are more likely to be targets of majority xenophobia than groups which are more assimilated into the dominant culture. For example, as anti-immigration sentiment grew in the United States in the 1980s, the East Asian community in New Jersey became a target of hate crimes by a Jersey City gang calling itself the *Dotbusters*. The epithet *dot*, a reference to the vermillion dot or bindi that some Indian women wear, became an anti-Indian racial epithet. Military actions also provide a window onto the changing nature of ethnic and racial insults, with new epithets arising to match the enemy. The twentieth century saw Americans fighting *krauts*, *nips*, and *gooks*; the twenty-first century has thus far yielded terms like *Ali Baba* and *hajji* for Muslims.

What seems clear overall is that the notion of offensive language is a variable one, shifting over time, relative to domain (the workplace, broadcast media, literature, political discourse, polite conversation), and affected by social, historical, political, and commercial forces. It is clear as well that the range of offensive language extends from usage that is simply offensive to the squeamish to language that is disruptive and harmful.

Offensive speech also parallels grammar in some ways. Like nonstandard grammar, offensive language positions its users with respect to the perceived mainstream. Avoiding coarse language in public signals an understanding of the boundary between public and private discourse and a tacit acceptance of that boundary. Another parallel to grammar is the ethical nature of language identified by George Phillip Krapp. To be a speaker of good English, one must think about usage. This entails using language reflectively as opposed to reflexively. For coarse language, that means deciding when offensive language advances a message, when it detracts from a message, and when it impinges on the rights of others. A sound personal ethic of language will ask of any usage whether it is effective, breaking this question down into components of emphasis, tone, frankness, distraction, politeness, and harmfulness.

I have also noted that coarse language can establish lower-order solidarity or mark sophistication. The boundary between coarse language and other language thus serves to include or exclude some speakers from the mainstream of polite discourse and to allow some speakers to transgress the mainstream boundaries for rhetorical effect. As with grammar and writing, we must ask what defines the mainstream of discourse and the boundaries of acceptability and politeness. Are they defined in terms of the public formal language of press conferences, speeches, and the classroom? Or are they defined in terms of the language of the common person? If so, which common persons? The issue is fundamentally one of language use being complicated by unconventional expression. This issue is also a characteristic of two other domains of usage—slang and political correctness. In the next two sections, I examine these phenomena.

Slang as Bad Language

When I was growing up, the received wisdom among my college-bound peers in the New Jersey public schools was never to use slang expressions in writing and to avoid them in speaking in front of adults. In fact, the use of slang was something that teachers and parents commented on and attempted to discourage—it was a type of bad language seen as undignified and unintelligible. Nevertheless, such writers as Whitman, Twain, and Sandburg have seen slang as a source of inventiveness and vitality in the language. The term *slang* seems to have originated in the eighteenth century. The earliest *Oxford English Dictionary* citation for it dates from 1756, and early uses of slang associated it with the language of the criminal underworld.[43] Modern slang is broader and includes some vocabulary that shows familiarity with special activities both illicit and innocent, some that challenges authority and propriety (often through irony), and some that simply celebrates the inventiveness of language. Slang differs from colloquial language, from jargon, from regionalism, and from vogue usage, yet there is no easy mechanism for identifying it since other types of word formation use the same formal processes of affixation, clipping, metaphor, borrowing, and blending. Neologisms like *dot com* are hard to distinguish formally from slang usage like *dot bomb*; however, the distinction is apparent from the intended irony.

The difficulty of defining slang does not mean that no one has tried. Harold Wentworth and Stuart Flexner, in their *Dictionary of American Slang*, simply consider slang to refer to "a body of words accepted as intelligible, . . . but not accepted as good formal usage."[44] Other lexicographers are more specific, proposing such definitions as "A type of language especially occurring in casual and playful speech usually made up of short-lived coinages and figures of speech deliberately used in place of standard terms for effects of raciness, humor, or irreverence."[45] This definition nevertheless requires further unpacking. Bethany Dumas and Jonathan Lightner, in their 1978 article "Is *Slang* a Word for Linguists?" suggest four characteristics for slang:

(1) Its presence will markedly lower, at least for the moment, the dignity of formal or serious speech or writing.

(2) Its use implies the user's special familiarity either with the referent or with that less satisfied or less responsible class of people who have such special familiarity and use the term.

(3) It is a taboo term in ordinary discourse with persons of higher social status or greater responsibility.

(4) It is used in place of the well-known conventional synonym, especially in order (a) to protect the user from the discomfort caused by the conventional item or (b) to protect the user from the discomfort or annoyance of further elaboration.[46]

These four characteristics—a lowering of seriousness, the presumption of familiarity with a topic or group, stigmatization in discourse with persons of higher status, and function as a shield for the user—help to elaborate the definition of slang. They also encapsulate both its social usefulness and its risks. Slang is used to create a kind of linguistic solidarity or status by identifying oneself with a group out of the mainstream or by setting oneself apart from conventional values through a style of toughness and ironic detachment.

Slang is often associated with adolescents and college students, groups making the transition into adulthood and thus negotiating new roles and identities. In her 1996 book *Slang and Sociability*, Connie Eble sees the key function of slang use among college students as that of establishing group identity and distinguishing student values from the values of those in authority. This function is consistent with the way in which slang borrows and adapts words from groups and topics perceived as falling outside of mainstream English. Eble's analysis of taped conversations among college students also reveals that slang is less commonly used among intimate friends but that the frequency of slang increases when someone new joins a close-knit group.[47] She suggests that students who are not especially close use slang to establish identity—their solidarity as students—while those who are already intimate friends have less need to demonstrate solidarity.

As noted earlier, creative writers have both recognized and exploited the vitality of slang—Carl Sandburg once commented that "Slang is language that rolls up its sleeves and spits in its hands."[48] Other writers, journalists, and teachers of academic writing have had a harder time dealing with slang, however, since their aim is often for a formal tone that addresses a hypothetical general audience. *The Associated Press Stylebook*, for example, recommends that journalists "in general, avoid slang, the highly informal language that is outside of conventional or standard usage."[49] And the *Harbrace Handbook* advises students that "On occasion, slang can be used effectively, even in formal writing. . . . But much slang is trite, tasteless, and inexact."[50] These guides hint at the relativity of slang usage but provide little help in understanding when slang might be effective. William Watt's 1957 *An American Rhetoric* is more helpful: Watt writes that "The trouble with slang is not, as many undergraduates assume, that it is always 'vulgar' or 'bad English.' The trouble is that much of it is (1) forced, (2) local, (3) overworked when alive, and (4) soon dead."[51] While the local currency of slang makes it attractive in speech, it can also make slang a distraction in formal writing.[52]

An understanding of the relativity of slang contrasts with folk attitudes that see slang merely as bad English used by bad people. Jonathan Lightner remarks that in the eighteenth and early nineteenth centuries "slang was seen as both emerging from and sustaining an undisguised baseness of mind that must lead to the coarsening of both language and civilization."[53] The sentiments of Oliver Wendell Holmes, Sr., were typical. In an 1870 address to the Harvard University Phi Beta Kappa Society, Holmes asserted that "the use of *slang*, or cheap generic terms, as a substitute for differentiated specific expressions, is at once a sign and a cause of mental atrophy."[54] Lightner sees attitudes toward slang as beginning to shift in the last quarter of the nineteenth century as writers like Mark Twain incorporated it in popular writing to define sympathetic and unpretentious literary characters.[55] In addition, H. L. Mencken cites the influence of cartoonists, sports writers and news columnists, writing approvingly that "Slang originates in the efforts of ingenious individuals to make the language more pungent and picturesque."[56] Giving examples like *stiff, flat-foot, smoke-eater*, and *yes-man*, Mencken argues that slang provides new shades of meaning. Nevertheless, in the early twentieth century, we still find the prevailing attitude that slang implies too much familiarity with or interest in vices and rough behavior.[57] John Burnham notes that the early twentieth-century attitude was that "Nice children did not have anything to do with users of slang, who identified themselves by their words."

As slang usage has become less associated with criminal behavior and more the object of study by scholars and the popular press, objections have sometimes been treated as questions of communication rather than character and criminalization.[58] The supposed vagueness of slang is, in turn, linked to habits of mind. This linking is apparent in the comment of Holmes, cited earlier. It was apparent as well in the concern of James Greenough and George Lyman Kittredge in 1901 that slang has "no fixed meaning" and that it would "gradually reduce one's thought to the same ignorant level from which most slang proceeds."[59] A hundred years later we find essentially the same view expressed by writer Linda Hall, who complains that her students do not worry about precision, so they do not see most of their speech as needing to be taken seriously.[60] She argues, for example, that the use of *cool* to refer broadly to that which is fashionable (*a cool blouse*) or personable (*a cool teacher*) creates a vagueness that hinders communication.[61] But there are many instances in which nonslang meanings are expansive as well. Consider the word *cup*, which can refer to a number of ounces, the container of a drink, or the drink itself (usually hot), a protective device for the male groin, or a size of brassiere or breast. The vagueness of *cup* is typically manageable through context and there is no reason to assume that the same is not the case for *cool* or to assume that slang reduces our abilities to make subtle distinctions vividly and effectively.

The argument is sometimes also made that slang is harmful to the language. For example, Jacques Barzun portrays slang as encroaching on the existing meanings of words. He writes that:

> Far from injecting vigor into the upper layers of speech, the slang of today has managed to destroy or make doubtful more good words than it could make up for a long time. Whole series—from earlier *fairy* and *pansy* to *queer, faggot, adult,* and *gay*—have done nothing but rob the language of irreplaceable resources. Others, such as *ball, bomb, blow, screw* have been left uncertain in slang and unexpectedly embarrassing elsewhere. Nowadays, slang rather preys on the straight vocabulary than feeds it new blood; and the loss is made worse by the general abandonment of the educated of *propriety* in every sense of the term.[62]

Barzun's objection focuses both on the character of slang users and on the effect of slang on the language, invoking the metaphors of theft and destruction. But his argument is far too general and ignores the fact that vocabulary changes to meet new needs and new shades of meaning. In some cases change is driven by new technical, political, medical, or social developments (as with the borrowing of the name *spam* to refer to bulk electronic junk mail). In other cases the change is cultural, as when a group reexamines its identity (as in the recent reemergence of *queer* as an assertion of gay pride) or when social attitudes change. In some cases the change is market driven, as when the media and advertisers follow linguistic trends to position themselves with consumers (using superlative expressions like *phat*, for example). The argument that slang "robs the language" and "preys on vocabulary" misses the point that the living language is a marketplace of ideas, nuances, and images. Barzun's concern that slang makes words doubtful, uncertain, and potentially embarrassing for speakers not in the know is revealing, however. Slang does not so much rob the language of resources as it reduces the security of speakers like Barzun to assume that their norms can be used without fear of embarrassment or misunderstanding. In other words, slang requires speakers of one variety to adjust and accommodate to the norms of another. It is this challenge to assumed norms that places slang in the category of improper usage for some speakers. It is not the language that is destabilized by slang. What is destabilized is the assumption that mainstream norms are shared by everyone. And part of the pleasure of slang for its users is belonging to an in-group that excludes the conventional mainstream.

In attitudes toward slang, we continue to find a contest between those who view nonstandard language as a danger and those who see it as having contextual utility. Critics of slang have associated it with lower order speakers and character defects, with social impropriety and looseness by standard speakers, and with damage to the precision of the standard. Defenders, on the other hand, stress the inventiveness of slang, its role in stylistic vitality and identity, and the parallel between the creation of slang and other forms of neology. For descriptivists, the issue of slang usage, however, is one of social appropriateness and utility, not abiding propriety and defense of the standard against debasement by false coinage. As with coarse language, the relativist view is that effectiveness is the measure of good language. On this view, speakers and writers need the background and experience to decide when jocularity, familiarity, inventiveness, and local color are useful and when they are an impediment.

Political Correctness

We now turn to a third type of stigmatized usage: political correctness. In recent years the term *politically correct* has emerged as a popular usage label, though not one adopted by dictionaries. Like vulgarity and slang, political correctness is difficult to define. The term is thought to have originated in self-mockery among the Left—as an ironic way of making light of its most doctrinaire and preachy members, presumably a marginal group within the larger set of social progressives. According to literary historian Ruth Perry, the phrase seems to have been adapted from earlier Soviet and Chinese usage where it indicated one who toed the party line. American use of the term is reported as early as the 1960s in the Black Power Movement and the New Left, and it has been suggested that the American adoption of the term reflects the prominence of Mao Zedong as a cultural icon of the 1960s.[63] By the 1980s, however, the term *political correctness* had become associated with so-called speech codes, which for critics included both the professional societies' guidelines for bias-free language and campus speech-codes such as those at the University of Wisconsin, Antioch University, and elsewhere.

Through its connection to universities, the term *political correctness* also became linked with debates over the place of the Western civilization model and the European canon of great books in the university curriculum. In recent decades, university curricula have paid increasing attention to non-European cultures, and scholars from a variety of disciplines have challenged the assumption that traditional Western forms of art, literature, culture, and social institutions are globally superior. In reaction, some critics have argued that this broadening of the curriculum entails a form of cultural relativism that precludes aesthetic or scholarly judgments. At the same time, the growth of ethnic studies, women's studies, and other fields that shifted disciplines away from earlier received perspectives to new concerns and new methods has provoked a similar reaction. Some have characterized diversity and multiculturalism in the curriculum as promoting a cultural and linguistic reverse discrimination, as a replacement of the search for truth with advocacy, and as a capitulation of standards to student interests and validation of students' experiences. Dinesh D'Souza, for example, writes that if one assumes that Western culture depreciates the accomplishments of women, people of color, gays, and other cultures, a series of consequences follow:

> [M]any minorities can explain why they had such a hard time with Milton in the English Department, Publius in political science, and Heisenberg in physics. These men reflected white male aesthetics, philosophy, and physics. Obviously, nonwhite students would fare much better if the university created more black or Latino or Third World courses, the argument goes. This argument leads to a spate of demands: Abolish the Western classics, establish new departments such as Afro-American Studies and Women's Studies, hire minority faculty to offer distinctive black and Hispanic "perspectives."[64]

Another consequence, in the view of critics like D'Souza, is a new vocabulary aimed at accommodating diverse constituencies, a vocabulary presumably reflected in the language that professors use in teaching, in the stylistic guidelines for students' assignments, and in campus codes of conduct. The end result, critics suggest, is a tide of intolerance on campuses toward views critical of multiculturalism. With this recasting of diversity as intolerance, a potential debate about the most appropriate curriculum for the global economy is transformed into a discussion about placating interest groups and silencing dissent. Here is how George H. Bush framed the issue in a 1991 commencement address at the University of Michigan:

> The notion of political correctness has ignited controversy across the land. And although the movement arises from the

laudable desire to sweep away the debris of racism, sexism, and hatred, it replaces old prejudices with new ones. It declares certain topics off-limits, certain expressions off-limits, even certain gestures off-limits. What began as a cause for civility has soured into a cause of conflict and even censorship. Disputants treat sheer force—getting their foes punished or expelled, for instance, as a substitute for the power of ideas. Throughout history attempts to micromanage casual conversation have only incited distrust. They've invited people to look for insult in every word, gesture, action. And in their own Orwellian way, crusades that demand correct behavior crush diversity in the name of diversity.[65]

Bush's remarks focus on the issue of tacit or overt speech codes. Others have also asserted a connection between political correctness and academic standards, focusing on such controversies as the Stanford University debate concerning changes in requirements from Western Culture to a sequence called Civilization, Ideas, and Values. Critics like D'Souza, Allan Bloom, William Bennett, and Lynne Cheney have associated a classical Western civilization curriculum both with traditional values and with academic rigor and have characterized other views of the curriculum as enforcing a primarily ideological rather than an intellectual agenda.[66]

Rhetoric about enforcement of ideologies gave the debate a contentious tenor, which was, in turn, sensationalized by the news media. For example, a December 24, 1990, issue of *Newsweek* with the words "Thought Police" on the cover included an article titled "Taking Offense: Is This the New Enlightenment on Campus or the New McCarthyism?" and the *Wall Street Journal*'s April 10, 1991, issue included an editorial titled "The Return of the Storm Troopers."[67] The media also focused on relativism as a source of political correctness, associating political correctness with French literary theory. In "Taking Offense," Jerry Adler characterized political correctness this way:

Intellectually, PC is informed by deconstructionism, a theory of literary criticism associated with the French thinker Jacques Derrida. This accounts for the concentration of PC thought in such seemingly unlikely disciplines as comparative literature. Deconstructionism is a famously obscure theory, but one of its implications is a rejection of the notion of "hierarchy." It is impossible in deconstructionist terms to say that one text is superior to another. PC thinkers have embraced this conceit with a vengeance. . . . It is not just in literary criticism that the PC reject "hierarchy" but in the most mundane daily exchanges as well.[68]

In addition, media portrayals of political correctness blended issues like campus speech codes, academic freedom, and literary theory with debates over the linguistic etiquette of naming and usage.[69] This is evident in accounts like John Taylor's January 1991 *New York Magazine* feature "Are You Politically Correct?" The magazine's cover graphic asked readers if they referred to Indians as *Native Americans* and pets as *animal companions*, juxtaposing two quite different examples, with the latter trivializing the former.[70] Such blending is also evident in various popular culture parodies, such as James Finn Garner's *Politically Correct Bedtime Stories*, which treat the issue of naming as one of rewriting convention and indoctrinating children. Conservative objections to bias-free language are typified by syndicated columnist John Leo, who refers to politically correct speech as a "remote campustongue" that is part of the "steady debasement" of English. Leo objects to the vagueness of terms like *nontraditional family, visually impaired,* and *substance abusers,* seeing political correctness as sacrificing precision not only for meaningless self-esteem but also in "conscious attempts to ratchet up a minor offense to a major one."[71]

Diane Ravitch, in her 2003 book, *The Language Police,* critiques the political pressures on K–12 textbook writers and publishers. As she notes, these arise from both the doctrinaire Left and the fundamentalist

Right. Both attempt to pressure publishers into using textbooks to present a particular worldview (either a nostalgically traditional picture of America or one that is an egalitarian utopia). Ravitch suggests that the extreme Right tends to object to certain role models and topics (such as witchcraft, magic, disobedience, and evolution) while the Left has more often focused on objections to biased language and stereotypes.[72] Among the many words proscribed by publishers' bias guidelines are *craftsmanship, crazy, bookworm, fat, Eskimo, Pollyanna, straw man*, and *wheelchair-bound*.[73]

Since its popularization in the 1990s, the label "politically correct" has broadened to include a wide range of ideological issues. Some current controversies involve language, such as the question of whether to refer to "partial-birth abortion" or "intact dilation and extraction," whether the government of Turkey should be called an "Islamic democracy" or just a "democracy," or whether the University of Illinois should drop its Native American mascot Chief Illiniwek. However, many contemporary critics of political correctness have extended the term to refer to any sort of categorization or practice that seems liberal. The political correctness label has been applied to nonlinguistic topics as diverse as affirmative action, Americans with Disabilities Act compliance, airline screening procedures, the use of women in combat, and the reality of post-traumatic stress disorder.[74]

Putting aside these broader issues, I will focus on complaints about political correctness *in language*, which see political correctness as imposing the usage preferences and agenda of social activists on the rest of society. On its face, the critique of political correctness is about censorship and enforced civility.[75] But the critique is largely rhetorical. Take, for example, the adoption of the term "political correctness" from the practices of prescriptive authoritarian regimes. In exploiting this usage, critics of political correctness themselves use language to shape the debate. This is unintentionally ironic since the objection to political correctness is that it manipulates language in order to shape attitudes and behavior.[76] There is also an unintentional irony (or perhaps hypocrisy) in critics' view that their language preferences are any less political than those of others. The unargued assumption is that the traditional naming practices are value-neutral while departures from them are ideologically motivated. But as art critic Robert Hughes notes in his book *Culture of Complaint*, the American Right has its own set of euphemisms (which Hughes refers to as "Patriotically Correct" language). Hughes notes, for example, that the use of the term *family values* to represent the cultural agenda of the American Right is certainly ideologically motivated. An amusing recent example of patriotically correct language was the proposal in 2003 by North Carolina Congressman Walter Jones and Ohio Congressman Bob Ney to rename french fries and french toast as *freedom fries* and *freedom toast* on cafeteria menus in the U.S. House of Representatives.[77]

Not all examples of renaming are so trivial, however. In 1990, the Republican organization GOPAC produced a pamphlet titled "Language: A Key Mechanism of Control."[78] The pamphlet listed a set of positive words for candidates to use to frame their message and a contrasting set of negative words to be used in referring to opponents. The positive terms included *activist, challenge, change, common sense, courage, crusade, freedom, hard work, moral, pioneer, pro-flag, pro-children, pro-environment,* and *tough*; among the negative were *anti-flag, anti-family, anti-child, anti-jobs, criminal rights, decay, ideological, intolerant, liberal, permissive attitude, radical, sick, traitors, unionized,* and *welfare.* Linguist George Lakoff has pointed out that political conservatives have invested for many years in creating language for their worldview while progressives have done much less.[79] Lakoff cites as an example the linguistic framing of taxation. Taxes can be viewed as an affliction needing "tax relief." But they could also be framed as a patriotic responsibility, as the "price of civilization" in Justice Holmes's phrasing. The use of naming and language choice to position ideas culturally is not exclusive to the political Left or Right. Many patterns of naming contain hidden assumptions and reflect contests of meaning and perspective.

Another rhetorical aspect of the critique of political correctness is the familiar characterization of relativism as nihilism. While the 1950s critique of relativism in grammar focused on the opposition between science and humanism, today's version often centers on the literary postmodernists' rejection of objectivity. Relativists, critics assume, deny the possibility of fixed meaning in language. And if language is without fixed meanings, it is a small step to the idea that all judgments are ideologically motivated. Critics thus see objectivity as replaced by a view of truth as whatever supports liberation and social transformation.[80] But as I illustrated in the opening chapter, this is not the only view of relativism. Relativism may simply refer to the realistic view that social conventions, canons, and usages are not beyond examination. On this view of relativism, its leading idea is that all interpretations and usages— novel or received—should be open to equal scrutiny, not that all are equally valid. As we shall see, the essence of linguistic etiquette and civility is that some choices *are* more useful than others.

Focusing on the issue of language, what remains is the criticism that so-called politically correct language attempts to soften reality and control thought. This criticism maintains that language change is both dangerously Orwellian in devaluing words and trivial in addressing language change rather than social change. For example, Robert Hughes argues that the real task of activists should be to better society rather than attend to relatively unimportant language issues:

> The notion that you change a situation by finding a newer and nicer word for it emerges from the old American habit of euphemism, circumlocution, and desperate confusion over etiquette, produced by fear that the concrete will give offence . . . No shifting of words is going to reduce the amount of bigotry in this or any other society. But it does create what the military mind so lucidly calls collateral damage in a target-rich environment—namely, the wounding of innocent language.[81]

Critiques of political correctness see it as (a) thought control; (b) nihilistic relativism; (c) damaging to the clarity, specificity, and precision of language; (d) trivial accommodation toward groups portrayed as cultural victims; and (e) a distraction from any serious agenda of social and economic progress. It is quite an indictment.

The extent to which language informs how we approach certain issues is an open question, of course, but the view that associates *all* socially motivated coinage with thought control, victimization, and damage to precision is much too simplistic. As with objections to slang, objections to social neology may arise less on linguistic merits than from the additional work that adapting to language change creates for some speakers. When naming becomes variable, speakers must decide what form to use. New usage reduces the privilege of one set of speakers to use their norms without fear of embarrassment or discomfort. Linguist John Baugh provides a telling example in his book *Out of the Mouths of Slaves.* Discussing public reaction when Jesse Jackson and others first called for use of the term *African-American* rather than *Black,* Baugh cites an April 1989 letter to Ann Landers in which a reader asks, "Why don't the blacks make up their minds? The whole subject is becoming tiresome. They chose black because they did not like Negro."[82] The letter writer's reaction reflects the way that changing terms of address makes language more problematic. But the complaint in this instance is personal rather than grammatical or social.

Let us consider the change from *Black* to *African-American.* It makes absolutely no sense to consider this change to be a form of thought control—there is no euphemism or manipulation of attitudes. Since the impetus for the change arose from within the African-American community, adopting it does accommodate the preferences of leaders of that community. But it is not a neologism based in an identity of victimhood. Rather, as Baugh suggests, the new terminology is part of a process of reexamining and reinvigorating group identity. He notes that ethnic groups use self-identification to challenge the status quo and that group introspection can result in new terminology. So periodic changes in self-identification are to be expected. With this in mind, it is a mistake to view change as a meaningless distraction from a more serious agenda. As for so-called collateral damage to the language, there is no substantive issue. The clarity and grammatical logic of the compound *African-American* is straightforward and parallel with *Italian-American, Mexican-American, Irish-American,* and so on. It involves identification by origin rather than racial classification or color. The casual indictment of socially motivated usage change as thought control does not apply in this instance.

Another example of the sort of case-by-case effort that is required to assess terminology can be found by looking at the set of terms *crippled, handicapped, disabled,* and *physically challenged.* As with *African-American,* usage ultimately decides what terms will be adopted, and usage, in turn, will be informed and shaped by the preferences of the group that a term refers to. But as a guide to usage, one can argue that *disabled* is the optimal choice on the basis of conciseness, accuracy, politeness, and connotation. The first two choices (*crippled* and *handicapped*) reflect views of disabilities that today have negative connotations. The term *crippled,* for example, focuses on the debilitating effect of an affliction on one's body and today is marked in dictionaries as "somewhat offensive" or "sometimes offensive." The term is also inaccurate in that afflictions that were once crippling are, in light of medical and social advances, often less debilitating today. Even organizations that have historically used the adjective in their name are dropping it. One recent reflection of this was the redesignation in 2001 of the Shriners Hospitals for Crippled Children as simply the Shriners Hospitals for Children. Announcing the change, the hospital board chair cited a desire not to label patients.[83]

The term *handicapped,* while less offensive than *crippled,* carries the connotation of being held back in some competitive enterprise (we talk of social handicaps, golf handicaps, and racing handicaps) and is unwelcome by some people with disabilities. As both public policy and social attitudes have shifted from seeing disabilities in terms of individuals' conditions (crippled) to their prospects (handicapped) to their situation (as requiring reasonable accommodation), language has evolved as well. What about the term *physically challenged*? This term seems less than optimal since it is both long and somewhat euphemistic, representing disability almost as an opportunity to test oneself. Euphemisms call attention to a speaker's connotation and so the term singles out the disabled in the same way that disparaging usage might.

In the American Association of University Presses' *Guidelines for Bias-Free Writing*, Marilyn Schwartz notes that in many contexts such alternatives as *physically challenged, physically* (or *mentally*) *different, differently abled, exceptional,* and *special* may suggest "that disabled people belong to a different or uncommonly rare species or that having a disability is an exciting adventure."[84]

Over time, naming etiquette evolves, like all other aspects of language. This evolution will often reflect preferences of those named (whether to be referred to as *Native American* or *Indian*, for example) and may also often aim at inclusiveness (such as using *they* as opposed to *he* for generic pronoun reference). While the initial phases of change often make language problematic, the end results of culturally neutral language can be to expand community with terms that are neither insults nor euphemisms. In any event, treating usage change as mere identity politics misses two key points: that usage changes as social attitudes, preferences, and situations do and that there is a distinction between new terms that attempts to be inclusive and ones that call attention to groups by euphemism. The practical problem is that different speakers draw the line in different places between what they perceive as inclusive and what they perceive as oversensitive euphemism. But the merits of various neologisms should be treated individually rather than merely dismissed as language manipulation. And as individuals, we use language best when we understand the alternatives, the logic, and the consequences of our choices.

Conventionalism and Comfort Levels

In this chapter I have looked at offensive language, slang, and politically correct speech. Each has the ability to disturb the comfort level of the mainstream. Coarse language divides speech communities by shocking its more puritan members and by establishing a low tone. Epithets and slurs divide speech communities by direct vilification or by sanctioning intolerance. Slang divides by creating usage problems for the uninitiated both in terms of meaning and tone. And social neology divides by politicizing language choices. Yet there is also a sense in which all of these foster solidarity within subgroups of speech communities. Coarseness creates a tough-guy solidarity among those disregarding convention. Slurs create a feeling of solidarity among the bigoted. Slang supports rebellious or avant-garde identity among its users. And politicized language identifies speakers as promoting or resisting certain social views. The bad language of cursing, slang, and political correctness, like bad grammar, exists outside of traditional norms and disrupts those norms, expanding discourse for some groups and making it problematic for others.

There is also an important parallel between good and bad vocabulary and good and bad grammar. In grammar, tradition overreaches when it ascribes an inherent value to the standard language and unrealistically prescribes against actual educated usage and dismisses groups that use certain forms. Like prescriptivism, conventionalism is an oversimplification strategy for treating usage. Complexities of appropriateness, audience, and utility are often glossed over in favor of attributions of vulgarity, taste, or ideology. Critics of coarse language and of slang sometimes portray that usage as reflecting a decline of standards, a lack of regard for tradition, and a danger to the stability of language. And critics of politically correct language see change as reflecting an ideological activism that makes language vague and uncertain. But coarseness, slang, and social neology cannot be understood in terms of the caricature of anything-goes relativism, but in terms of linguistic realism. Effective language does not rely on a fixed and unchanging vocabulary but depends on particulars of usage and audience. So we need to ask, case by case, what is really offensive, what is appropriate verbal license, when informality is useful, and whose sensibilities have a right to be respected.

Five Bad Citizens

In a 1917 speech, Theodore Roosevelt famously made the link between speaking the English language and good American citizenship, saying that

> We must have one flag. We must also have one language. . . . The greatness of this nation depends on the swift assimilation of the aliens she welcomes to her shores. Any force which attempts to retard that assimilative process is a force hostile to the highest interests of our country.[1]

For Roosevelt, language was both a symbol of national unity, like the flag, and a means of creating that unity, by swift assimilation of immigrants to American language, customs, and values. For many, the foreign languages of immigrants, to the extent that they were maintained rather than given up, were a form of bad language that got in the way of their adoption of American speech and values.

In previous chapters I have examined how differences of grammar and vocabulary lead to judgments about speakers. The same is true of retention of foreign languages, which has often been seen as unpatriotic, uneducated, or separatist. In this chapter I focus on American attitudes toward languages other than English, beginning with some history and case studies and moving forward to contemporary issues of English-only and bilingual education. In looking at the urge to assimilate other languages, my aim is to explore why some see foreign languages as making bad citizens.

Birth of a Nation

The United States began as a developing nation. Much early American discussion of language issues focused on the relative merits of American versus British usage and whether British English should continue to be the standard in the United States. Writers like Benjamin Franklin, who helped to set standards for American prose style—and who were successful writers in part because their prose style satisfied English critics—argued for British standards. As historian Daniel Boorstin notes, Franklin wrote to his friend David Hume in 1760 that he hoped that "we in America make the best English of this Island our standard."[2] John Pickering likewise argued that attention to English standards was necessary for literary appreciation, scientific communication, and international respect. Pickering cited English criticisms of American usage and remarked that, while the American language had changed less than might have been expected, "it has in so many instances departed from the English standard, that our scholars should lose no time in endeavoring to restore it to its purity, and to prevent further corruption."[3]

On the other hand, writers like Thomas Jefferson and Noah Webster were proponents of an American language. Jefferson argued that language planning should look to the future by expanding the vocabulary so that English would be an appropriate vehicle for new knowledge. In a letter of 1813 stressing usage and innovation over grammar and tradition, Jefferson suggested that the new United States would require a certain amount of new vocabulary and that language, like government, ought to follow the will of the people.[4] Jefferson's own writing was criticized for using novel words and, in an 1820 letter to John Adams, Jefferson wrote, "I am a friend to neology. It is the only way to give a language copiousness and euphony," adding that "Dictionaries are but the depositories of words legitimated by usage."[5]

Noah Webster had a businessman's interest in creating an independent American economy. He also had a revolutionary's interest in creating a unified and independent American culture and language.[6] He wrote that "Custom, habits, and *language*, as well as government, should be national. America should have her *own* language distinct from all the world."[7] In addition, Webster saw American usage as reflecting a conservatism that had been given up by British grammarians. In his view, the best speech was that of the American gentleman farmers, whom he saw as different from the English peasants—as better educated, landowning, and independent.

Webster also feared that copying British manners would mean carrying over British linguistic vices to the new American nation. As literary scholar David Simpson emphasizes, Webster saw the establishment of an American language as a way to recapture the former purity of the English language before its corruption by the London court and the English theater.[8] This view arose in part from Webster's Puritan suspicion of ornamentation, though disdain for the language of the court was also characteristic of reformers like Bishop Lowth. Webster's distaste was particularly aimed at the language of writers like Samuel Johnson, which he viewed as pompous and antiquated. He believed that freed of British vices, educated usage in America would reflect principles of rational analogy and would preserve a uniformity of American speech against both literary affectation and dialect variation. And he hoped that adopting such a version of English, together with access to land and an egalitarian commercial environment, would preserve the social and moral health of America. As Simpson explains, Webster worried that Americans who adopted contemporary British speech habits would create disharmony in their own communities by introducing the class distinctions of England. Historian Kenneth Cmiel notes that such attitudes were common—many expressed a "fear of aristocratic overrefinement, of using civil forms solely to maintain social distinctions."[9] But fears of refinement were balanced by a sense that eloquence was necessary for participation in political affairs. Cmiel notes that "even radicals understood that entrance to public life demanded verbal felicity."[10]

The dispersion of the population in America and the distance from British cultural standards also raised concerns that linguistic corruption would follow from the lack of a cultural center. Standardization of usage was a concern to some of the political founders of the United States. One solution entertained was the establishment of a legal authority to govern language, with John Adams advocating that Congress establish a national academy to standardize usage and pronunciation. Adams feared a natural degeneration of English and saw a national academy promoting the study of English (and other languages) as key to diplomatic goals.[11] Adams, who was often characterized as a monarchist, was careful to stress the democratic effect of a common standard. In 1780 he wrote that, with a public standard in place, "eloquence will become the instrument for recommending men to their fellow citizens, and the principal means of advancement through the various ranks and offices of society."[12] Adams also stressed that he was not advocating a new American language. He wrote that "[w]e have not made war against the English Language, any more than against the old English character," and he suggested that an academy would be an American accomplishment of something that England had not succeeded in doing.[13] The Continental Congress, however, did not place a high priority on a national academy, and the proposal never emerged from the committee studying it. While an official English Academy was never established, there does not seem to have been much doubt that English was intended as the de facto standard language. As John Jay noted in the *Federalist Papers*: "Providence has been pleased to give this one connected country to one united people—a people descended from the same ancestors, speaking the same language, professing the same religion, attached to the same principles of government."[14]

In colonial and post-Revolution discussions of language, we find the familiar theme of choosing a standard. Here the choice was between British and American styles and involved considerations of simplicity, commonness, and refinement. The discussion of an American language was embedded in larger discussions of American and British culture, and language played an important role in defining an American identity that could be linked to the best of English values and culture yet remain separate from perceived English vices. A separate American language was seen as a means of representing and maintaining international status and of accommodating new knowledge and situations.

Native American Languages

The founders of America understood the need to accommodate various European linguistic groups, as a means of fostering support for the revolution and as a means of encouraging settlement. While many of the founders were sympathetic toward the learning of other languages, broader public attitudes toward foreign and minority languages have often been indifferent or hostile. In this section and the next, I look at two case studies of attempts at assimilation—Native American languages and the sign language of the deaf. While these cases are very different, what stands out is the way that language differences are seen as a social problem.

From colonial times, European settlers' attitudes toward Native Americans often focused on civilizing and Christianizing, in part by forcing Native Americans to speak English. From the early 1800s, Congress provided funds for missionary Indian schools that promulgated official government views about land holding and resettlement. By the late 1800s, as the military was more capable of policy enforcement in the West, the government became much more directive toward Native

Americans. As John Reyhner notes, when Congress ended treaty making in 1871, policy shifted from relocation to assimilation, and the government became involved in the operation of Indian schools.[15] A report of the Commissioner for Indian Affairs in 1878 advocated removal of children from the influence of reservation life (and from parents) and proposed the creation of boarding schools. Prototype schools were developed in 1878 at the Hampton Institute in Virginia and in 1879 at the Carlisle Indian School in Pennsylvania, a converted army barracks. By 1902 almost 10,000 children had been relocated to twenty-five Indian boarding schools where English-only rules were enforced by corporal punishment. Also during this period, mission schools that had been instructing students in Bible studies using their native languages were forced to conduct instruction only in English in order to retain federal funds.

Federal policy of the late 1800s was exemplified by the views of J. D. C. Atkins, Commissioner of Indian Affairs. In his 1887 annual report, Atkins cited the report of a commission on Indian conditions the previous year, which advocated that "barbarous dialects should be blotted out, and the English language substituted." The report also linked assimilation of language to assimilation of thought and behavior, in language that foreshadows Orwell's theme of language as a mechanism of conformity and social control:

> Through sameness of language is produced sameness of sentiment, and thought; customs, and habits are moulded and assimilated in the same way, and thus in process of time the differences producing trouble would have been gradually eliminated.[16]

Adopting the majority language, in his view, would assimilate Indians to the majority perspective. Atkins went on to say that Indians "must be taught the language which they must use in transacting business with the people of this country. No unity or community of feeling can be established among different peoples unless they are brought to speak the same language."[17]

Assimilationism remained the main policy direction in Indian affairs well into the twentieth century, though a shift away from the assimilationist perspective did occur in the 1930s. The Meriam Report of 1928, an extensive survey of social and economic conditions sponsored by the Institute of Government Research, criticized the practice of breaking up Native American families and the practices of the boarding schools. The report led to such federal legislation as the Indian Reorganization Act of 1934, which promoted self-determination and cultural pluralism. Federally sponsored day schools were also established to provide English training with less disruption of the family and community. During World War II, however, funding was reallocated to the war effort. After the war, assimilationism reemerged as a way of encouraging Native American urbanization, and a policy of terminating reservations emerged in the 1950s.

During the New Frontier and Great Society era, termination efforts were challenged and policy again shifted to ways of combining federal assistance with self-determination. President Lyndon Johnson called for the end to termination efforts in his March 1968 Special Message to Congress, "The Forgotten American," and won passage of the Indian Civil Rights Act of 1968. The Nixon administration continued efforts to support self-determination, with the Indian Education Act of 1972 strengthening Indian control of education in their communities. In addition, the tribal college movement begun in the 1960s expanded Native American higher education. Most recently, the 1990 Native American Languages Act made it policy to "preserve, protect, and promote the rights and freedom of Native Americans to use, practice, and develop Native American languages."[18] Among other things, the act encouraged Native American language survival and recognized the rights of tribes to use Native American languages as a medium of instruction in federally funded schools.

The support for Native American languages is a case in which the policy of assimilation and termination was recognized as counterproductive in a variety of ways—socially, educationally, and culturally. Earlier policies of relocation to boarding schools, restraint of language traditions, and termination of reservations have been supplanted by perspectives that give communities more voice in how schools educate youth and that encourage the use of native languages and cultures to strengthen educational opportunities for Native American students.

Manualism versus Oralism

Education of the deaf in the United States provides an interesting parallel to the assimilationist theme apparent in attitudes toward Native American languages. As historian Douglas Baynton points out in *Forbidden Signs: American Culture and the Campaign against Sign Language*, attitudes toward sign language changed dramatically at the end of the nineteenth century. Deafness had been viewed as an affliction that isolated the deaf from religion and prayer. But after the Civil War period, it came to be seen as a social condition, isolating groups from the nation as a whole.[19] Baynton remarks that "the ardent nationalism that followed the Civil War—the sense that the divisions or particularisms within the nation were dangerous and ought to be suppressed—provided most of the initial impetus for a new concern about what came to be called the 'clannishness' of deaf people."[20] The deaf were treated essentially as immigrant communities and sign was referred to as a foreign language by Alexander Graham Bell and others. Bell in fact warned of the dangers of intermarriage of deaf adults creating a separatist race of deaf people.

The sentiment that deafness was a social problem as well as an individual affliction was reflected in a shift in the methods of teaching the deaf from manualism to oralism. Manualism, the use of sign language as a means of communication, had arisen from the work of reformers like Thomas Gallaudet, an evangelical minister who founded the American Asylum for the Deaf and Dumb in Hartford, Connecticut, in 1817. Gallaudet and others believed that the deaf could not acquire moral understanding without taking part in group religious exercises, which sign made possible. Gallaudet's manualism reflected a somewhat romantic view of the deaf as in need of salvation, but at the same time it acknowledged that the deaf were a cohesive community. By contrast, oralists tended to see community among the deaf as a danger and viewed sign as encouraging the deaf to communicate primarily among themselves. As Baynton notes, the focus of oralism was not on the individual but, as with the assimilation of Native Americans, on "national unity and social order through homogeneity in language and culture."[21]

Oralism focused instruction on the goal of speaking. It drew support from popular ideas from the emerging theory of evolution: sign language was seen as reflecting lower orders of communication and oral language as one of evolution's higher achievements. In fact, the view that oral language had arisen from gesture was taken as evidence that sign represented an evolutionary step back.[22] With its apparent progressive flavor and with advocates like Alexander Graham Bell, the oralist position took hold in the education system. According to Baynton, by 1899 sign was prohibited in about 40 percent of schools for the deaf and by 1920, in about 80 percent, establishing a pattern that held for the first half of the twentieth century.[23]

During the twentieth century, advocates of oralism also stressed pedagogical and psychological factors. Alexander and Ethel Ewing's 1964 *Teaching Deaf Children to Talk*, for example, argued that "the highest priority for deaf children is learning to talk, this not only in terms of speech as a means of communication, but because the spoken language is a prime factor in social development (from its very beginning with the mother child relationship) in thought-patterning and the development of intelligence."[24] And as Marc Marschark notes, until the late 1960s many hearing people still saw sign as "a relatively primitive communication system that lacked extensive vocabulary and the means to express subtle or abstract concepts."[25]

Like Native American languages, sign has enjoyed a resurgence in the last forty years. One factor in this was a critical mass of studies in the 1960s and 1970s confirming that oralism had failed. Education researcher Herbert Kohl, for example, in his 1966 study *Language and Education of the Deaf*, described deaf education as dismal. Kohl drew on government statistics showing that of the 1,104 sixteen-year-old students leaving deaf schools in 1961–1962, 501 graduated (with a mean grade level of 7.9) and 603 left without graduating (at a mean grade level of 4.7). He characterized the deaf child as isolated from the start of life, likely to show "outbursts of anger, rage, and frustration" in school, and to be "further frustrated by their failure in language" due to oral instruction.[26]

There may be other factors as well in the renewed viability of sign. Marschark notes that the number of deaf children experienced a tremendous growth in the 1960s due to the rubella epidemic of 1962–1965, which left close to 40,000 infants born deaf. This undoubtedly focused attention on improving deaf education. In addition, linguistic researchers from the 1970s on have emphasized the affinities of sign with spoken language. And members of the deaf community themselves have become very effective at making the case for sign language and deaf culture and at pointing out the failures of oralism.[27] Federal legislation has also benefited sign users: the Rehabilitation Act of 1973 required programs receiving federal aid to provide access to individuals with disabilities, with sign interpretation as a possible way of doing this for the deaf. And the 1990 Americans with Disabilities Act required comparable access in all state and local government schools, regardless of whether or not the schools get federal assistance.[28] For a variety of reasons, sign language has survived the assimilationist efforts of the oralist movement. Sign is accepted by many universities as meeting a second language requirement and major sign research centers exist at the Rochester Institute of Technology, the Salk Institute, and of course Gallaudet University. As with Native American languages, issues of access, education, and culture have reversed an earlier trend toward assimilating language communities.

Restrictions on Foreign Languages

So far we have seen how late nineteenth-century thinking reflected the assimilationist ideology of "one nation—one language." The national language impetus of colonial times evolved so that minority languages such as sign language and Native American languages came to be treated as diversity problems—as barriers to efficiency, national unity, and civic participation. The tension between assimilation and pluralism also provides a context from which to consider language issues that arise from immigration and settlement. In the early twentieth century, concerns about assimilation reached a fever pitch after the influx of immigration that lasted from 1880 to 1919. Some reactions, such as literacy tests and proposals for the deportation of immigrants who failed to learn English, were clearly exclusionary.[29] Other initiatives, such as those that focused on Americanization, were motivated by concern for the newcomers' welfare, as well as for promoting American ideas.

During this period public schools increasingly focused on Americanization and civics, and civics instruction included fostering certain attitudes toward language. There was an increased pressure to ensure that English was the language of the classroom by restricting foreign language instruction. The most famous incident of this sort is the case of *Meyer v. Nebraska*.[30] The *Meyer* case arose in the context of anti-German sentiment following World War I. Several states adopted laws that restricted the use of foreign languages in public, that prohibited foreign language parochial schools, and that proscribed the teaching of modern foreign languages to young children. Nervous about its state's German-speaking population, the Nebraska legislature passed two laws restricting foreign languages. In 1919 legislators passed an open meeting law which required that meetings concerning "political or nonpolitical subjects of general interest . . . be conducted in the English language exclusively." The other law, known as the Siman Law after its legislative sponsor, prohibited the teaching of any foreign language before the completion of the eighth grade and provided for a fine of up to $100 and a jail sentence of up to 30 days.[31]

The Siman Law was challenged when parochial school teacher Robert Meyer was fined for teaching German during the school's lunch hour. Meyer, who had been reading a Bible story in German to a student, claimed that he was merely providing religious instruction outside of normal school hours. While extracurricular religious instruction was allowable under the law, state prosecutors noted that the school had extended its lunch recess specifically to permit the lunchtime study of German. The Nebraska Supreme Court, voting 4–2, ruled that the school curriculum was within the state's jurisdiction and took the view that the teaching of foreign languages was harmful to the country and to young children. The Nebraska Court wrote:

> To allow the children of foreigners, who had emigrated here, to be taught from early childhood the language of the country of their parents was to rear them with that language as their mother tongue. It was to educate them so that they must always think in that language, and, as a consequence, naturally inculcate in them the ideas and sentiments foreign to the best interests of this country.[32]

The case was appealed to the United States Supreme Court, which ruled in 1923 that the restrictions on foreign language instruction were unconstitutional abridgements of liberty. Justice James McReynolds wrote the majority opinion voiding the Siman Law on the basis of the Fourteenth Amendment. McReynolds wrote that "the protection of the Constitution extends to all,—to those who speak other languages as well as to those born with English on the tongue."[33] He agreed that all citizens needed to be literate in English, writing that the Court appreciated "the desire of the legislature to foster a homogeneous people with American ideals, prepared readily to understand current discussions of civic matters." But he maintained that English literacy could not be promoted through an unconstitutional ban on foreign language instruction. McReynolds argued in addition that the state could not interfere with parents' natural duty to provide for the education of their children. The decision was not unanimous, however. Justice Oliver Wendell Holmes, Jr., dissented in the concurrent case of *Nebraska District of Evangelical Lutheran Synod v. McKelvie*, drawing on the idea that childhood is a critical time in establishing language skills:

Youth is the time when familiarity with a language is established and if there are sections in the State where a child would only hear Polish or French or German spoken at home I am not prepared to say that it is unreasonable to provide that in his early years he shall hear and speak only English at school. But if it is reasonable it is not an undue restriction of the liberty of either of teacher or scholar.

Meyer v. Nebraska provides a good illustration of the way in which foreign language issues were seen by policy makers in the first quarter of the twentieth century. Foreign languages were seen as promoting a heterogeneity at odds with good citizenship. Even as it accepted the rights of parents to have foreign languages taught to children, the Court asserted the desire of the majority for English literacy and for, in McReynolds's words, "a homogeneous people."

Bilingual Education

Just as earlier controversies about the teaching of foreign languages prefigure some of today's English-only debates, the issue of bilingualism and bilingual education has an interesting history as well. Though some of us may associate debates over bilingualism with issues arising in the last forty years, it has actually been a policy concern since the founding of the nation. In fact, the eighteenth-century and early nineteenth-century discussions of the role of German in Pennsylvania are similar to discussions heard today regarding Spanish. Benjamin Franklin worried about the third of the state's population who were German-speaking, fearing that Pennsylvania would become a German-dominated colony. Fears of political and cultural domination—and of possible sedition—led to proposals for Americanization of German areas and for English requirements for public discourse. But some early policy makers also advocated bilingual education as a means to assimilate the German population to English political and religious ideas, while at the same time providing them with an education in a language they could understand. Bilingualism came to be an important issue in the Pennsylvania Constitutional Convention of 1837–1838, at which Charles Ingersoll proposed that schools provide education in both English and German. According to linguist Dennis Baron, objections to Ingersoll's proposal included the fear that other languages would need similar provisions. Concerns were also expressed that bilingual teachers were generally less qualified and that bilingual education would corrupt schoolroom English. Some delegates also argued that there was little need for bilingual education because most Germans had been already assimilated to English and that educated Germans themselves favored assimilation. The Pennsylvania Constitutional Convention rejected Ingersoll's bilingualism proposal by fewer than ten votes.[34] As we will see, similar objections recur today in debates about bilingual education and English-only legislation.

The impetus for modern bilingual education efforts came from studies in the 1960s showing that schools were ignoring the language barrier between Spanish-speaking children and English-speaking teachers, and in some cases even punishing children for speaking Spanish. The 1968 Bilingual Education Act, sponsored by Senator Ralph Yarborough of Texas, was originally proposed as part of President Lyndon Johnson's Great Society programs aimed at improving school success and economic opportunity. In his January 1967 speech introducing the act, Senator Yarborough spoke of the disparities in the education of Mexican-American children in the Southwest in language echoing that of the Supreme Court's 1954 *Brown v. Board of Education* decision outlawing school segregation:

> Little children, many of whom enter school knowing no
> English and speaking only Spanish, are denied the use of their
> language. Spanish is forbidden to them, and they are required
> to struggle along as best they can in English, a language
> understood dimly by most and not at all by many.

Thus the Mexican American child is wrongly led to believe from the first day of school that there is something wrong with him, because of his language. This misbelief soon spreads to the image he has of his culture, of the history of his people, and of his people themselves. This is a subtle and cruel form of discrimination because it imprints upon the consciousness of young children an attitude which they will carry with them all the days of their lives.[35]

The 1968 Bilingual Education Act established federal jurisdiction over bilingual education and provided financial assistance for new programs, though without specifically defining what bilingual education was. Later amendments to the act, in 1974 and 1978, emphasized assimilation but also promoted language maintenance as well. Equally important in determining educational policy was Title VI of the 1964 Civil Rights Act, which prohibited discrimination on the basis of race or national origin in federally funded programs.

The view that equal treatment alone did not address the needs of students with limited English proficiency led to lawsuits such as *Lau v. Nichols* in 1974. In the Lau case, parents of about 3,000 students in San Francisco filed a class-action suit that argued that the city of San Francisco had not provided sufficient supplementary instruction in English to students whose primary language was Chinese. The U.S. Supreme Court ultimately reversed a Federal District Court ruling that having access to the same curriculum entailed lack of discrimination.[36] However, the Supreme Court's opinion did not provide a specific remedy; it only required that the Board of Education solve the problem. The Lau decision was extended to all public schools as part of the 1974 Equal Educational Opportunity Act but again without identifying solutions. In 1975, the Department of Health, Education, and Welfare began outlining so-called Lau remedies, which included a requirement that students' native languages be used in instruction and that native cultures be taken into account as well. Compliance to the Lau ruling was monitored by the

U.S. Office of Civil Rights. But as many states adopted bilingual education measures, school systems often were compelled to develop bilingual programs whether or not they had any expertise in doing so. As linguist Lily Wong Fillmore has noted, many programs that arose this way were perfunctory and understaffed, leading to poor results.[37]

As English language education became more central to the work of schools, various types of programs developed. English as a second language instruction is typically geared to classes that are made up of students from many different languages and often focuses specifically on English skills. By contrast, transitional bilingual education programs involve classes of students who share the same second language. In such cases, instruction in school subjects takes place in the native language but time is also spent on English. English immersion approaches are ones in which instruction is entirely in English (often simplified) and which focus both on English skills and on other academic subjects. Still another approach is dual-immersion (or two-way bilingual education), where instruction is given in two languages. Here classes include native speakers of two languages, for example, English and Spanish, with the goal being dual proficiency.

Transitional bilingual education came under increasing attack in the 1980s as Hispanic and Asian immigration increased and as social programs lost federal funding. Such critics as Education Secretary William Bennett argued that there was no evidence that bilingual education programs helped students learn English. In 1980, an English-only Lau remedy had been approved in Virginia because the number of language groups made bilingual education less feasible than intensive English instruction. Soon Congressional amendments began to focus on the possibility of adding English-only immersion methods to Lau remedies, and a 1988 reauthorization designated up to 25 percent of the federal funding for immersion methods. Amendments to the Bilingual Education Act in 1994 increased emphasis on bilingual education, bilingual proficiency, and language maintenance, but funding was then cut by over 30 percent in 1996.

The broad policy goal of bilingual education programs remains educational opportunity and assimilation of minorities to English. Opponents of bilingual education often see it as unnecessarily delaying the learning of English and as unrealistically assuming that minority children can be comfortable in both cultures. Arguments are often focused on the effectiveness of bilingual programs and the claim that they are costly diversions from English instruction that reduce incentives to learn English. Opponents also argue that bilingual education serves more as a means of preserving ethnic cultures than of assimilating speakers to English and American culture. Bilingual education has been characterized by some as a cultural program for minorities rather than an educational program aimed at fluency in English. In a 1985 opinion piece in the *New York Times*, writer Richard Rodriguez argued that bilingual education efforts, despite the outward focus on learning English, reflect ethnic identity movements that romanticize dual culture. In Rodriguez's view, the cost of bilingual efforts is the embarrassment and silence of working-class immigrant children who do not succeed in mastering English.[38]

In June of 1998, 61 percent of California voters approved Proposition 227 (*English Language in the Public Schools*), which required that students from non-English backgrounds be taught in intensive immersion classes rather than bilingual programs. The initiative was part of a broader "English for the Children" campaign initiated by California activist Ron Unz. As a result, California law now requires that schools place children with limited English skills in an English immersion program for at least a year. As the name of Unz's campaign suggests, the rationale is that early literacy in English is fostered by rapid exposure to native speakers of English in mainstream classrooms. In 2002 Massachusetts voters followed, overwhelmingly rejecting bilingual education in favor of English immersion classes. Massachusetts had been the first state to enact bilingual education in 1971, but 70 percent of voters approved ballot Question 2, funded by Unz.[39] Like the California measure, Question 2 called for placing most non-English-speaking students in English immersion classes for a year. Under the Massachusetts bilingual education plan that had existed, about 30,000 non-English-speaking students took subjects like math or science in their native languages, easing into English over time. In California, bilingual programs served about 30 percent of that state's 1.3 million limited-English-proficiency students. Critics of these measures have expressed concern about inflexible, state-mandated curricula and about the potential difficulty of obtaining waivers for parents who choose not to have their children participate in immersion. Educators have concerns as well. One is the effect that mainstreaming limited English speakers after just one year of English instruction might have on the broader learning environment. Another is the consequence of grouping students by English proficiency rather than age.

Proponents of transitional bilingual education often view sink-or-swim approaches as ineffective and unfair, arguing that non-English-speaking children fall behind in early learning and cognitive development when they are unable to comprehend classroom language. Supporters of bilingual education may also argue that rejection of the home language in English-only immersion affects children's self-perception, as Senator Ralph Yarborough did in introducing the act. In addition, proponents often stress bilingual education as a positive factor in developing a workforce competent in languages other than English, and see support for bilingualism in childhood as a way to foster adult second-language proficiency.

Does bilingual education work? Is it better or worse than immersion programs? A review commissioned by the National Research Council and the Institute of Medicine assessed the success of various types of bilingual and second-language learning efforts. Chaired by Stanford University psychologist Kenji Hakuta and directed by Diane August of the National Research Council, the study was unable to answer the question of what type of program was best. Hakuta and August found beneficial effects to both bilingual programs and structured immersion programs, and noted that successful bilingual and immersion programs had elements in common. They concluded that questions of effectiveness needed to be community based. Equally significant, the study condemned the "extreme politicization" of the research process by advocates, noting that "most consumers of the research are not researchers who want to know the truth, but advocates who are convinced of the absolute correctness of their positions."[40]

English-Only

In the background of the debate over bilingual education and immersion is the recent campaign to make English the official language of many states. The origins of this English-only effort began with California Senator S. I. Hayakawa's unsuccessful English Language Amendment to the U.S. Constitution. In the early 1980s, Hayakawa and others believed such an amendment was necessary to prevent language differences from becoming divisive. Following the defeat of that amendment, Hayakawa and John Tanton of the Federation for American Immigration Reform founded the group U.S. English in 1983.[41] This group saw a number of political successes including initiatives that made English the official language of various states (in Virginia, Indiana, Kentucky, Missouri, Alaska, Tennessee, California, Georgia, Arkansas, Mississippi, North Dakota, North Carolina, South Carolina, Arizona, Colorado, Florida, Alabama, New Hampshire, Montana, Utah, South Dakota, Iowa, and Wyoming). Some of these initiatives were characterized by proponents as merely symbolic. Others, however, were intended to curtail demands for bilingual services. As linguist Geoffrey Nunberg reports, English-only advocates have petitioned for limits on the number of licenses for foreign-language radio stations and have attempted to halt the publication of such resources as the *Hispanic Yellow Pages*.[42]

While the U.S. English group has been successful in promoting English-only legislation at the state level, restrictive legislation has been challenged in courts. Arizona's 1988 English-only amendment, for example, was struck down in 1990 because it required the use of English by state employees on the job. Judge Paul Rosenblatt ruled that by prohibiting state legislators from speaking to their constituents in languages other than English, the state amendment abridged First Amendment rights. Judge Rosenblatt noted that while the government may regulate the speech of public employees in the interests of efficiency, "a state may not apply stricter standards to its legislators than it may to private citizens, . . . nor may a state require that its officers and employees relinquish rights guaranteed them by the First Amendment as a condition of public employment."[43] Rosenblatt stopped short, however, of ruling that the plaintiff had a First Amendment right to speak Spanish at work.

The arguments of English-only proponents draw on the idea of English as having an economic and civic value, but also on fears about linguistic diversity.[44] English-only rhetoric casts English as the bond that unites us as a nation and sees that unity as threatened by bilingual services, foreign-language mass media, and the preservation of heritage languages. Such services and efforts are seen as a disincentive to the transition to English and as serving the interests of separatist ethnic leaders. For example, a U.S. English fundraising brochure from the mid-1980s describes English as being "under attack" and raises fears of "institutionalized language segregation and a gradual loss of national unity."[45] The brochure also refers disapprovingly to "new civil rights assertions" such as bilingual ballots and voting instructions, to "record immigration . . . reinforcing language segregation and retarding language assimilation," and to the availability of foreign-language electronic media as providing "a new disincentive to the learning of English." In addition to the English-only constitutional amendment, the brochure called for elimination of bilingual ballots, curtailment of bilingual education, enforcement of English language requirements for naturalization, and the expansion of opportunities for learning English.[46]

English-only rhetoric also draws on the fears of the kind of violence and fragmentation that have affected Canada. In the 1960s the Canadian province of Quebec became the focus of militant efforts to establish a separate French-speaking nation. Beginning in 1969, a series of riots and terrorist acts, including the kidnapping and murder of Quebec's minister of labor and immigration, led the Canadian government to temporarily suspend civil liberties in 1970. After a political accommodation was reached, French became the official language of Quebec in 1974. In 1976 Quebec separatists won the provincial election and soon passed a charter that restricted education in English-language schools, changed English place-names, and established French as the language of government and public institutions. While Quebec voters rejected referenda to make the province an independent country in 1980 and again in 1995, the earlier pattern of violence, legislation, and separatism has made many Americans nervous about heritage language retention, especially in the Southwest where there are large numbers of Hispanic speakers.

English-only rhetoric incorrectly assumes that today's immigrants refuse to learn English and that official status is an effective means of fostering identification with the majority culture. Sociologist Carol Schmid has summarized a number of surveys of immigrant attitudes which suggest that there is little danger of English losing its desirability for nonnative speakers, and which dispel the fallacy that Spanish speakers don't want to learn English.[47] She notes that surveys of Hispanics find that they overwhelmingly support the idea that speaking and understanding English is necessary for citizenship and economic success, a fact that is also supported by the robustness of advertisements for English training on Spanish-language television. And there is also evidence that speakers of other languages shift to English over time. Schmid cites the well-known study by Calvin Veltman which found that about three-quarters of Spanish-speaking immigrants were speaking English regularly after about fifteen years of residence.[48] She also emphasizes that language loyalty rates of Spanish speakers in the Southwest actually declined between 1970 and 1990. The idea that English is in danger from Spanish is not supported by such data.

The English-only movement of the 1980s and 1990s has been counterbalanced to some extent by the work of groups such as the English Plus Clearinghouse and the English Plus Coalition, both of which were established in 1986. These groups see the learning of languages as a resource and argue that English-only restrictions are counterproductive both economically and politically. They have also argued that English-only laws are unnecessary as a means of fostering assimilation. As linguist Robert King has emphasized, linguistic diversity does not necessarily entail political violence.[49] The English-only rhetoric ignores the many linguistically heterogeneous nations that lack the separatist violence that has existed in Belgium, Sri Lanka, and Canada. Switzerland, for example, has a long tradition of language rights, decentralization, and power sharing among groups, and the Swiss very successfully accommodate multilingualism. Schmid sees the Swiss adaptation to multilingualism as an instructive model for both the United States and Canada.[50] Switzerland arose from a military confederacy of German states dating from 1291, which gradually added French, Italian, and Romansch allies. Though German remained the alliance's official language until 1798, there was little linguistic conflict among the various cantons, and a tradition of local autonomy and diversity was an important factor in attracting new groups to the confederation. An 1848 constitution established the equality of French, German, and Italian in the Swiss confederation by making them all national languages. And while today's French-speaking minority in Switzerland has a strong linguistic identity, the intensity of that identity is attenuated by Swiss national pride and the allegiance of French and German speakers to a common civic culture. There are also important differences between the language situations in the United States and in Canada which suggest that the Canadian experience is not likely to be repeated in the United States. Schmid emphasizes that the dominance of English has historically been much stronger in the United States than in Canada, and she notes the strong interest that nonnative speakers in the United States have had in learning English. She attributes the interest in separatism in Canada to French-Canadians' worries over assimilation, to optimism about the sustainability of a separate existence, and to the failure of Canadian political institutions to accommodate the collective identity of a French-speaking region. These different conditions suggest that the United States is in no danger of being overcome by linguistic separatism.

One Flag, One Language

The ideology of language assimilation arises from several factors. It is motivated by the belief that a common language is necessary for national unity and for economic productivity. It is also motivated by the assumption that a common language resolves social differences and builds understanding among those of different backgrounds. And it is motivated by the fear that language diversity will lead to political disunity and potential violence. In the United States there have also been sustained periods in which foreign and minority languages have been stigmatized, suppressed, and seen as problems to be overcome rather than resources to be fostered. As a result, foreign languages and minority languages have been the focus of social engineering that often attempts to legislate a process of assimilation already underway and to dictate its nature as monolingual rather than bilingual. The acceptance of sign language and the preservation and revitalization of Native American language are areas where progress has been seen. But the perception of foreign languages seems to have changed little since Theodore Roosevelt's 1917 statement extolling language as the symbol of national unity.

Six Bad Accents

In the early days of television broadcasting, many people wondered whether exposure to national standards of speech would soon obliterate regional dialects. If you watch any television at all, you've probably noticed that this has not happened. First-language English speakers—even newscasters—don't all sound alike, and dialect variation not only persists but in many cases has even become more noticeable in many areas. But while many speakers see their dialects as indications of regional or ethnic pride, many also see dialects as bad English. The ideology of assimilation discussed in the last chapter is also a factor in the way people respond to dialect variation—regional and ethnic accents are often treated as deviating from a desired national standard. People characterize dialects in negative ways: as harsh, flat, nasal, heavy, thick, slow, fast, or ignorant, and as having a twang, drawl, brogue, or lilt. Dialects are also labeled in relation to cultural symbols, as the speech of rednecks, surfers, Yankees, Valley girls, immigrants, yuppies, or "the street." And, of course, the labeling of dialects is related to region and ethnicity: we talk about Southern, New England, New York, Midwestern, or Texas accents, and we talk about Black English, Cajun, Spanglish, and Pennsylvania Dutch, to cite just a few examples.

The line between languages and dialects is notoriously difficult to draw, and one of the fundamental principles of modern linguistics is the fact that all dialects—like all languages—are linguistically equal. As I noted in chapter 1, this is because dialects themselves are systematic and regular and their differences are regular as well. Take, for example, the pronunciation of *ten* and *pen* as "tin" and "pin" in some southern speech. The contrast between *e* and *i* is often lost when a nasal consonant follows (*n, m,* or *ng*). So we find an *i* in words like *Ben, Ken, Wendy, feminine,* and *when*. But we are unlikely to find it in words such as *bet, wet, let, Kelly, well,* and *February*. We say that the dialect variation is systematic because the distinction between short *e* and short *i* tends to merge according to a pattern or rule—it occurs before the nasal consonants *m, n,* and *ng*. It's not the case that Southerners find this a hard distinction to make.

This is the important fact about dialect differences. They are due to pronunciation regularities of a region or group, rather than to a failure to acquire language correctly. Another example of the systematic nature of dialects involves the pronunciation of short *a*. The initial vowel of *coffee, sausage, chocolate,* and *Florida* for many American speakers is a short back *a* so that they are pronounced *cahffee, sahsage, chahcolate,* and *Flahrida*. For many speakers in the East, however, these words have a slighter higher and more rounded pronunciation so that they are pronounced *cawffee, sawsage, chawcolate* and *Flawrida*. The *aw* is especially common, for example, before *f, s,* and *th* as in the words *off, cough, offer, officer, coffee, boss, loss, broth,* and *moth*. Again the variation reflects a regular pattern of correspondence among sounds rather than something random and irregular.[1]

Because all dialects have systematic patterns of usage, none can be said to be more regular than others. It is equally true, however, that dialects are not all socially equal. The social inequality of dialects arises in part from the belief that many differences in American speech have been leveled out by expansion and migration and from the conviction that leveled, homogeneous speech is desirable. Historian Daniel Boorstin, for example, reinforced these perceptions when he claimed that "The linguistic uniformity of American English is geographic (without barriers of regional dialect) and social (without barriers of caste or class). Both types of uniformity have had vast consequences for the national life; they have been both symptoms and causes of a striving for national unity."[2] The association of national unity and social equality with leveling of dialects parallels the assimilationist ideology that has been applied to minority and foreign languages. Dialect is often seen as bad language to be eliminated in favor of a national standard.

Broken English

In the last chapter we looked at the perception that English is necessary for unity, efficiency, and success and the concern that foreign language maintenance is inefficient, divisive, and costly. Before we turn to regional and ethnic dialects of English, it is worth spending some time thinking about attitudes toward foreign accents.

In chapter 1, I mentioned the 1952 episode of *I Love Lucy*, in which Lucy Ricardo says to her husband, Ricky, "Please, promise me you won't speak to our child until he's nineteen or twenty." Lucy was concerned enough about her own "lousy English" to hire a speech tutor (an Englishman). But she was even more worried about Ricky's Cuban accent. The episode poked fun at Lucy's attitude, but the concern over catching the accent of nonnative speakers remains today. While foreign languages are not necessarily bad, the nonnative English of immigrants is still seen as "broken." This metaphor of broken English suggests language that does not do its job well and is in need of repair. In fact, the characterization of broken English reflects three familiar themes—accents as contaminating, accents as confusing, and accents as a barrier to success.

In her book *English with an Accent*, linguist Rosina Lippi-Green recounts the controversy that ensued in 1992 in Westfield, Massachusetts, over the reassignment of two bilingual teachers to nonbilingual classrooms. Over 400 people signed a petition, spearheaded by Westfield's mayor, which urged that first- and second-grade teachers be "thoroughly proficient in the English language in terms of grammar, syntax, and—most important—the accepted and standardized use of pronunciations."[3] The petition was rejected by the full school board, but the controversy illustrates public concern over accent and its potential to shape the speech of children. Westfield's mayor, himself an immigrant, reflected this concern when he remarked that immigrants like him should not be teaching five- or six-year-olds speech because they would only pass along "confusion" and "defects." However, research on language acquisition shows that the development of children's accents depends much more on their interaction with peers than on the models provided by parents, teachers, or the media, so such concerns are misplaced.[4] Teachers must understand their subject material and be understandable to their students, but there is no danger of students catching their accents.

In the early part of the twentieth century, teacher certification guidelines in some states required speech and pronunciation tests that routinely excluded nonnative speakers from teaching careers.[5] While speech tests are no longer widely used, current teacher certification guidelines in most states require that teachers be proficient in Standard English. For example, Massachusetts Department of Education regulations as of 2003 require a demonstration of fluency for all teachers in English-language classrooms. But they require a test only when the determination cannot be made by a supervising school official observing a teacher.[6]

In higher education, the concerns expressed are less about the potential of accents to affect speech than about students' perceived difficulties in learning from nonnative speakers. Perhaps the most notable complaints arise in large research universities, where students sometimes complain about the comprehensibility of nonnative teaching assistants. An opinion column in the *Johns Hopkins Newsletter*, for example, aired a freshman's complaint that "There stands a wall of confusion between many international teaching assistants (TAs) and their students" and that "in a standard Hopkins physics sections, students learn more about Chinese syntax than about the interactions between subatomic particles."[7] A September 2000 national news story reported "a fresh wave of complaints about the speaking ability of TAs," citing student complaints at almost a dozen universities including the University of Missouri at Columbia, Northeastern University, and Princeton. After a similar wave of complaints in the 1980s, many states began to require English proficiency for university teaching assistants, and many universities, in turn, adopted standardized oral exams to assess spoken English proficiency of nonnative speakers.[8] However, it is difficult to determine exactly how much of a problem really exists. A study by Harvard economist George Borjas looked at differences in the grade point average of large economics classes taught by native English speakers and nonnatives. Borjas found a .2 grade point difference between sections, but he cautioned that his study was quite limited. An earlier study by education researcher Donald Rubin suggested that students' perceptions of accent and ethnicity can affect their performance on comprehension tests even when the English samples are native.[9]

A third concern about accent is one often raised by nonnative speakers themselves. This is the worry that accented English will be a barrier to success. According to a March 2002 U.S. Census Bureau report, about 11.5 percent of the U.S. population was foreign-born.[10] Employees worry about being misunderstood, being stereotyped, and losing jobs and promotions. As one speech teacher comments, "Accents breed biases. Some people mistakenly hear laziness, or stupidity, in an accent."[11] The concern is apparent from the way that advertisers of accent reduction courses position their products by noting that "accents can hamper performances, can adversely influence advancement and promotion, and may be a source of concern and embarrassment."[12] Employers, in turn, worry about accents in terms of efficiency, customer relations, and image, and high-tech companies such as Microsoft, Texas Instruments, and Toshiba often contract with private firms to offer accent reduction courses for international employees. Accent bias has become a legal issue as well. The Equal Employment Opportunity Commission (EEOC) addresses accent under the guidelines prohibiting national origin discrimination. The EEOC guidelines do permit employers to take accent into account when effective oral communication in English is required for the job, but only in such cases.[13] But while such legal protections are in place, the growth of accent reduction services suggests that both nonnative speakers and employers take a functional view of English and see a strong connection between language and economics.[14]

Attitudes toward Regional Dialects

Many second-language speakers feel social and economic pressures to modify their accents. Similar pressures are often felt by speakers of regional, social, and ethnic dialects. Their speech may be seen as a real or potential communication barrier. It may be seen as indicating lack of access to quality education or to correct information. And it may be seen as an impediment to economic and social success or a reflection of a parochialism to be educated away as speakers become more cosmopolitan.

How do these attitudes come about? As Gavin Jones points out in his book *Strange Talk: The Politics of Dialect in Gilded Age America*, in the period after the Civil War, dialect literature like Mark Twain's *Huckleberry Finn* assumed an increasingly important role in the public consciousness. While dialect literature was part of the movement toward realism and became a staple of novels and plays, it was at the same time a way of satirizing regional speakers and ethnic minorities, a tradition that continued later in vaudeville and television. Many nineteenth-century writers and literary opinion-makers viewed speech as characterizing properties of mind, with problems of verbal culture sometimes even seen as reflecting physiological and moral degeneration. Dialect was a means of spreading degeneration into the standard language—a metaphorical infection of a healthy standard.[15] For example, Henry James, in an address to the Bryn Mawr class of 1905, advised his audience of young women to learn to speak well and to follow the model of articulate careful speakers. Careless speech, he said, was a form of bad manners that produced social discord and cultural decay. James portrayed the English language as needing to be rescued from the influences of the schools, the press, and particularly immigrants—"the American Dutchman and Dago . . . [to whom] we have simply handed over our property."[16] James and others saw the foreign accents of immigrants as influencing American dialects negatively. In fact, satire of the dialects of immigrants was a staple of humor in the early twentieth century. Jones, for example, points out that works such as *Choice Dialect and Vaudeville Stage Jokes*, a 1902 manual of jokes and sketches, relied heavily on Irish, Italian, African-American, German, Yiddish, and Chinese caricatures. Of more than fifty sketches in the books, only two focused on regional American speech.[17]

Today, attitudes toward dialect are more likely to be fixed and reinforced by television and movies than by the written word or stage.[18] Yet the idea remains strong that dialects reflect the personality, character, and education of speakers (with "education" often a polite way to refer to intelligence). Attitudes are reflected to some extent in the popular descriptions of dialect speech (Boston Brahmin, hillbilly, cracker, street talk) and in stereotypes such as the rude New Yorker, the stoic New Englander, the naive Midwesterner, the shallow California valley girl or boy, the wily Southern belle, the slow-moving good old boy, and so on.[19] Television and film stereotypes often represent dialect characters as having particular social class backgrounds and experiences. For example, in the 1959 film *Pillow Talk*, Rock Hudson's character adopts a fake Texas accent (and the name Rex Stetson) in order to woo Doris Day. Responding to the accent, Day's character finds the faux Texan unpretentious and down-to-earth compared to the men she normally deals with. Similarly, the Dead End Kids and "Bowery Boys" films of Leo Gorcey, Huntz Hall, and Bobby Jordan used a working-class New York dialect for both realism (as in their introduction in the 1937 film *Dead End*) and increasingly for humor (as in the later Bowery Boys films where accent was combined with malapropism and urban parochialism).[20] A version of a New York working-class accent was even used by animator Mel Blanc to provide the speech patterns for the cartoon character Bugs Bunny. Attitudes toward dialects are also reflected in airport and rest-stop booklets on regional dialects, which exaggerate and reinforce stereotypes of dialect speakers. For example, Steve Mitchell's *How to Speak Southern* leads off with the entries *aint, airish, airs, argy,* and *arn* ("aunt," "drafty," "mistakes," "argue," and "iron") and includes others such as *mite could* ("might could") and *tawk* ("talk"). The respelling reinforces the idea that the dialect is fundamentally incorrect and that it leads to misunderstandings (such as "aint" for "aunt" and "airs" for "errors"). At the same time, however, the booklet takes ironic pride in the dialect with its dedication to "all Yankees in the hope that it will teach them to talk right."[21]

The popular stereotypes are not, however, just amusing examples of our ability to poke fun at regional differences. The view of dialect as metaphoric infection perhaps no longer predominates, but regional speakers still perceive that their abilities and social class are judged from their speech. In the documentary *American Tongues*, for example, a sales representative from New York complains that when she attends meetings elsewhere in the country people don't listen to what she says but instead focus on how she speaks. Reflecting on reactions to her dialect, she remarks that "Automatically when they hear this Brooklyn accent, they think like you grew up in a slum, hanging out on a corner, and you know, they get the wrong impression."[22] Research by Patricia Cukor-Avila and Dianne Markley tested the idea that accent creates an impression of ability. Cukor-Avila and Markley asked 56 human resource professionals to assess the education, initiative, and personality of potential employees based on a 45-second reading sample and to recommend the best type of job for the speaker. They found that job seekers with identifiable accents, such as a heavy Southern or New Jersey accent, were more often recommended for lower-level jobs with little customer interaction. Those with less identifiable accents were more often recommended for high contact and high profile jobs.[23]

Just as teachers with nonnative accents have been referred for speech correction, it was not so long ago that teachers with regional dialects were subject to the same regimen. Linguist Raven McDavid, in his essay "Linguistics, Through the Kitchen Door," reported that in 1937 when he was teaching at the Citadel, the college president ordered him to summer school to take refresher courses in elocution to lose his accent.[24] Today, many native speakers still invest in accent-reduction courses with the idea of suppressing a regional accent. A 1998 *New York Times* report on accent reduction, for example, refers to the many executives in major corporations who have sought out voice training to combat monotony, nasality, shrillness, rapidity, and accents. In the story, a Julliard-trained voice coach stresses that "Certain accents—not just foreign either—can give a negative impression."[25] The broadcast media has also reinforced the idea of a more desirable general American dialect. Manuals of pronunciation for broadcasters link efficient communication with "Western, Middle Western, or General American" speech.[26] The view that the regional dialects of the South and East are leveled in the Midwest is also a factor in other communications industry choices, such as the concentration of telemarketing firms in certain areas and the selection of the voice of directory assistance. In *American Tongues*, Ramona Lenny, who was for many years the voice of directory assistance, remarks that the telephone company was "looking for generic speech. Or some people call it homogenized speech. Speech that would float in any part of the country and didn't sound like it came from somewhere in particular, perhaps the voice from nowhere."[27]

Studies on language attitudes, such as those by linguist Dennis Preston and others, have found that speakers tend to prefer the dialect of their own region. Preston has also found that respondents surveyed in places like Michigan viewed Southern speech as generally less correct and less pleasant than that of the rest of the country. The speech of New York City and New Jersey is also viewed as low in correctness and pleasantness. In fact, the New York area working-class accent and the Southern rural accent are probably the two most stigmatized and stereotyped regional variants.[28] New York speech might once have been associated with the upper-crust speech of Franklin Roosevelt; today, it is more likely associated with Fran Drescher's portrayal of *The Nanny* or *Saturday Night Live*'s "Cawfee Tawk" skit. In the *Saturday Night Live* skit, a fictional cable morning show host uses a stigmatized variant of the eastern short *a* mentioned earlier in which the AW of *coffee* is followed by an UH sound (cAWUHfee). Stereotypes of New York metropolitan speech also often draw on features such as r-lessness (for example, *nawth* or *nawt* for *north* or *fought* for *fourth*), the replacement of *th* with *d* and *t* (*den* for *then* or *nuttin* for *nothing*) and addition of an UH sound to the front *a* of words like *bad* (bAUHd). Perceptions of the working-class dialects of New York and New Jersey sometimes reflect the idea that speakers are always in a hurry or that crowded urban areas provoke loud and rude speech. Attitudes may also be shaped by the assumption that nonstandard urban speech is associated with urban poverty. As the Brooklyn speaker quoted above notes, listeners may infer that a speaker with a certain urban accent "grew up in a slum" and they may draw conclusions from speech about speakers' backgrounds, experiences, and reliability.

Negative associations are also reflected in perceptions about Southern speech. There are, of course, many different kinds of Southern speech—the dialects of the South vary socially and regionally from the Gulf of Mexico to the Shenandoah Valley and from urban setting to rural. But such variation often merges in popular stereotypes, just as the variation of urban New York speech is merged. The rest of the country tends to see the South as a single population that is distinct from the North, Midwest, and West.[29] The salient image of the South is a historical one, rooted in perceptions that remain from the Civil War and Reconstruction. While the North is tied to associations of industry and progress, the South is seen as agricultural and nostalgic. And while Northerners are stereotyped as hard-working, reliable, and serious, Southerners are patient, friendly, and folksy. The image of Southern speech portrays it as more parochial and less educated than other varieties as well. In part, this may be due to the prevailing stereotypes about the region and their reinforcement in films and other media. It may also in part be due to a reinterpretation of regional dialects as social ones. In the past as many poorer and less-educated workers migrated from the South in search of jobs in other parts of the country, their differences of speech would have distinguished them. Differences of speech would have been associated with their educational and economic status as well, reinforcing non-Southerners' preconceptions and prejudices about the region. In the last quarter of the twentieth century as many national businesses moved to the South, dialect also became an issue for Southerners seeking economic opportunity within their own region. The themes of Northerners' perceptions and of miscommunication between Southerners and others are common, and myths remain about Southern speech—for example, that the Southern drawl is due to the heat in the South or that it somehow represents a more relaxed and less serious approach to life.[30] Humorist Dave Barry, for example, worries about flying because he doesn't like to be in a "complex piece of machinery controlled by someone with a southern accent" and the *Chicago Tribune*'s Mike Royko jokes that President Bill Clinton attended Yale and Oxford but "still talk[s] like a Hillbilly."[31]

Perceptions of rural Southern dialects, like views of urban working-class dialects, reflect mainstream assumptions about the relation between dialect and education. Dialects are often stereotyped as the result of poor learning and (presumably) poor schools. Much dialect usage is thus characterized as bad speech from two perspectives. First, it is local rather than national, so it falls together with foreign accents and minority languages. Second, it is nonstandard and consequently viewed as substandard and error-based. It the first case, dialects are bad English because they are thought to inhibit communication, betray one's origin, and compete with a national standard for the loyalty of speakers.

In the second, dialects invite assumptions about education and intelligence.

If dialects have these social disadvantages, why do they persist? Why doesn't exposure to Standard English—delivered via television or travel, for example—level out regional speech in favor of a national usage? The question assumes that regional speech perseveres simply because of the old-fashionedness of speakers or because of their geographical or social isolation.[32] In other words, it assumes that speakers would give up their dialects if they knew better and worked at it. Actually, however, regional accents are often retained and even intensified as a means of asserting local identity, particularly with younger people who stay in or return to their communities. In a classic study of variation, sociolinguist William Labov made this point in the 1960s. Labov studied the speech of Martha's Vineyard, a New England island with a tourist population several times the size of its small permanent population. The island is divided into an eastern part that is popular with tourists and a more rural western part that is the center of the island's fishing trade. Labov studied the vowel sounds AW and AY in words like *house* and *height*. He found that younger speakers native to the island seemed to be shifting their pronunciations of such words away from the standard and toward dialect pronunciations associated with fishermen of the western part of the island. He found, in fact, that the heaviest users of this nonstandard pronunciation were young men wanting to identify themselves with the traditional values of the island as opposed to tourists. Included in this group were many college-educated young men from the island who were well-exposed to the norms of the education system and to speakers from other areas. Here the value of the traditional island pronunciation as representing island virtues was a stronger factor than conformity to the educated standard.

Another example, perhaps involving a more familiar setting, comes from Penelope Eckert's study of the speech of groups of students in a suburban high school. Studying student social groups in a school near Detroit, Michigan, in the early 1980s, Eckert found the high school population to be defined by two groups, the more conventional "jocks" and the counterculture "burnouts," with a large population of students falling between these. Jocks and burnouts were intentional in creating their group identities by adopting different styles of dress, music, habits, activities, and language. Looking at the speech of groups, Eckert found that burnout girls tended to take the lead in certain pronunciation changes. For example, they led in adopting a pronunciation of words like *mother* and *something*, which standardly have an *uh* vowel in the first syllable, with the sound of the *oo* of *foot*.[33] It is clear that the burnouts are exposed to Standard English, given the school situation and the use of the more standard pronunciation by other students and adults. Rather, their speech variation is intentional and purposeful in terms of group identity.[34] So the idea that dialects are inexorably being leveled out may reflect wishful thinking that variation will merge as speakers gain more information about what the norm is. Such wishful thinking ignores the important social role of variation. Sources of cosmopolitanism such as television, literature, and travel are of little use if there is no social incentive or opportunity to put that information into practice. We adjust our speech to fit in with our peers or those that we want to be our peers. In everyday life, good English is not the voice from nowhere—it is the voice of our peers.

Ebonics

Perhaps no ethnic variety of English has been as high profile as African American Vernacular English, or Ebonics. In recent years, Ebonics has twice captured national attention for short but intense periods. The first time was after a 1979 federal court decision involving the Ann Arbor, Michigan, public school system. The second time was nearly twenty years later after a controversial resolution passed on December 18, 1996, by the Oakland, California, School Board.

The study of African-American speech has a rich history, with differences in black and white speech noted even in colonial times. In the nineteenth century, the tradition of dialect literature included the work of such writers as George Washington Cable and Joel Chandler Harris. In the twentieth century, pioneers in the study of African-American speech included Lorenzo Dow Turner, author of *Africanisms in the Gullah Dialect*, a book that documented the contribution of thousands of African words to the Gullah dialect spoken on the Sea Islands off the coast of South Carolina and Georgia. Linguists Beryl Bailey and William Stewart extended this work by noting similarities among African-American English, African-based creoles such as Krio (spoken in Sierra Leone), and the Caribbean creoles of Barbados and Jamaica. Their work suggested an African-Caribbean-North American language continuum and a creole origin for African-American Vernacular.[35] In a different vein, William Labov's sociolinguistic work of the 1960s helped to demonstrate the regularity of African-American English and led to many other important studies of African-American urban speech. Other key researchers include Geneva Smitherman, whose work has provided a larger discourse and social context for African-American English; John Baugh, who has analyzed many of the syntactic patterns of African-American English and applied sociolinguistic research to educational policy; and John Rickford, who focuses on patterns of diffusion, contact, and divergence. The work of these scholars reflects the range of contributions of modern sociolinguistics.

In earlier times and earlier work, however, African-American English had fared badly. Some nineteenth-century writers, such as William Francis Allen in his 1867 introduction to *Slave Songs of the American South*, treated African-American dialects as arising from "phonetic decay," "corruption in pronunciation," and "extreme simplification."[36] James Harrison, whose essays in the 1880s perceptively noted the influence of African-American English on the speech Southern whites, nevertheless attributed features of the dialect to "thick lips" and "aural myopia."[37] While the scholarly tradition has moved ahead in the last century, popular views of African-American English, both in the white and black communities, have not kept pace. Many people still dismiss African-American English as merely being informal, sloppy speech or as a kind of ethnic slang. Prescriptive commentators and others unfa-

miliar with the complexity of language tend to focus on the easily identifiable features of African-American English such as the pronunciation of voiceless *th* as *f* at the end of words (as in *both* or *mouth*),
variation in word endings or verb forms (such as the omission of *is* and
the possessive in examples like *She a mamma girl* (for *She's a mamma's
girl*), or the use of *be* as in *He be late every time.*[38] Such differences are
offered up as evidence of lazy incorrectness or mislearning. Similarly,
discussion of vocabulary differences often focus on slang expressions
such as *bling bling, chill out, threads, fresh, phat,* and *homeboys,* many
of which cross over into mainstream casual usage. However, such slang
is often treated as evidence of the inappropriate informality of African-
American speech.

The differences between African-American English and other dialects extend far beyond the existence of an African-American accent,
grammatical differences, and slang vocabulary. Discussions of African-
American English often gloss over the nonslang vocabulary of African-
American experience, such as historical and church usages like
Juneteenth and *Amen corner* or everyday terms like *ashy.*[39] Similarly,
subtle systematic differences between African-American English and the
mainstream are often ignored. As an example, consider the use of the
word *steady* as in *He steady be tellin em how to run they lives.* As John
Baugh notes, *steady* functions as a predicate adverb in this and other
examples like *Ricky Bell be steady steppin in them number nines; And you
know we be steady jammin all the Crips; Them fools steady hustlin every-
body they see; Her mouth is steady runnin;* and *All the homeboys be rappin
steady.*[40] Baugh points out that *steady* parallels features of Standard
English *steadily* but is also unique in that its use in African-American
vernacular requires animate subjects that are specific. So speakers of African-American vernacular would not find examples like *A man be rappin
steady* natural since the subject is generic rather than specific. In addition, the difference between *be* and *is* signals habitual versus simple
present tense for most speakers, so many speakers of African-American
vernacular will distinguish between the meanings of *His mouth is
steady runnin* (present) and *His mouth be steady runnin* (habitual).

Even looking at just the examples of *steady* and *be*, we can see that it is a mistake to view African-American vernacular language differences simply as grammatical irregularities and errors. The usage of words like *steady* and *be* reflects the unique and regular patterns of African-American vernacular speech. There are many other differences as well, ranging from pronunciation and vocabulary to grammar and meaning.

The study of African-American English has often been controversial and it has been dominated by a contentious debate over whether African-American English is just a dialect or really a separate language.[41] However, the debate about whether African-American English is a separate language has overshadowed what should be the key issue: the consequences of that dialect. The educational issues related to African-American vernacular are similar to those raised in connection with other minority languages and dialects. To what extent does a language barrier exist that impedes progress in learning to read and write? And to what extent do language differences prejudice listeners (especially teachers and employers)?

Using foreign language methods to address a potential language barrier among students whose primary language is African-American vernacular was first suggested in the 1960s. The basic idea was to teach children to read by first using African-American vernacular texts and later introducing standard school English. So-called bridge readers provided readings in African-American vernacular along with contrastive and situational exercises. Advocates of such bidialect programs cite a pilot project by psychologists Gary and Charlesetta Simpkins in which fourteen teachers and twenty-seven classes of students in four different parts of the country tested the idea that reading skills could be improved by using these methods.[42] Students in the study improved reading skills (as measured by the Iowa Test) by 6.2 months in the four-month period of the study while students in the control group improved by only 1.6 months. Some critics have argued that such methods as bridge readers are ill-considered because they can interfere with the learning of Standard English (paralleling arguments used against bilingual education). Other skeptics, such as Berkeley linguist John McWhorter, see bidialectal approaches as largely unnecessary. McWhorter argues that African-American students are often more adept at switching among dialects than are speakers with true foreign language barriers and he sees the differences between African-American vernacular and other dialects as relatively minor—that is, not as great as those between English and other languages or between very divergent dialects of German.[43]

Another educational concern is the relative status of African-American vernacular vis-à-vis Standard English. When African-American vernacular is seen as bad English, what is the effect on students' attitudes toward school and teachers' attitudes toward students? And, more generally, what is the effect on patterns of discrimination, hiring, and advancement? One approach taken by educators can be found by looking at the 1974 resolution by the Conference on College Composition and Communication, the "Students' Right to Their Own Language." This resolution resulted from the group's discussions of African-American speech in the late 1960s and early 1970s, and was published in a special issue of *College Composition and Communication* in the fall of 1974:

> We affirm the students' right to their own language patterns
> and variety of language—the dialects of their nurture or
> whatever dialects in which they find their own identity and
> style. Language scholars long ago denied that the myth of a
> standard American dialect has any validity. The claim that any
> one dialect is unacceptable amounts to an attempt of one social
> group to exert its dominance over another. Such a claim leads
> to false advice for speakers and writers, and immoral advice for
> humans. A nation proud of its diverse heritage and its cultural
> and racial variety will preserve its heritage of dialects. We
> affirm strongly that teachers must have the experiences and
> training that will enable them to respect diversity and uphold
> the right of students to their own languages.[44]

The intent of the resolution was to establish a position against correctionism in speaking and against dialect prejudice in the classroom. The resolution also highlighted the importance of dialects as part of the national heritage and recommended training teachers to recognize the nature of language diversity. Needless to say, however, aspects of the resolution provoked reaction by commentators: John Simon, for example, asserted that "Not only is ignorance going to be defended on the grounds of the sacred right to nonconformity, but it will also be upheld on the still more sacred grounds of antiracism and antielitism."[45] And Arn and Charlene Tibbetts, in their book *What's Happening to American English?*, describe the resolution as denying Standard English to students and as "preach[ing] reverence for poverty-stricken usage."[46]

Issues related to African-American English were tested in the legal system in the late 1970s, in the so-called King lawsuit mentioned at the beginning of this section. In 1977, the parents of about a dozen African-American public school students in Ann Arbor, Michigan, sued the school board, arguing that the school had failed to properly educate their children by not taking into account social, economic, cultural, and linguistic differences. The children had been placed in special classes, held back, and disciplined although their speech and language evaluations showed no limitations in language or cognitive abilities. Judge Charles Joiner focused the case narrowly under the relevant law and ruled that the schools were not required to take students' social, economic, or cultural circumstances into consideration. The case proceeded on the basis of language barriers alone.

Testimony by a team of experts that included linguists Geneva Smitherman, William Labov, J. L. Dillard, and Richard Bailey convinced Judge Joiner that African-American vernacular was systematically different from other varieties and that both the linguistic differences and the attitudes of teachers needed to be addressed. In his July 12, 1979, opinion, Joiner wrote:

[I]t is clear that black children who succeed, and many do, learn to be bilingual. They retain fluency in "black English" to maintain status in the community and they become fluent in standard English to succeed in general society. . . . [N]o matter how well intentioned the teachers are, they are not likely to be successful in overcoming the language barrier caused by their failure to take into account the home language system, unless they are helped . . . to recognize the existence of the language system used by the children in the home community and to use that knowledge as a way of helping the children to learn to read in standard English.[47]

As a result of the King decision, Ann Arbor teachers underwent additional in-service training in the nature of African-American dialect.

The King case also became a major focus of negative media attention. Commentator Carl Rowan wrote that classifying "the bad English of the ghetto blacks as a separate language" would "consign millions of black children to a linguistic separation that would guarantee they will never 'make it' in the larger US society." His opinion piece called for tough standards, asserting that "What black children need is an end to this malarkey that tells them they can fail to learn grammar, fail to develop vocabularies, ignore syntax, and embrace the mumbo-jumbo of ignorance." However, Rowan ignored the key educational issue. He focused on linguistic separation and economic marginalization rather than the potential use of African-American vernacular in teaching reading or in making teachers aware of the nature of students' language.[48] Commentators like Rowan found it easier to complain about separatism and marginalization than to address the underlying issues of educational policy and practice. The titles of many editorials and news stories from the summer of 1979 show a similar negative focus on identity politics and economic consequences: "If Black English is a Distinct Language, then What about Cracker Talk?" "What We Think: Black English Must Go," "Black English: Dialect Can Be Dead End," "Dis Ain't Right," "The Menace of 'Black English,'" "Dialects Stunt People's Growth and Development," "English, Not 'Black English,'" and "Black Students Don't Need an Alibi."[49] It was during this time that expatriate writer James Baldwin published his *New York Times* op-ed piece "If Black English Isn't a Language, Then Tell Me What Is?" Baldwin's essay, widely reprinted, focused on the important role of African-American English in the lives of black Americans. He argued that its role goes beyond linguistic differences, emphasizing the power of vernacular language to create identity, describe local realities, and create community.[50] However, Baldwin's voice was drowned out by the negative reaction to the decision by the public and other press commentators. Official reaction to Judge Joiner's decision was also negative, with a 1981 federal regulation prohibiting bilingual education or limited-English-proficiency funds from being used for African-American English.[51]

Almost twenty years later, African-American English again held the nation's attention, when in December of 1996 the Oakland, California, school board adopted a resolution declaring that Ebonics was a unique language and the "predominantly primary" language of African-American students. There has been much speculation about the wording of the school board's resolution and its later clarifications, but the force of the resolution was a mandate for school administrators to set up a program of instruction for African-American English in order to help students maintain their cultural heritage and acquire English skills. The press coverage was broad and, as Geoffrey Nunberg notes, largely accurate, in its treatment of the linguistic and educational issues.[52] However, editorialists, politicians, and commentators again weighed in on the issue in ways that distorted the nature of African-American English and the school board resolution. Most significant was the way in which commentators continued to equate African-American English with mere informal speech. The *New York Times*, for example, editorialized that "The School Board in Oakland, Calif., blundered badly last week when it declared that Black slang is a distinct language that warrants a place of respect in the classroom."[53] Echoing Carl Rowan's perspective from 1979, the *Times* went on to suggest that the Oakland decision would stigmatize African-American children and validate "habits of speech that bar them from the cultural mainstream and decent jobs."

African-American opinion leaders and commentators were similarly negative about the Oakland resolution. Writer Maya Angelou, comedian Bill Cosby, and NAACP leader Kweisi Mfume, for example, all denounced the Oakland resolution.[54] Writer Earl Ofari Hutchison provides an example of African-American reaction to the Oakland resolution. Writing in a special issue of *The Black Scholar* devoted to Ebonics, Hutchison argued that the Oakland resolution was racially divisive and counterproductive, saying that what is needed instead are higher standards and more dedicated, determined teaching. Hutchison viewed calls for special programs as reinforcing negative stereotypes that "blacks are unstable, uncooperative, dishonest, uneducated, and crime-prone and not fit to be heard." While Hutchison is correct about the attention reinforcing negative stereotypes, his characterization of African-American vernacular, like that of the *Times*, misses the mark. He writes that "Some young blacks, heavily influenced by rap, hip-hop culture, slang, and street talk, mispronounce words, misplace verb tenses, or 'code switch' when they talk to each other."[55] But he ignores the grammatical regularity of African-American English and simply equates it with slang and street talk. The view that African-American English is merely bad grammar, street talk, and identity politics is evident as well in the headlines of editorials surrounding the Oakland resolution: "Call It Bad Grammar, not a Language," "Hey Bubba, Whut Chew Think a' Dis Ebonics Nonsense?" "Ebonics: If We Can't Teach 'em, Join 'em?" "Hooking Them on Ebonics," "An Ebonics Plague on Race Relations," "Will Appeals to Fund 'Hillbillyonics' be Next?" "Black English Is Merely a Form of Bad English," "Ebonics Decision a Cynical Ploy," "Ebonics Is a Crippling Force," "Teaching Down to Our Children," "Ebonics Is the Latest Educational Sham," "'Ebonics' a False Promise of Self-Esteem," "Oakland's Ebonics Farce," and "Triumph of Black English Gives New Cred to Street Talk."[56]

Comedians seized on the controversy as well, with Jay Leno, for example, featuring a segment on the "Ebonic Plague," invoking the now-familiar theme of nonstandard language as disease. Other satires and cartoons, such as spoofs of Hebonics, Bubbuhonics, Yankeeonics,

Bronxonics, and Dilbertonics, implicitly characterized discussion of African-American English as part of identity politics rather than educational policy or multicultural heritage. And in October of 1998, the *New York Times* ran a quarter-page free public service ad commissioned by a group called Atlanta's Black Professionals. The ad urged readers to "SPEAK OUT AGAINST EBONICS" and showed a silhouette of Martin Luther King, Jr., along with the headline "I has a dream."[57]

Politicians and policy makers also weighed in. Albert Shanker, president of the American Federation of Teachers, wrote that "As the Oakland board is using it, Ebonics is basically a self-esteem strategy, a pat on the head for African-American students. If Black English is a *real* language, and not just a dialect or slang, then students are not wrong when they use it in class, just different. This is supposed to help kids feel better about themselves, but it will make raising their proficiency in mainstream English harder, not easier."[58] Education secretary Richard Riley cited the 1981 regulation prohibiting the use of federal funds for Black English bilingual education, commenting that "Elevating black English to the status of a language is not the way to raise standards of achievement in our schools."[59] Back in California, state legislator William Haynes introduced a bill in the 1997–98 legislative session aimed at terminating California's Standard English Proficiency program for African-American students. The bill asserted that "districts are attempting to convince students that poor communication skills are acceptable speech patterns and writing skills, and that these students cannot learn to speak correct English due to social or cultural forces outside their control."[60] Such comments focus on the presumed role of African-American vernacular as a barrier to skill development and as a self-esteem strategy as opposed to an aid to scholastic achievement.

Defenders of African-American vernacular continued to emphasize the role of different linguistic codes in navigating among diverse audiences. California English professor Ron Emmons, writing in the *Baltimore Sun*, noted the ambivalence he had growing up as a member of the African-American middle class: "Like thousands of middle-class and middle-class-aspiring African-Americans, I was taught throughout childhood to loathe black English. I was taught it was a lazy tongue, used by people too 'low class' to learn the proper way to speak. Speaking black English would lower me in the eye of society, and would deprive me of ever getting a good education or good job." Nevertheless, he noted that, in the hallways and playgrounds, speaking African-American vernacular was necessary to have a voice.[61] Emmons's comments reinforce a key idea: just as Standard English speakers shift styles to be effective in a range of settings, so too do African-American English speakers. A *New Yorker* article on a speech class at the Julliard School finds a student there making the same point.[62] African-American vernacular, she says, "makes us feel stronger, together—the fact that we can talk in a way that other people wouldn't understand." But the student acknowledged the need for Standard English as well adding, "If I only knew slang, how far could I go?" Observations such as these return us to the theme of relativity of usage by emphasizing that African-American vernacular is socially useful in some circumstances while Standard English is socially useful in others. The observations also highlight the complexity of African-American attitudes toward Ebonics. Teachers, policy makers, and the public should understand the issue of African-American vernacular in terms of appropriateness to audience rather than the simplistic attitude that Ebonics is a plague to be eradicated.[63]

Accommodating to the Idealized Mainstream

In the public discussion of African-American vernacular and other types of dialect difference, we often find language variation characterized as bad English. Mainstream perceptions of ethnic, regional, and social dialects frequently reflect stereotypes about the intelligence and industriousness of dialect speakers. These perceptions also reflect assumptions about dialects creating communication barriers and having negative economic consequences. And we sometimes find a politicization of language difference, particularly in the case of African-American English, where support for vernacular usage may be seen as identity politics.

While there is a degree of mainstream acceptance of variation, the dominant viewpoint advocates assimilation to an idealized Standard English rather than accommodation of mainstream discourse to bidialectism and vernacular discourse. Assimilationism treats the speech of certain mainstream groups as setting the standard for language and, by extension, other cultural and social values as well. Assimilationism also assumes that a single Standard English is socially good—fostering mobility, political unity, and common values. But it avoids the question of how Standard English is defined and how open the standard ought to be to variation and change. The issues raised by dialect variation have that as a focus: determining an appropriate openness to variation and a balance between language diversity and language standardization.

Much is glossed over in the most heated rhetoric of dialect assimilation. One crucial point that is often ignored is that many code switchers acknowledge the value of Standard English—though many also value other language traditions as means of group and individual identity. Also overlooked is that the intent of dialect awareness and bridge programs is to provide opportunities to participate in the mainstream, not to encourage separatism. What remains to be more widely recognized is that nonstandard varieties are systematic and socially useful in a variety of contexts. Recognizing dialects as regular, expressive, and appropriate in many situations does not entail a splintering of national culture or an abdication of efforts to teach mainstream forms. Rather, it is an attempt to teach and analyze language more effectively, honestly, and realistically by coming to grips with dialect variation.

Seven Images and Engagement

What, then, is bad language? In the preceding chapters I have examined some of the overlapping themes that arise in discussions of grammar, usage, accent, and dialect. The picture that emerges is one in which "good" language often reflects social desires for uniformity, conformity, and perceived tradition. Bad language is characterized with a range of qualities opposed to these. Public attitudes about good and bad are influenced by correctionism, conventionalism, and assimilationism, which together define much variation as bad language. Language policy often follows these themes as well with tacit or explicit goals of promoting correctness, convention, and assimilation.

In this concluding chapter I have three goals. First, I consolidate and revisit some of the common objections to so-called bad language. Second, I summarize the key images about language that arise in much everyday thinking about usage. Finally, I highlight a few successful language awareness projects and describe some of what modern linguistics is doing with schools and communities. These examples suggest avenues for a more productive dialogue about language and more productive civic engagement with language issues.

Bad Assumptions about Language

We have looked at some of the ways in which people think about good and bad language and at some of the assumptions or premises that underlie that thinking. One assumption is that the standard language is a delicate organism or fragile artifact. Another is that language is primarily a tool for social efficiency and economic advancement. A third is that language variation is a threat. When we reason from these premises, a variety of misconceptions arise. The most prevalent are the following seven:

- Language is a reflection of intelligence—nonstandard language deviates from an ideal standard of clear, correct thinking.
- Departures from standard language are a reflection of weak character.
- Nonstandard language will corrupt the language (and morals) of the innocent and will generally debase polite society.
- Speaking Standard English is necessary to having one's voice heard.
- A common language is a necessary condition for a common viewpoint.
- Language differences divide society and encourage separatism.
- Descriptive linguistics is a permissive, nihilistic discipline.

Consider the first bad assumption—that language reflects intelligence. Features of language do not directly reflect intelligence. Rather, they reflect the background of individuals and the language of their peers and families. Language also reflects the usage that people perceive to be socially and economically valuable. Nonstandard language of various sorts can certainly be the vehicle of clear thinking and correct reasoning, though it is not typically the vehicle of mass publication, broadcasting, and education. And standard language can certainly be the vehicle of muddy reasoning and stupidity.

The second bad assumption concerns language and character, and reflects the idea that nonstandard speakers are too lazy to master the standard language. But while usage may provide insight into an individual's background, views, sensibilities, prejudices, and even self-image, that is all. There are many reasons that speakers might decide not to conform to the standard. These include a desire to set one's self apart from convention, the sense that the standard is arbitrary and confusing, and the idea that conformity is futile to advancement. It might also involve the conviction that conformity to the mainstream standard means giving up something else of value. But we have seen no reason to assume that departures from standard language are an indication of bad character or laziness.

The third misconception is the idea that nonstandard language will corrupt the speech of those who hear it and that in doing so it will debase the language of polite society. The fear is that dialects, nonstandard grammar, slang, and other variation will compromise the standard forms and even replace them. But this fear arises from the assumption that speakers and society are unable to tolerate or manage variation without confusing standard and nonstandard forms or merging the two. However, the most effective language users among us are very often those who can manage several codes at once, shifting among languages, dialects, styles, or registers to communicate vividly, broadly, and appropriately. Certainly, most newspapers and magazines employ a range of styles for different topics. What *is* problematic is fixation on a single variety of language in a world in which effective communication requires navigation among different backgrounds, classes, ethnicities, and styles. But this suggests advocating greater tolerance for language diversity rather than less.

The three misconceptions discussed so far reflect bad assumptions about individuals and their language. A second set of bad assumptions politicizes norms and language variation. This set includes the assumption that language change and diversity encourage separatism and political division. It also includes the belief that having a common language is a necessary condition for a common national viewpoint. And it includes the belief that speaking Standard English is necessary to having one's voice heard.

Think for a moment about the assumption that Standard English is necessary to civic life. It seems clear that speaking Standard English is not necessary in order to have a voice in national affairs. Many professionals and policy makers speak in nonstandard or nonnative English. In the 1960s and 1970s, for example, Henry Kissinger and Zbigniew Brzezinski occupied high-level diplomatic and national security positions despite nonnative English. More recently, actor Arnold Schwarzenegger's Austrian accent was no barrier to his election as California governor. Of course, most of us are not influential enough that others will accommodate to our speech. To have our ideas taken seriously in school, work, and civic affairs, we need to avoid stigmatized forms and to use mostly Standard English in writing and public speaking. What is needed for broad public influence is the ability to use standard forms or society's indulgence to use non-standard forms. But what is needed for local influence may well be another sort of language that is dialectal or unconventional. Effective speakers must be able to switch to an appropriate style for a situation. So the idea that one's language needs to be consistently standard as a prerequisite for success is an oversimplification.

The assumptions that a common language is required for a common national viewpoint and that diversity is divisive are also oversimplifications. Many, perhaps most, citizens would agree on the need for a common set of national values—equality, fairness, security, dignity, education, and so forth. The myth of divisiveness is based on the idea that one cannot simultaneously be committed to national values and to maintaining language diversity. It is also based in the premise that the language one speaks governs one's loyalties. Countries like Switzerland, however, provide models of ways in which a variety of languages and cultures can unite around a common flag and national culture. In addition, embracing a variety of languages can strengthen citizens' understanding of international issues, global economics, and history, and can foster both economic and cultural opportunities.

A variant of the myth of divisiveness is the idea that common values require a fixed and standard set of names for our social reality. This underlies the complaint that changes in usage often reflect an illegitimate political agenda that subverts language and thought. From Orwell's worries about the language of politics to contemporary complaints about political correctness and incorrectness, the worry is that different ways of describing experience draw society away from basic shared values. However, there is no reason that everyone should understand or describe experience in the same way. Language represents the distinctions that speakers feel are important and the verbal styles that enable them to be effective and comfortable. Conventional standard usage makes language convenient for those whose viewpoints it reflects. But an enforced standard that suppresses the distinctions, styles, and perspectives of many speakers is unlikely to foster a true consensus, especially if it ignores the ideological differences underlying language variation and choice.

The final mistaken assumption is that descriptive linguistics is nihilistic and permissive. As we have seen, this arises in part from misrepresentation of what linguists have been saying. Among other things, descriptive linguistics is about the fact that language is constantly changing, the fact that all dialects and languages are regular and rule governed, the fact that standards rest on usage, and the fact that usage is relative. These facts are sometimes characterized as an agenda of grammatical permissiveness and communicative anarchy. Linguists' recognition that nonstandard language is regular and systematic is often translated into the claim that all dialects are equal for any situation. This misconstrual is evident in critiques of linguistics ranging from Jacques Barzun's dismissal of Fries to the most recent debate over Ebonics. What is overlooked is how knowledge of linguistics can help teachers to understand students' language backgrounds and plan effective lessons that bridge the gap between nonstandard and standard forms. And knowledge of linguistics can help all of us to appreciate and manage language variation.

Imagining Language

Why do such misconceptions persist? No doubt there are many reasons. One that I see as central, however, is the ease with which views of language are framed by metaphors. Images and metaphors help to structure the way that we view reality. We talk about ideas as organisms (they are given birth to, die off, and are even resurrected). We talk about physical orientations as having values (people feel up or down; markets can go south; compliments can be left-handed). We talk about personal relationships as involving physical forces (as having electricity, magnetic attraction, or chemical reaction). We work at computers that have desktops and trash cans and perform operations such as "cut" and "paste." As philosopher Mark Turner has emphasized, metaphor also plays a role in the way in which we reason socially and politically. In the 1950s, for example, the metaphor of "urban blight" blended together the problems of the inner city with the idea of agricultural disease to justify large-scale urban renewal. Another example is the association of the nationality English with the canine breed bulldog during World War II. This blended metaphor, which arose through both the personality and jowly looks of British wartime leader Winston Churchill, provided a mascot suggesting the tenacity of the English people. It was an image that was both popular and useful during wartime, appearing, for example, on posters urging American support of the British war effort. Meaning-making in culture often seems to involve the use of metaphor to create mental frameworks that structure people's reasoning about social issues.[1] This is certainly the case for language. We find a number of ways in which metaphoric images of language establish perceptions of linguistic variation and foster assumptions about language and speakers. Five metaphors seem to present the most pervasive and ingrained images: language as a living organism, language as an artifact, language as capital, language as nation, and language as thought.

The metaphor that *language is a living organism* is most apparent in the many discussions that focus on the decay, degeneration, or infection of language by improprieties, novelty, variation, and vulgarity. The image is found in arguments that see a need to "protect" the language from bad influences or in indictments of some usage as "killing," "infecting," or "corrupting" good usage. This metaphor is evident in the views of nineteenth-century American critics like George Perkins Marsh, Richard Grant White, and Henry James, who saw bad speech as reflecting physiological disorders. The metaphor persisted in the twentieth century in the hard-boiled rhetoric of article and book titles like "Stop Murdering the Language" and *Who Killed Grammar?*[2] It is also apparent in some of the Ebonics humor (such as the reference to an Ebonic Plague) and in the idea that one can catch bad language, like a virus. The metaphor of language as an organism can also be developed ecologically, with language as an aspect of nature in need of protection from corruption.[3] Even linguists sometimes rely on the organic or ecological metaphor, treating language as an aspect of nature out of grammarians' control. Thus, when linguists talk about the growth and development of a language or talk about language change as being as "ineluctable and impersonal as continental drift," they too draw on this imagery.[4]

The second metaphor is the image of *language as an artifact*. This metaphor involves both high culture and social efficiency. The cultural aspect is one of the standard language as a finished work of grammatical art—intricate, polished, sophisticated, and capable of appreciation by the most refined, perceptive, and disciplined among us. This image is reflected in the phrase "the king's English," with its suggestion of royal lineage. The image is apparent, too, in such prescriptive book titles as *Strictly Speaking, Paradigms Lost,* and *The Writer's Art*, among others, which allude to their authors' focus on supposed discipline, literalness, and history. The complementary image of practical efficiency has a different focus. Here language is a tool for communication, and correct language use is skill in using a particular tool. The metaphor is apparent in the very notion of "standard language" itself with its association of standard time, standard weights and measures, and other precisely defined physical standards. Without the efficiency and precision provided by standardization, the analogy goes, communication will drift to uncertainty and chaos.

The image of *language as capital* also functions in two complementary ways. First, there is the image of language as cultural capital that speakers must obtain (through birth or bootstrapping) to advance economically or socially. When writers like E. D. Hirsch, Joseph Williams, and Ernest Gellner portray language as part of an individual's economic self-interest, they are drawing on this image. When Carl Rowan and others portray African-American vernacular as guaranteeing economic marginalization, they draw on this image as well. The other aspect of *language as capital* is the image of departures from the norm destabilizing the standard, just as inferior goods and services might destabilize and devalue a currency. Economic imagery was apparent when sixteenth-century writer John Cheke objected to borrowed words by invoking the image of bankruptcy by borrowing. And it was apparent when Jacques Barzun argued that slang devalues good words and robs the language of resources.[5]

At the civic and political level, we find the intertwined metaphors of *language as nation* and of *language as thought*. The first, which is central to discussions of English-only and language assimilation, involves the idea that Standard English is patriotically unifying. The leading idea of the image of *language as nation* is that Standard English holds the nation together. We find it in colonial views stressing the need for an American language, in verbal images such as Theodore Roosevelt's "one flag—one language," and in the image of the "melting pot."[6] We find it today in the official stances of organizations like U.S. English, whose slogan is "Toward a United America," and in the biblical imagery of multilingualism as a babel of languages.[7] We find it, too, in the treatment of language variation as a kind of separatism that is at times—as in *Meyer v. Nebraska*—portrayed as inimical to national security.

The metaphor of *language as thought* functions in a parallel way and the idea that language reflects and shapes thought can be found in various incarnations. It is reflected in nineteenth-century comments about the language of nations reflecting the moral character of their speakers. George Perkins Marsh, for example, condemned the Italian language, writing that "A bold and manly and generous and truthful people would not choose . . . to call every house with a large door, *un palazzo* a palace."[8] The connection of language to thought is also reflected in nineteenth-century Indian Affairs Commissioner J. D. C. Atkins's remarks that Indians must be taught the national language to establish a "community of feeling." The image is implicit in twentieth-century claims that speaking other languages inculcates foreign values. The metaphors of *language as nation* and *language as thought* thus work in tandem to provide an apparent rationale for assimilationism. Today the image of *language as thought* is also a salient metaphor of discussions of political correctness, with its rhetoric of indoctrination and thought-police. At the heart of the political metaphor, of course, is George Orwell's fictional Newspeak, which presents language as a mechanism of social control.

Images of language reinforce majoritarian assumptions about the motivations and attitudes of different groups. Each of the images discussed here situates language in a certain way and provides a basis for assumptions about the presumed values, character, and goals of language users. If language is a refined artifact, then some speakers can be characterized as poor stewards of this treasure. If language is organic, speakers may be characterized as doing harm to that organism. If language has an economic value, speech may be treated as impoverished. And if language creates community, then some speakers can be characterized as creating discord. By understanding the mental images that frame variation, we can better understand the gulf between a mainstream standard and language outside of that mainstream. We can also better understand the perspective of individuals and groups outside the mainstream. For many, language is part of a social identity that lies outside of majoritarian values. People's unconscious usage and conscious stylistic and rhetorical choices allow them to stake out a position socially—as grammatically correct or not; as rhetorically simple, sophisticated, or ornate; as regional, ethnic or nonnative; as coarse, avant-garde, or politicized.

English Made Hard

The second important reason that misconceptions about language persist is our failure to take language issues seriously. Language is part of the symbolism of success and social mobility in America. But often public discussion of language is left to controversialists and amateurs who write about falling standards, the dangers of euphemisms and political correctness, or the importance of the distinction between *shall* and *will.* The prevalence of correctionism, conventionalism, and assimilationism has also made it easy for linguists to be characterized as laissez-faire, permissive, and out of touch with social reality. This is particularly so when language is merged with broader clashes such as those between egalitarianism and elitism or the politics of Right and Left. Linguists are treated as the enabling and indulgent catalogers of usage, while traditionalists, assimilationists, and conventionalists are represented as advocates of high standards, hard work, and efficient communication.

The rhetorical positioning of linguistics is not the only cause of such misunderstandings, of course. Linguists are occasionally clumsy or hyperbolic in discussing the inevitability of change, the doctrine of usage, and the regularity of dialects. Too much effort has been focused on the easy work of challenging traditional grammar, fussy prescriptivism, and official English and less on the hard work of providing and justifying alternatives.

For many people, linguistics is English made hard. Key concepts such as the relativity of usage and the regularity of nonstandard languages run counter to the prevailing mainstream images of good language as involving a fixed standard. The research focus of linguistics also sometimes places work out of the scope of what is immediately accessible to the public and directly useable by teachers, policy makers, and scholars in other fields.[9] Unlike the study of accounting, psychology, or technical writing, it is often not immediately obvious how a particular linguistic concept is important and how it will help people in their lives and careers. And while people may accept that all dialects are equal as an intellectual point, it remains hard to shake the gut reaction that relativity of usage does not reflect how the world really works.

There is nevertheless a long tradition of linguists' working with schools, communities, and national groups on problems of education and policy.[10] This tradition is often overlooked in the characterization of linguistics as too theoretical and as permissive. Following the lead of Sterling Leonard and Charles Fries, many linguists have been active in both the National Council of Teachers of English and the Linguistic Society of America, and have helped to build important bridges between professional linguistics and practitioners of language arts. In addition, the leadership of the Linguistic Society of America has steadily committed that organization to supporting a wide range of connections with other disciplines and with local and national policy makers. The society has added committees on linguistics in the schools and linguistics in the undergraduate curriculum, and its annual meetings have increased the number of sessions devoted to issues in educational linguistics, to the effective dissemination of information on language variation, and to involvement with educators and policy makers. Similarly, the Center for Applied Linguistics, founded in 1959, has worked for over forty years to provide information to educators and policy makers, to develop effective language curricula, texts, and materials, and to help evaluate language education programs. The center provides resources for teachers working in English as a second language, bilingual education, immigrant education, foreign language education, and proficiency assessment, and it has been a leading force in fostering understanding of the role of dialect in education and society. The center's publication

What Teachers Need to Know about Language, for example, provides a set of questions about language that teachers should be able to answer and also outlines a set of possible courses in educational linguistics. The questions range over the basic units of language; the nature of variation; and reading, spelling, and writing.[11]

In terms of work with schools and communities, there is too much being done to attempt a systematic listing. Instead, I will just highlight three projects that I think illustrate how linguistics can effectively make connections with the public interest. First, the efforts of sociolinguist Walt Wolfram and his students at North Carolina State University suggest what can be done at the state and community level.[12] Wolfram and his students are involved in research on the English spoken in various parts of North Carolina: in the endangered dialect community of the Outer Banks of North Carolina, in diverse Robeson County (a county that includes Lumbee Indian, African-American, and European American communities), and in the isolated coastal region of Hyde County. Wolfram's North Carolina Language and Life Project researches historically isolated dialects in areas such as these. Its goals combine preservation, linguistic research, and education, and the Language and Life Project team works with local communities to promote language traditions and to develop popular materials that can be used in preservation efforts. The project also works with local officials to develop cultural plans for sharing research and it works with local school systems to incorporate dialect materials into curricula on local history.[13] Wolfram and his colleagues have established about twenty research sites in the state, have produced scholarly articles and popular books and videos, and have developed new interest in language among social science educators in North Carolina with school outreach activities.

The work of Massachusetts linguist Maya Honda and her colleagues provides an example of a somewhat different sort.[14] Under the auspices of the Harvard University Graduate School project on the Nature of Science/Scientific Instruction and Method, Honda and others worked with teachers at the Watertown, Massachusetts, public schools to introduce linguistics to pilot groups of seventh-grade life science students and eleventh/twelfth-grade anatomy and physiology classes. The students participated in a two-week unit on linguistics in which they were asked to develop and evaluate hypotheses about relatively accessible aspects of language. These included such tasks as puzzling out the nature of English plural formation, the conditions under which contraction is possible, and the formation of various types of questions from declarative forms. Before and after the nine-lesson unit, researchers from Harvard's Educational Technology Center assessed the students' understanding of the nature of science using a standard interview procedure. All of the students showed improvement in the Nature of Scientific Inquiry interview. Honda notes that the experience of studying linguistics also improved students' metalinguistic awareness—that is, their ability to talk about language phenomena—and that it sparked their interest in language and their ability to reflect on their second-language learning experiences as well.

Our third example is a student competition organized by the University of Oregon. A United States Linguistic Olympics was piloted at the University of Oregon in 1998, 1999, and 2000. It was based on the Russian Linguistic Olympics, which has been a part of education in that country since 1965 and which attracts hundreds of students to competitions in Moscow and St. Petersburg. Aimed toward secondary school students, the U.S. Linguistic Olympics allowed students to attempt to solve language puzzles. As with the Russian version, the puzzles were based on real but exotically unfamiliar languages like Quechua, Hawaiian, Chickasaw, or Babylonian. The puzzles could be solved without special background knowledge about the languages. Thus, they challenged students' pattern recognition, reasoning, and analytic skills while at the same time providing a window into the diversity of language in the world. According to organizer Thomas Payne, the Linguistic Olympics has several benefits:

> The puzzles . . . require the students to "enter into" the minds
> of speakers of some of the most exciting languages on earth,
> and to think carefully through different hypotheses and

problem-solving strategies. The most successful students are those who are able to extend themselves beyond their usual thought patterns to discover ways in which different languages approach reality. In the process, students discover linguistics, and learn something about the global language situation.[15]

What these projects in North Carolina, Massachusetts, and Oregon show is that it is possible to introduce linguistics into schools and communities in ways that foster careful language description and that reinforce awareness of the regularity and integrity of the different varieties and patterns that speakers use. Each of the examples takes a slightly different approach but collectively they suggest fruitful ways to open connections with social science educators, science educators, and community groups interested in local heritage and culture. Such public education efforts and partnerships show great promise for the future. As respect for the complexity and variety of language grows, the conditions will arise for misconceptions about language and speakers to be more easily dispelled and for a more reasoned discussion of language issues.

Beyond Simplistic Characterization

In this book we have seen that simplistic notions of good and bad language fail because they are too often based on mistaken assumptions about language and speakers. We have also seen that language variation serves a number of functions in society and that the characterization of some speakers as bad often has as much to do with who they are as with their language. And we have seen that relativism does not entail, as some critics would have it, that anything goes. But if simple notions of good and bad language are not adequate, how should we think about language?

As suggested earlier, I think that the correct model for making intelligent language choices is the model of law or practical ethics.

Understanding language is a matter of asking questions, finding balance, and solving problems pragmatically. We have seen throughout this book that educational, social, and civic issues related to language are more nuanced and complex than they first appear. The topics presented in the preceding chapters provide the beginnings of the sort of analysis needed to understand language issues. They suggest that there is much more to language policy than a professed dedication to high standards and a commitment to assimilation, convention, and correctness. Successful language policy will balance tradition and appropriate innovation. Sound language policy must also be well-informed by history and research rather than driven by metaphors about language and misconceptions about speakers. In public policy debates such as those concerning Ebonics or bilingual education, citizens need to be able to judge whether claims about language and learning are valid or questionable. Thus, when commentators refer to African-American vernacular as "a language that has no right or wrong expressions, no consistent spellings or pronunciations, and no discernible rules," it is important to know that all dialects are rule governed and that African-American English *is* a consistent dialect with its own grammatical rules. When opponents of bilingual education make the generalization that "young immigrant children can easily acquire full fluency in a new language such as English, if they are heavily exposed to that language in a classroom at an early age," it is important to know that the effectiveness of a language program depends on the community and the school and that both immersion and bilingual education can be successful.[16]

Language choices are also made by individuals. Since usage questions are really about appropriateness, speakers and writers must continually think about and reassess usage. This is harder work than simply getting an inoculation against bad language by memorizing a set of *do's* and *don't's*. Intelligent language use involves deciding which of various principles applies, and it means explaining choices, not simply invoking authority. Well-educated speakers are ones who can think and decide for themselves and who can reflect on the effects usage will have on an audience. We will look at two final usage examples to illustrate how speakers can assess the effect of usage.

Consider first the use of generic *he* and its alternatives. A careful writer or speaker must determine what pronoun to use in such examples as *Every medical student can decide for _____ whether to dress formally in the hospital setting.* Contrast the approaches of, say, prescriptivist John Simon, who sees the pronoun choice as a question of politics and ideology, with the analysis of linguists Francine Frank and Paula Treichler in their book *Language, Gender, and Professional Writing.* Frank and Treichler suggest that language users consider several factors in deciding usage. They suggest that speakers think about recasting the subject as a plural.[17] They also suggest considering the appropriateness of singular *they* or the felicity of the compound form *himself or herself* (and the possibility of clumsy repetition later in the text). And they point out nuances of meaning that arise (thus the example under consideration has different semantic requirements from the sentence *The Mount Holyoke student of 1900 knew that _____ wanted an education,* because Mount Holyoke is a women's liberal arts college). Understanding the rhetorical consequences of different options provides writers and speakers with a basis for making their own decision and for defending their usage. My choice in the above example would be to rephrase it as *Medical students can decide for themselves whether to dress formally in the hospital setting* or perhaps as *Each medical student can decide whether to dress formally in the hospital setting.* The operative principles for me are inclusion, brevity, and seamlessness. My suggested revision does not imply that only males are medical students, it avoids the possible clumsiness of *for himself or herself,* and it does not distract readers from the exposition by inviting them to comment on my pronoun selection.

I end with the lowly apostrophe, concluding where Strunk and White's *Elements of Style* begins. Recall that Strunk and White suggest forming the possessive singular by adding '*s* regardless of the final consonant. But they follow their suggestion with a long list of exceptions: "ancient proper names in -*es* and -*is,* the possessive *Jesus'* and such forms as *for conscience' sake, for righteousness' sake.*" My usage, however, is to almost always add the apostrophe plus *s*, even to their suggested exceptions. Why? One reason is consistency and efficiency—using *'s* in all cases frees me from having to ponder about names like *Arkansas* or *Katz* and from having to worry about whether the Hispanic name *Jesus* is treated the same as the biblical *Jesus*. And it frees me from having to worry that readers will misinterpret as carelessness any variation between the apostrophe plus *s* and the bare apostrophe (if for example I write *Ulysses'* in one place and *Thomas's* in another). At the same time, it does not seem worth my while to comment on bare apostrophes like *Ulysses'* or *Thomas'* in the writing of students or colleagues, since they may have come to a different conclusion. For me, these examples represent how individuals should think about grammar—one rule at a time as active participants in their own usage rather than as bystanders. I end where Stunk and White begin to emphasize that a critical and realistic attitude toward grammar can be fostered by attention to language even at the smallest of levels. But whether we begin at the broadest level—with the history of correctionism, conventionalism, or assimilationism—or at the narrowest—with the analysis of adverbs, possessives, and infinitives—it is attention to the history of the language and the relativity of usage that must be the goal.

Notes

1. Bad Language: Realism versus Relativism

1. Molly Ivins's comment is from the documentary *American Tongues*, produced by Louis Alvarez and Andrew Kolker (Hohokus, NJ: Center for New American Media, 1986). The World War II squad theme, for example, is apparent in films like *A Walk in the Sun* (1946), which featured a dependable but slow Southern medic. The theme is still alive in films like *Saving Private Ryan* (1998), which features a religious Southern sharpshooter. For a fuller treatment of the combat film conventions, see Jeanine Basinger's *The World War II Combat Film: Anatomy of a Genre* (New York: Columbia University Press, 1986).

2. "Lucy Hires an English Tutor," originally aired on Dec. 29, 1952.

3. These examples are from *The Sherwin Cody 100% Self-correcting Course in English Language* (Rochester, NY: The Sherwin Cody School of English, 1918).

4. *What said he?* is from *As You Like It* (3.2.221), *Came he not home to night?* is from *Romeo and Juliet* (2.4.2), and *And did you not leave him in*

this contemplation? is from *As You Like It* (2.1.64). Other examples are easy to find.

5. The restriction is quite regular: we can compare two things by saying *This book is better than that one is* but not *This book is better than that one's.* We can say *I found Mary but I don't know where John is* but not *I found Mary but I don't know where John's.* For further discussion of contraction, see Ellen M. Kaisse, "The Syntax of Auxiliary Reduction in English," *Language* 59.1 (March 1983), 93–122.

6. On *like*, see Kathleen Ferrara and Barbara Bell's "Sociolinguistic Variation and Discourse Function of Constructed Dialogue Introducers: The Case of Be + Like," *American Speech*, Fall 1995, 265–90, and Muffy E. A. Siegel's "*Like*: The Discourse Particle and Semantics," *Journal of Semantics* 19.1 (2002), 35–71.

7. There are further restrictions and subtleties as well; see Walt Wolfram's "Dialect Awareness Programs in the School and Community," in *Language Alive in the Classroom*, ed. Rebecca Wheeler (Westport, CT: Praeger, 1999), 47–66.

8. The usage note in the eleventh edition of *Merriam-Webster's Collegiate Dictionary* (Springfield, MA: Merriam-Webster, 2003) also comments that *anymore* is regularly used in negatives, interrogatives, conditionals, and certain constructions such as comparatives ("too sophisticated to believe *anymore* in solutions").

9. See Michael Adams's *Slayer Slang* (New York: Oxford University Press, 2003) for a more complete glossary of slang words introduced by this program. Language-play like that of *Seinfeld* and *Buffy The Vampire Slayer* creates humor aligned with a storyline (in the former) or attracts attention by using casual language in dramatic contexts (in the latter).

10. The pronunciation *or-uh-GUN* is used chiefly by natives and those familiar with natives' preferences. Outsiders, particularly Easterners, tend to pronounce the name *or-uh-GAWN*. In the case of *Uranus*, we cannot rely on natives' preferences.

11. Sydney J. Harris, "Good English Ain't What We Thought," *Chicago Daily News*, Oct. 20, 1961.

12. National Council of Teachers of English, Commission on the English Curriculum, *The English Language Arts* (New York: Appleton-Century-Crofts, 1952), 277.

13. Versions of Cody's ad can be found in Richard Bailey's *Images of English* (Ann Arbor: University of Michigan Press, 1991), 14, and in Maxwell Sackheim's *My First Sixty Years in Advertising* (Englewood Cliffs, NJ: Prentice Hall, 1970), 79. As Erin A. Smith notes in *Hard-Boiled: Working-Class Readers and Pulp*

Magazines (Philadelphia: Temple University Press, 2000), 68, the ads in pulp magazines likely were aimed at working-class and immigrant men. There are also many appeals to women as well: a quiz titled "If You Think You Speak Good . . ." in the March 1983 issue of *Mademoiselle* (66–68) asked readers ten questions concerning grammar and usage. In the answer key, the writer warns readers that wrong answers mean "you can probably forget about the job," and that "the listener might wonder why your ideas need so much dressing up."

14. William Morris and Mary Morris, *Harper Dictionary of Contemporary Usage* (New York: Harper and Row, 1975), 349–50, from the panel comments on *hopefully*.

15. Philosopher James Rachels suggests that cultural relativism in ethics actually involves several subideas: that societies have different moral codes; that there is no objective standard for judging differences in codes; that the morality of our society enjoys no special status; that there is no universal ethical truth and that for any society its moral code determines what is right; and that it is intolerant to try to judge the actions of others. Rachels points out that a view embodying *all* of these ideas would make morality simply internal to a society and would make moral progress problematic. But he also points out that weaker versions of relativism are useful in that they emphasize that cultural preferences and received notions are not all necessarily based on reason. This moderated relativism is the one that underlies descriptive linguistics. See James Rachels, *The Elements of Moral Philosophy* (New York: Oxford University Press, 1986), ch. 2., esp. pp. 14–15.

16. Another critique is that of Allan Bloom, in his best-selling *The Closing of the American Mind*. Bloom's characterization seems to be simply this: relativism posits that different cultures treat moral, cultural, and social issues in different, culturally determined, ways. Hence, values are relative and for a relativist one choice is as good as another. The antidote to relativism for Bloom and for others such as Victor Davis Hanson and John Heath (in their *Who Killed Homer? The Demise of Classical Education and the Recovery of Greek Wisdom*) is a recommitment to a Judeo-Christian foundation for education and a return to Greek literature and philosophy. Hanson and Heath, for example, see Greek wisdom as providing a model of an ordered society with proven social and political values. They argue that the modern curriculum, with its focus on interdisciplinary study (including critical theory and multiculturalism) has compromised standards and rigor. As a remedy, they recommend the classics as a core curriculum and a revival of requirements for Greek and Latin.

17. Henry also sees such cultures as fostering education and administrative meritocracy, expanding by trade or imperialism, and organizing to reduce

divisive local control. See William Henry III, *In Defense of Elitism* (New York: Doubleday, 1994), 29–31.

18. Henry, 2–3.

19. E. D. Hirsch, *Cultural Literacy* (New York: Houghton Mifflin, 1987), 73.

20. Ernest Gellner, *Nations and Nationalism* (Ithaca: Cornell University Press, 1983), 35.

21. Hirsch, xiii.

22. Llewellyn's classic article on the canons of legal construction, "Remarks on the Theory of Appellate Decision and the Rules or Canons about How Statutes Are To Be Constructed," appeared in the *Vanderbilt Law Review* (3 *Vand. L. Rev.* 395, 401–6, 1950). Llewellyn notes that "When it comes to presenting a proposed statutory construction in court, there is an accepted conventional vocabulary. As in arguments over points of case-law, the accepted convention still, unhappily, requires discussion as if only one single correct meaning could exist. Hence there are two opposing canons on almost every point . . . . Plainly to make any canon take hold in a particular instance, the construction contended for must be sold, essentially, by means other than the use of the canon." In addition, as Geoffrey P. Miller notes in his "Pragmatics and the Maxims of Interpretation" (*Wisconsin Law Review* [1990], 1179), canons of legal interpretation have a long history and parallel the indeterminacy of rules of religious interpretation. Miller cites the *Mimamsa* of Jaimini from 500 B.C., which provided principles for interpreting Hindu texts, the hermeneutical rules of Judaism provided by the Talmudic commentary of Rabbi Ishmael ben Elisha, and the summary of Roman law from the Digest of Justinian, all of which contain point-counterpoint maxims of interpretation.

23. Henry, *In Defense of Elitism*, 176.

24. Henry Louis Gates, Jr., *Loose Canons: Notes on the Culture Wars* (New York: Oxford University Press, 1992), 21.

25. Gates, 33.

2. Bad Writing

1. The quote from Charles William Eliot is cited in Stephen Judy's *The ABCs of Literacy* (New York: Oxford University Press, 1980), 33–34. Merrill Sheils's cover article "Why Johnny Can't Write" appeared in the Dec. 8, 1975, issue of *Newsweek* (pp. 58–65). He leads with this example from an 18-year-old freshman's essay: "It's obvious, in our modern world of today theirs a lot of impreciseness in expressing thoughts we have." Sheils noted that the decline in student reading and writing skills was attributed to the increase in television viewing and that classroom time for writing instruction had decreased.

He also cited linguists' views (on speech versus writing) and the qualifications of teachers as factors.

2. Thomas Bartlett, "Why Johnny Can't Write, Even Though He Went to Princeton," *Chronicle of Higher Education* 49.17 (Jan. 3, 2003), A39.

3. Commentators in the United States have routinely romanticized earlier times as periods of more robust literacy. In his 1980 book *The ABCs of Literacy*, Stephen Judy catalogues a number of these complaints by American educators from the mid-nineteenth century on. See *The ABCs of Literacy*, 33–36.

4. For an overview, see Robert Connors, "The Abolition Debate in Composition: A Short History," in *Composition in the Twenty-First Century: Crisis and Change*, ed. Lynn Z. Bloom, Donald A. Daiker, and Edward M. White (Carbondale: Southern Illinois University Press, 1996), 47–63.

5. The 1986 version of the *Harbrace College Handbook*, for example, has initial sections titled Grammar, Mechanics, Punctuation, and Spelling. These are followed by sections called Diction, Effective Sentences, and Larger Elements, which contain information on usage, repetition, and conciseness; on sentence style, emphasis, and variety; and on organization, unity, development, and coherence. (See John Hodges, Mary Whitten, and Suzanne Webb, *The Harbrace College Handbook*, 10th ed. (New York: Harcourt Brace, 1986).

6. William Strunk, Jr., and E. B. White, *The Elements of Style*, 3rd ed. (New York: Macmillan, 1979), viii.

7. Peter Elbow's perspective is elaborated in his book *Writing with Power* (New York: Oxford University Press, 1981).

8. In *Common Ground: Dialogue, Understanding, and the Teaching of Composition* (Englewood Cliffs, NJ: Prentice Hall, 1993), 108, rhetorician Kurt Spellmeyer emphasizes that the personal essay highlights the process of constructing meaning:

> The literary critic, the philosopher, the political scientist, and to some degree even the novelist, tender versions of experience in which their own ordeal of uncertainty, the ordeal that every writer endures, and from which no one ever escapes, has unfolded beforehand, behind the scenes, and it is the reader who must catch up in order to be instructed. By contrast the [personal] essay foregrounds the speaker's movement from presentation to representation, from experience as "fact" to experience invested more fully with personal, and with social, meaning.

9. Rudolph Flesch, *The Art of Readable Writing* (New York: Harper and Row, 1974), 4. Flesch was the author of the 1955 study *Why Johnny Can't Read*

and What You Can Do About It (New York: Harper, 1955), which developed the phonics method and which spawned the many "Why Johnny Can't" titles of later books and articles.

10. Lester Faigley, "What Is Good Writing? Views from the Public," in Sidney Greenbaum, ed., *The English Language Today* (Oxford: Pergamon, 1985), 99–105.

11. Other researchers have surveyed the reaction of business writers to various sorts of traditional errors, noting that some are taken more seriously than others. See Maxine Hairston's "Not All Errors Are Created Equal: Nonacademic Readers in the Professions Respond to Lapses in Usage," *College English* 43 (1981), 794–806, and Larry Beason's "Ethos and Error: How Business People React to Errors," *College Composition and Communication* 53.1 (2001), 33–64.

12. George Orwell, *Nineteen Eighty-four* (New York: Knopf, 1992), 312; the descriptions of the ministries ("the Ministry of Peace . . .) is from text p. 6.

13. Orwell's essay "Propaganda and Demotic Speech" was published in the journal *Persuasion* (Summer 1944) and is reprinted in *George Orwell* (London: Secker and Warburg, 1980), 636–40. Orwell saw the divide between written and spoken language as a key element in the ineffectiveness of news reading.

14. George Orwell, "Politics and the English Language," in *Shooting an Elephant and Other Essays* (London: Secker and Warburg, 1950), 96.

15. Alan Sokal, "Revelation: A Physicist Experiments with Cultural Studies," *Lingua Franca*, May–June 1996; reprinted in *The Sokal Hoax* (Lincoln: University of Nebraska Press, 2000), 52.

16. Simon Winchester, "Word Imperfect," *Atlantic Monthly*, May 2001, 55. For empirical research on denseness of style, see Rosemary Hake and Joseph Williams's essay "Style and Its Consequences: Do as I Do, Not as I Say," *College English* 43 (Sept. 1981), 443–51.

17. B. R. Myers, "A Reader's Manifesto," *Atlantic Monthly*, July–August 2001, 104–22. The observations on McCarthy, Proulx, DeLillo, Auster, Guterson, and Bellow are from pp. 108, 105, 112, 116, 118, and 122, respectively.

18. Myers, 122.

19. Albert Baugh and Thomas Cable's *A History of the English Language* (Englewood Cliffs, NJ: Prentice Hall, 1978) was a resource for the discussion of inkhorn terms and is the source for the quotes from Sir John Cheke (p. 216), Sir Thomas Caloner (p. 217), and Thomas Wilson (p. 217), and the opinions of Elyot, Dryden, Mulcaster, and others.

20. J. H. Francis's *From Caxton to Carlyle: A Study of the Development of Language, Composition and Style in English Prose* (Cambridge: Cambridge University Press, 1937) was a useful source in the discussion of prose style.

21. From William Hazlitt, *Essays*, ed. Charles H. Gray (New York: MacMillan, 1926), 76; Thomas Babington Macaulay, *Selected Writings*, ed. John Clive and Thomas Pinney (Chicago: University of Chicago Press, 1972), 4; and Thomas De Quincey, "The Palimpsest of the Human Brain," *Collected Writings*, ed. David Masson (London: A. and C. Black, 14 vols., 1889–90), vol. 13, p. 349.

22. See Kenneth Cmiel, *Democratic Eloquence* (New York: William Morrow, 1990), 250. Ochs promised "language that is parliamentary in good society" ("Business Announcement," *New York Times*, August 19, 1896, 4).

23. Jack Rosenthal's observations are from his essay "So Here's What's Happening to Language," *New York Times*, Nov. 14, 2001, K38.

24. The discussion of *Time* magazine style is from Lance Morrow's account "The Time of Our Lives" in the *Time* 75th anniversary issue (March 9, 1998), 84–91; the 1936 *New Yorker* satire is excerpted on page 193 of that issue in a piece titled "The Reviews Are In."

25. Peter Tiersma, *Legal Language* (Chicago: University of Chicago Press, 1999), 33–34.

3. Bad Grammar

1. William Zinsser, *On Writing Well*, 5th ed. (New York: Harper, 1994), 26, 33.

2. The definition is from George Lyman Kittredge and Frank Edgar Farley, *Advanced English Grammar* (Boston: Ginn, 1913), 2.

3. Other musical examples include "That don't impress me much," "We don't need no education," "Them there eyes," "You done lost your good thing now," "Ain't no woman (like the one I got)," "Ain't that a shame," "I ain't never gonna let you down," "Ain't nobody's business if I do," and "Ain't misbehaving."

4. *The MLA Handbook for Writers of Research Papers* (New York: Modern Language Association, 1984), 34. Other sources for discussion of the apostrophe include the *UPI Stylebook* (Lincolnwood, IL: National Textbook, 1992), 222; William Strunk and E. B. White's *The Elements of Style* (New York: Macmillan, 1979), 1. For more on the apostrophe, see my article "s's" in *The SECOL Review* 17.2 (1993), 127–41.

5. The quote from Thomas Sheridan is from the preface to his 1780 *General Dictionary of the English Language*, cited in Charles Fries's *American English Grammar* (New York: Appleton Century, 1940), 17.

6. The method of providing examples of faulty syntax was a technique borrowed from the pedagogy of teaching classical languages.

7. It is worth noting that English literature entered the curriculum first as a source of textual examples for grammatical analysis. The tradition of liter-

ary appreciation was essentially still outside of the school curriculum in the late 1800s. Today, of course, the situation is just the opposite, with literature forming the center of English studies and grammar its periphery. For discussion of the introduction of literature into English studies, see Gerald Graff's *Professing English* (Chicago: University of Chicago Press, 1987).

8. The quote from Joseph Priestly's 1761 *Rudiments of English Grammar* is cited in Albert Baugh and Thomas Cable's *A History of the English Language*, 282–83.

9. George Campbell, *The Philosophy of Rhetoric* (Carbondale: Southern Illinois University Press, 1963 reprinting), 139. The discussion of reputable, national, and present usage is found on page 141–51.

10. The American verbal critics of the nineteenth century included such men as William Mathews, George Perkins Marsh, and Richard Grant White in the post–Civil War era. White, for example, was much concerned about the misuse of words by the educated, noting that "the mental tone" of a community could be affected by "loose, coarse, and frivolous phraseology" and censuring usages like *donate* and *photographer*, among others (*Words and Their Uses*, 19th ed. [Boston: Houghton Mifflin, 1890], 5). William Mathews saw the character of the American people as reflecting their penchant for grammatical improprieties, writing that "In America, this scorn of obedience, whether to political authority or philological, is fostered and intensified by the very genius of our institutions" (*Words: Their Use and Abuse* [Chicago: Griggs, 1876], 328). Perhaps the most direct expression of this link between grammar and moral corruption is from George Perkins Marsh, who maintained that "To deny that language is susceptible of corruption, is to deny that races or nations are susceptible of depravation; and to treat all its changes as normal, is to confound things as distinct as health and disease" (*Lectures on the English Language* [New York: Scribner, 1860], 649). As his comment suggests, Marsh viewed language not as a set of conventions for expressing ideas but as a direct reflection of thought and character. Use of the wrong language would lower one's moral status. Moreover, the language habits of nations were indicative of their citizens' collective moral qualities. Marsh's condemnation of the Italian language, for example, asserts that "A bold and manly and generous and truthful people would not choose . . . to apply to a small garden and a cottage the title of *un podere*, a power; to call every house with a large door, *un palazzo* a palace" (224–25).

11. See George Philip Krapp, *Modern English: Its Growth and Present Use* (New York: Charles Scribner's Sons, 1909), 325–34.

12. George Philip Krapp, *The Knowledge of English* (New York: Holt, 1927), 178.

13. Krapp, 182.

14. Krapp, 173.

15. See William Morris and Mary Morris, *Harper Dictionary of Contemporary Usage* (New York: Harper and Row, 1975), 348–50.

16. Proponents of *hopefully* as a propositional modifier point out just the opposite—that the use of *hopefully* is parallel to that of sentence adverbs such as *evidently, frankly, doubtlessly, clearly,* and *happily.* See William Safire, *On Language* (New York: Avon Books, 1981), 134–36, for an example.

17. See Linda Perlstein's "Grammar Glitch Pushes PSAT to Rethink, Rescore," *Washington Post,* May 14, 2003, A1.

18. For example, the claim that this construction is faulty appears in Jacques Barzun's *Simple and Direct: A Rhetoric for Writers* (New York: Harper and Row, 1984), 77. He writes that "The proper linking of pronouns with antecedents includes one commandment that may seem superfluous because it is difficult to remember: there can be no logical link between a proper name in the possessive case and a personal pronoun. 'Wellington's victory at Waterloo made him the greatest name in Europe' is all askew, because there is in fact no person named for the *him* to refer to. *Wellington's* is not a noun but an adjective." The claim that this usage is incorrect also appears in Diana Hacker's *A Writer's Reference,* 4th ed. (New York: St. Martin's Press, 1999), 192.

19. Simon, *Paradigms Lost,* 210. Simon remarks that if we lose the objective case *whom* (he calls it accusative) "our language will be the poorer for it." He goes on to argue that "Obviously, 'The man, whom I had never known, was a thief' means something other than 'The man who I had never known was a thief.' Now, you can object that it would be just as easy in the first instance to use some other construction; but what happens if *this* one is used incorrectly?" See also Hacker, who simply writes that *who* "can only be used for subject and subject complements" (*A Writer's Reference,* 187).

20. The television program *Who Do You Trust?* ran from 1956 to 1963 (with hosts Edgar Bergen for the first season and Johnny Carson from 1957 to 1962); the supposed grammatical incorrectness was part of the promotional strategy for the show.

21. Robert Burchfield, ed., *The New Fowler's Modern English Usage,* 3rd ed. (New York: Oxford University Press, 1996), 848; Elizabeth Jewell and Frank Abate, eds., *New Oxford American Dictionary* (New York: Oxford University Press, 2001), 1926; *Merriam-Webster Collegiate Dictionary* (Springfield: Merriam-Webster, 2003), 1430. As early as 1928, the *Oxford English Dictionary* listed *whom* as "no longer current in natural colloquial speech" (see James A. H. Murray et al., *A New English Dictionary on Historical Principles* [Oxford: Clarendon Press, 1928]).

22. The joke comes from comedian Lily Tomlin's character Ernestine the telephone operator, which appeared on NBC's *Rowan and Martin's Laugh In* (1968–1973) and was reprised in a 2003 ad campaign for telephone company WebEx. The use of *who* is illustrated in examples like the catch phrase of the movie *Ghostbusters*: "Who ya gonna call? Ghostbusters!" Here the informality is reinforced by the pronoun choice.

23. Leonard reported that judges—linguists, authors, editors, business people, and members of professional societies—rated the usage as established. The linguists rated the usage higher than others but all groups except the authors and business people gave majorities for acceptance. See Leonard, *Current English Usage* (Chicago: Inland Press, 1932), 111.

24. A fuller description of usage would note that the nominative use of *whom*, as in *I'll help whomever arrives* or *Give this to whomever arrives*, is an overcorrection.

25. For some discussion of debates within the English profession, see Raven McDavid, Betty Gawthrop, C. Michael Lightner, Doris C. Meyers, and Geraldine Russell's *An Examination of the Attitudes of the NCTE toward Language* (Urbana, IL: National Council of Teachers of English, 1965).

26. Jacques Barzun, *The House of Intellect* (New York: Harper, 1959), 243. A measure of Barzun's influence was his selection for the cover of *Time* magazine's 1956 issue "America and the Intellectual." Another important critique of *The English Language Arts* was Harry Warfel's *Who Killed Grammar?* (Gainesville: University of Florida Press, 1952), which accused linguists of destroying respect for grammar and of fostering a rebellious attitude toward the study of language.

27. National Council of Teachers of English, Commission on the English Curriculum, *The English Language Arts* (New York: Appleton-Century-Crofts, 1952), 278.

28. Charles C. Fries, *American English Grammar* (New York: D. Appleton–Century, 1940), 287.

29. Robert C. Pooley, *Teaching English Usage* (New York: Appleton-Century-Crofts, 1946), 180–81, 194–98, and 218–23.

30. Jacques Barzun, "What Are Mistakes and Why," in *A Word or Two before You Go. . . .* (Middleton, CT: Wesleyan University Press, 1988), 7. In the same quote he elaborates that the language of professionals is "inherently clumsy and ponderous [with] words misunderstood and misapplied, idioms distorted, prepositions used at random, jargon and imagery blanketing thought, novelties multiplying without need, grammar and syntax defied to no purpose." See also *The House of Intellect*, 232–40.

31. Some writing aimed at the general public (such as Robert A. Hall's) was particularly easy to flog as permissive. Other linguists of the mid-twentieth century recognized that their efforts would be characterized as politically subversive. W. Nelson Francis, for example, remarked in a 1954 article in the *Quarterly Journal of Speech* that "Those of us who try to get the new concepts of grammar introduced into the curriculum are tagged as 'liberal' grammarians—the implication being, I suppose, that one has a free choice between 'liberal' and 'conservative' grammar, and that the liberals are a bit dangerous, perhaps even subversive." Francis refers to a "smear campaign" associating linguistics with lack of standards. See his "The Revolution in Grammar," reprinted in *Linguistics for Teachers*, ed. Linda Miller Cleary and Michael D. Young (New York: McGraw Hill, 1993), 441.

32. See C. P. Snow, *The Two Cultures and the Scientific Revolution* (Cambridge: Cambridge University Press, 1959).

33. This quote is from Barzun's essay "After Fowler's Generation," which originally appeared in *The American Scholar* in 1957 and is included in Barzun's *A Word or Two before You Go. . . .*,105–14. Barzun expanded on this view in his 1959 book *The House of Intellect*, writing that "For the state of the language as we find it in the centers of culture, certain modern linguists bear a grave responsibility. In wanting to prove their studies scientific, they went out of their way to impress the public with a pose and set of principles that they thought becoming: a true science, they argued, only records, classifies and notes relations; it never prescribes" (240).

34. Barzun, *The House of Intellect*, 243. In his 2000 book *From Dawn to Decadence*, he continues to view linguistics as misguided (see pp. 657–59).

35. See Fries's *American English Grammar*, 289–92.

36. Later critics recycled Barzun's views. Thus Dwight Macdonald, writing about *Webster's Third* in the *New Yorker* in 1962, remarks that:

[A] revolution has taken place in the study of English grammar and usage, a revolution that probably represents an advance in scientific method but that certainly has had an unfortunate effect on such nonscientific efforts as the teaching of English and the making of dictionaries—at least on the making of this particular dictionary. The scientific revolution has meshed gears with a trend toward permissiveness, in the name of democracy, that is debasing our language by rendering it less precise and thus less effective as literature and less efficient as communication. (Dwight Macdonald, "The String Untuned," *New Yorker*, March 10, 1962, 130)

Nearly two decades after this statement, Barzun's influence is still apparent in comments like John Simon's characterization of linguistics as "that statistical, populist, sociological approach, whose adherents claimed to be merely recording and describing the language as it was used by anyone and everyone, without imposing elitist judgments on it" *Paradigms Lost*, xiv). A recent example is from Mark Halpern, writing in a 1997 *Atlantic Monthly* essay titled "A War That Never Ends" (*Atlantic Monthly*, March 1997, 19–22). Halpern's essay reacts, somewhat belatedly, to Geoffrey Nunberg's 1983 essay "The Decline of Grammar," which argued in response to Simon and others that the real decline in grammar was in the standard of public discussion of language rather than in the tolerance of colloquial and informal usage. In a longer essay in *The American Scholar*, Halpern portrays linguistics as being simultaneously too broad and too specialized and sees it as losing its status as a source of expert judgment about language. He writes that "Questions of usage—judgments as to how we should write and speak today—will be recognized as lying within the purview of the general educated public, with philosophers, literary critics, and poets perhaps seen as leaders. We, the new usage arbiters, may occasionally turn for assistance to the findings of what is now called linguistics, if we judge such information to be relevant to our own objectives, but if we do we will be looking not for judicial rulings but for expert testimony on technical points, whose values we will assess by our own lights" ("The End of Linguistics," *The American Scholar*, Winter 2001, 25–26).

37. Herbert Morton, *The Story of Webster's Third: Phillip Gove's Controversial Dictionary and Its Critics* (Cambridge: Cambridge University Press, 1994), 135–38. In addition, *Webster's Third* reassessed the slang and colloquial words of *Webster's Second* in light of then-current usage. Morton notes that Gove dropped the labels *correct* and *incorrect, proper* and *improper, humorous, jocular, poetic, ludicrous, Gallicism,* and *contemptuous,* restricting the dictionary to such labels as *nonstandard, substandard, obsolete, archaic,* and *slang* and to indications of regional usage. For other discussion of *Webster's Third,* see James Sledd and Wilma Ebbitt's *Dictionaries and* That *Dictionary* (New York: Scott, Foresman, 1962).

38. Finegan, *Attitudes toward English Usage* (7), and Morton, *The Story of Webster's Third* (309, n. 23), cite Richard Emrick's *Detroit News* article "New Dictionary Cheap, Corrupt" (Feb. 10, 1962) as calling the dictionary "a kind of Kinsey Report in linguistics." See Morton, chs. 9 and 10, for a review of press coverage. On the comparison of Charles Fries with Kinsey, see John Sherwood's "Dr. Kinsey and Professor Fries," *College English* 23 (1962), 275–80.

39. Edwin Newman, *On Language* (New York: Galahad, 1992), 9. This volume combines his *Strictly Speaking* (1974) and *A Civil Tongue* (1975).

40. John Simon, *Paradigms Lost: Reflections on Literacy and Its Decline* (New York: Clarkson N. Potter, 1980), 39.

41. For example, Simon writes (149) that "There is, I believe, a morality of language: an obligation to preserve and nurture the niceties, the fine distinctions, that have been handed down to us."

42. Simon, 165–66.

43. Simon, 147.

44. Some traditionalists recognize the mean-spiritedness of the conservative critique. See, for example, Paul Robinson's "Lost Causes," *The New Republic*, Jan. 26, 1980, 25–27, which sees "complementary traps of vindictiveness or mindless modernity."

45. Geoffrey Nunberg, "The Decline of Grammar," *Atlantic Monthly*, Dec. 1983, 34.

46. Joseph Williams, "Linguistic Responsibility," *College English* 39.1 (1977), 13.

47. Robert Claiborne, *Our Marvelous Native Tongue* (New York: Times Books, 1983), 294. He blames bad writing on "educationalists" and on "well-meaning but muddled-headed experts on linguistics, incompetent teachers and the unions that protect their jobs, tight fisted school boards and taxpayers, short-sighted college admissions officers, and the designers and marketers of aptitude tests." Claiborne quotes linguist Robert A. Hall's statement that "there is no good or bad in language," citing Hall's *Leave Your Language Alone!* which first appeared in 1950 under that title (Ithaca, NY: Linguistica, a private printing) and was later reissued in 1960 as *Linguistics and Your Language* (New York: Doubleday). Hall was not naïve about the role of grammar, however. In the 1960 reprint, he writes that "Often enough, we may find we need to change our usage, simply because social and financial success depends on some norm, and our speech is one of the things that will be used as a norm. In a situation like this it is advisable to make an adjustment; but let's do so on the basis of the actual social acceptability of our speech, not because of the fanciful prescriptions of some normative grammarian or other pseudo-authority" (29).

48. John Updike's review of Burchfield's *The New Fowler's Modern English Usage*, titled "Fine Points," appeared in the *New Yorker* (Dec. 23/Dec. 30, 1996, 142–49). Another recent example is writer Jacob Heilbrunn's characterization of linguistic research (on Ebonics) as "professional crackpotism, well within the pedagogical mainstream." See his "Speech Therapy," *New Republic*, Jan. 20, 1997, 18.

49. Finegan, *Attitudes toward English Usage*, 125.

50. David Foster Wallace, "Tense Present," *Harper's*, April 2001, 39–58. See esp. pp. 44–47 and 57–58. Wallace also sees descriptivism as the basis of a

misguided pedagogy of writing instruction as self-expression rather than communication. And he views it as a source for the "language in which today's socialist, feminist, minority, gay and environmentalist movements frame their sides of the political debate," a connection he attributes to a descriptivist belief that traditional English is perpetuated by a privileged class.

51. Ironically, Wallace criticizes structural linguistics for relativism arising from its scientific method while at the same time suggesting that its faith in science has been supplanted by poststructuralist views of knowledge that relativism helped to create.

4. Bad Words

1. Walter Mosley, *Always Outnumbered, Always Outgunned* (New York: W. W. Norton, 1998), 18.

2. Paul Boyer, *Purity in Print: The Vice Society Movement and Book Censorship in America* (New York: Scribner's Sons, 1966), 258.

3. The observation about James Kelman's *How Late It Was, How Late* is from Martha Nussbaum's *Cultivating Humanity* (Cambridge, MA: Harvard University Press, 1997), 98.

4. Timothy Jay's *Cursing in America* (Amsterdam: Benjamins, 1992), 231–34, is the source for the discussion of cursing in film.

5. Tad Friend, "You Can't Say That: The Networks Play Word Games," *New Yorker*, Nov. 19, 2001, 44–49.

6. Jim Rutenberg, "Hurt by Cable, Networks Spout Expletives," *New York Times*, Sept. 2, 2001, 1, 19.

7. The example "You backstabbing son-of-a-bitch" is from NBC's *Just Shoot Me* (originally broadcast April 9, 1998) and is not particularly atypical. And in the Sunday comics, we find an umpire being called a "scumbag" in the comic strip *Blondie* (May 16, 2004).

8. Jim Rutenberg, "Hurt by Cable, Networks Spout Expletives."

9. See "Court Convicts Cursing Canoeist under Century-old Michigan Law," *St. Louis Post Dispatch*, June 12, 1999, 29. It should be noted that a Michigan appeals court ruled the law unconstitutional in April of 2002.

10. The stereotyping involved in the conjunction "women and children" in the Michigan law would take us somewhat far afield, but see Mary Ritchie Key's discussion of the "notion that women should be 'protected' from rough language" together with "the Madonna/Whore syndrome" (*Male/Female Language, with Comprehensive Bibliography*, 2nd ed. [Lanham, MD: Scarecrow Press, 1996], 49–50). Timothy Jay documents gender stereotyping when he observes that "the overwhelming majority of media portrayals of men and women cursing show that men curse more often than women" and that

"women who curse tend to represent 'bad' characters (e.g., whores, drunks, drug users)." See his *Why We Curse?* (Amsterdam: Benjamins, 2000), 166–67.

11. The observations from Paul Boyer are from *Purity in Print*, 3–5.

12. Data from the American Library Association Office for Intellectual Freedom is available on its website for "Challenged and Banned Books." http://www.ala.org/Content/NavigationMenu/Our_Association/Offices/Intellectual_Freedom3/Banned_Books_Week/Challenged_and_Banned_Books/Challenged_and_Banned_Books.htm#backgroundinformation.

13. *FCC v. Pacifica*, 438 US. 726 (1978).

14. David Paletz and William Harris, "Four-Letter Threats to Authority," *Journal of Politics* 37.4 (1975), 965.

15. The Equal Employment Opportunity Commission guidelines define sexual harassment as "verbal or physical contact of a sexual nature [having] the purpose or effect of unreasonably interfering with an individual's work performance or creating an intimidating, hostile, or offensive work environment." See the Code of Federal Regulations, Title 29, volume 4, parts 900 to 1899, 29CFR1604.11, available at http://www/eeoc.gov/facts/fs-sex.html.

16. The Supreme Court's *Chaplinsky v. New Hampshire* decision is at 315 U.S. 568 (1942), and the Court's decision in the St. Paul Bias-Motivated Crime Ordinance of 1990 appears at *R. A. V. v. City of St. Paul*, 505 U.S. 377 (1992).

17. Material on the 1997 debate over ethnic slurs in the *Merriam-Webster Collegiate Dictionary* can be found in the *Washington Post* story "Furor Erupts over Racial Epithet: Activists Seek to Drop or Redefine 'Nigger' in Merriam-Webster Dictionary" (Oct. 8, 1997, A16), and in the *New York Times* story "Dictionary Will Revise Definition of 200 Slurs" (May 3, 1998, 20).

18. See Randall Kennedy, *Nigger: The Strange Career of a Troublesome Word* (New York: Pantheon Books, 2002). The quote from Patricia Williams is from David D. Kirkpatrick's "A Black Author Hurls *That* Word as a Challenge," *New York Times*, Dec. 1, 2001, A15–16. See also Anita Henderson's "What's in a Slur?" *American Speech* 78.1 (2003), 52–74.

19. Erroll McDonald was quoted in David D. Kirkpatrick's "A Black Author Hurls *That* Word as a Challenge."

20. The Supreme Court's *Cohen v. California* decision is found at 403 U.S. 15 (1971) and its decision concerning the musical *Hair* is found at *Southeastern Promotions, Ltd. v. Conrad et al.* 420 U.S. 546 (1975).

21. James Ledbetter, "Making Booker: James Kelman Fucks With Literature," *Village Voice Literary Supplement*, March 7, 1995, 9.

22. "Female Lawyers See Bias in Their Arrests," *ABA Journal*, 81 ABAJ 28, March 1995.

23. Renatus Hartogs and Hans Fantel, *Four-Letter Word Games: The Psychology of Obscenity* (New York: Evans, 1967), 15.

24. Geoffrey Hughes, *Swearing: A Social History of Foul Language, Oaths, and Profanity in English* (London: Blackwell, 1991), 38. Hughes (pp. 40–163) is the source for the general overview of how English swearing has changed.

25. Hughes, 79. Hughes (88) also points out that the Parson's tale discusses swearing at length and suggests that it was most common "among the aristocracy and the lower orders."

26. Hughes, 96.

27. For discussion of Shakespeare, see Eric Partridge's *Shakespeare's Bawdy: A Literary and Psychological Essay and a Comprehensive Glossary* (New York: E. P. Dutton, 1948).

28. See Ashley Montagu, *The Anatomy of Swearing* (New York: Macmillan, 1967), 154–65, and Hughes 116–17. Montagu (156) notes that Jonson, John Marston, and George Chapman were briefly jailed for a passage in their 1605 play *Eastward Ho* that was judged to be derogatory to the Scots.

29. Hughes, 102.

30. Ashley Montagu, *The Anatomy of Swearing* (New York: Macmillan, 1967), 162, is the source for the quote from the 1623 act fining swearers.

31. Montagu, 159.

32. Hughes, 142.

33. Hughes is the source for the observations concerning Jeremy Collier's *A Short View of the Profaneness and Immorality of the English Stage* (146), Swift (143), and Nathaniel Bailey's and Samuel Johnson's dictionaries (157–58). As Hughes notes, *fuck* was also among the words omitted from the *Oxford English Dictionary*, though Farmer and Henley's 1890 dictionary of *Slang and Its Analogues* reported that the word was commonly used (158–62).

34. John C. Burnham, *Bad Habits: Drinking, Smoking, Taking Drugs, Gambling, Sexual Misbehavior, and Swearing in American History* (New York: New York University Press, 1993), 208. Burnham writes that "The stereotyped deviant identity had always alluded to the rebellious use of profane and obscene expressions" that are "part of the ritual of antisocial behavior" and symbolize "lower-order parochialism." More broadly, Burnham sees swearing as associated with what he calls the minor vices (drinking, smoking, drugs, gambling, and sexual misbehavior).

35. Burnham, 213.

36. Burnham is also the source of the citations to Edwin Whipple's 1885 "The Swearing Habit" (355, n. 16).

37. Burnham, 219.

38. H. L. Mencken, *The American Language* (New York: Knopf, 1937), 313, is the source for the quote from L. W. Merryweather's 1931 *American Speech* article.

39. Allen Walker Read, "An Obscenity Symbol," *American Speech* 9.4 (1934), 264–78. Read suggested that "the ordinary reaction to a display of filth and vulgarity should be a neutral one or else disgust; but the reaction to certain words connected with excrement and sex is neither of these, but a titillating thrill of scandalized perturbation." For current research on contemporary attitudes, see Robert S. Wachal's "Taboo or Not Taboo: That Is the Question," *American Speech* 77.2 (2002), 195–206.

40. The quote from John Brophy and Eric Partridge's *Songs and Slang of the British Soldier, 1914–1918* (London: Scholartis Press, 1930) is from Mencken, 315.

41. Montagu (279) is the source for the quote from Norman Vincent Peale's 1942 sermon.

42. Burges Johnson, *The Lost Art of Profanity*, 75.

43. See Richard Bailey's *Nineteenth-Century English* and Farmer and Henley's *Slang and Its Analogues* for details.

44. Harold Wentworth and Stuart Berg Flexner, *Dictionary of American Slang* (New York: Thomas Y. Crowell, 1960), xvii.

45. *American Heritage Dictionary* (Springfield, MA: Merriam-Webster, 1997), 1279.

46. Bethany Dumas and Jonathan Lightner, "Is *Slang* a Word for Linguists?" *American Speech* 53.1 (1978), 14–16.

47. See Connie Eble, *Slang and Sociability: In-group Language among College Students* (Chapel Hill: University of North Carolina Press, 1996), 99–129.

48. The quote from Carl Sandburg is from the profile "Minstrel of America: Carl Sandburg," *New York Times*, Feb.13, 1959, 21.

49. Norm Goldstein, ed., *The AP Stylebook and Libel Manual* (Reading, MA: Addison-Wesley, 1996), 191.

50. John Hodges, Mary Whitten, and Suzanne Webb, *The Harbrace College Handbook* (New York: Harcourt Brace, 1986), 198.

51. William Watt, *An American Rhetoric* (New York: Holt, 1957), 270.

52. For an example of the advice given to broadcasters, see Stuart Hyde's *Television and Radio Announcing*, 8th ed. (New York: Houghton Mifflin, 1998). Hyde also emphasizes the relativity of slang. He writes that "To some 'slang' means corrupted speech; to others it means a creative and effective use of language. Slang is condemned by language purists, but most of us use it without apology in some settings and contexts" (144). He adds that broadcast

announcers should nevertheless be sensitive to the effective and ineffective use of nonstandard language: "Slang that might be appropriate in a commercial may be out of place in a newscast. Although sports announcers, talk-show hosts, and popular music announcers often use slang to good effect, it's usually avoided by news commentators and analysts" (147).

53. Jonathan Lightner, "Slang," *The Cambridge History of the English Language: 6, English in North America*, ed. John Algeo (Cambridge: Cambridge University Press, 2001), 227.

54. Oliver Wendell Holmes, Sr., "Mechanism in Thought and Morals," *Pages from an Old Volume of Life* (Boston: Houghton Mifflin, 1891), 275.

55. Lightner, 227. Among others, Lightner sees George Ade, Peter Dunne, Ring Lardner, and Jack London as influential.

56. H. L. Mencken, *The American Language* (New York: Knopf, 1937), 563.

57. Burnham, 215. Dennis Baron emphasizes the association of slang with linguistic disease, social poverty, and decay (*Grammar and Good Taste* [New Haven: Yale University Press, 1982], 216–17). An example of this in early twentieth-century psychological research can be found in Gladys Schwesinger's "Slang as an Indication of Character," *Journal of Applied Psychology* 10 (1926), 245–63. Schwesinger performed what she described as an attempt at "character detection and management" by surveying delinquents and nondelinquents for knowledge of slang terms.

58. An exception seems to be the characterization of African-American English, which is sometimes mischaracterized as "street slang" by commentators reacting to both the 1979 King school decision and the 1996 Oakland School Board resolution, and an unsuccessful California Senate bill referred disapprovingly to school programs that "teach that slang is an appropriate alternative to correct English in some situations" (cited in John Baugh's *Beyond Ebonics* [New York: Oxford University Press, 1999], 79). I return to the question of African-American vernacular in the next chapter.

59. See James Bradstreet Greenough and George Lyman Kittredge, *Words and Their Way in English Speech* (New York: Macmillan, 1901), 73.

60. Linda Hall, "Coolspeak," *Hudson Review* [2002], 414.

61. For an analysis of the meaning and use of *cool* see Robert Moore's essay "We're Cool. Mom and Dad Are Swell: Basic Slang and Generational Shifts in Values," *American Speech* 79.1 [2004], 59–86.

62. Jacques Barzun, "What Are Mistakes and Why," in *A Word or Two before You Go. . . .*, 8–9. Barzun also suggests that slang ignores "the really working part of words drawn on" (6), citing *workaholic* and arguing that –*aholic* is being misused.

63. Ruth Perry, "A Short History of the Term *Politically Correct*," in *Beyond PC: Toward a Politics of Understanding*, ed. Patricia Aufderheide (St. Paul: Graywolf, 1992), 72. For a survey of definitions, see Robin T. Lakoff's *The Language War* (Berkeley: University of California Press, 2000), 93.

64. Dinesh D'Souza, "The Visigoths in Tweed," in Aufderheide, *Beyond PC*, 19.

65. George H. Bush, May 1991 commencement address, in Aufderheide, *Beyond PC*, 227.

66. John K. Wilson, *The Myth of Political Correctness* (Durham: Duke University Press, 1996), provides useful background on the mythologization of campus events. See also Annette Gomis van Heteren's *Political Correctness in Context* (Almería: Universidad de Almería, 1997) and the special issue of the *Partisan Review* "The Politics of Political Correctness" (60.4 [1993]).

67. Other examples of media include articles such as the *National Review*'s squib "Sensitivity Fascism" and Richard Bernstein's "The Rising Hegemony of the Politically Correct" in the *New York Times*, among many others.

68. Jerry Adler, "Taking Offense," *Newsweek*, Dec. 24, 1990, 53.

69. The idea that language created and reinforced generalizations about people and groups was not a new idea of the 1960s, 1970s or 1980s. Gordon Allport's 1954 book *The Nature of Prejudice* (Reading, MA: Addison-Wesley) had emphasized this point.

70. John Taylor, "Are You Politically Correct?" *New York Magazine*, Jan. 21, 1991, 32–40. Taylor's story struck a theme similar to that of Adler's *Newsweek* piece, seeing political correctness as arising from the entrenchment of a 1960s political vision in universities, with French critical theory providing the vehicle for a critique of established cultural norms. Taylor writes that "Semiotics and Lacanian psychoanalysis argued that language and art conveyed subliminal cultural prejudices, power configurations, metaphorical representations of gender. Deconstruction declared that texts, to use the preferred word, had no meaning outside themselves"(36).

71. John Leo, *Two Steps Ahead of the Thought Police* (New York: Simon and Schuster, 1994), 40–42. Columns like Leo's fall into the category of easy journalistic satire.

72. See Diane Ravitch, *The Language Police: How Pressure Groups Restrict What Students Learn* (New York: Alfred A. Knopf, 2003), 62–96.

73. The examples are from appendix 1 of Ravitch's *Language Police*, "A Glossary of Banned Words, Usages, Stereotypes and Topics," 171–202.

74. Claims about political correctness in medicine, for example, can be found in Sally Satel's book *P. C., M. D.: How Political Correctness Is Corrupting*

Medicine (New York: Basic Books, 2001). For comments on political correctness as undermining anti-terrorist efforts, see Paul Craig Roberts's essay "U.S.S. Cole Torpedoed by Political Correctness," *Capitalism Magazine*, online, Oct. 28, 2000, and Michelle Malkin's "Racial Profiling: A Matter of Survival," *USA Today*, Aug. 17, 2004, 13A; Malkin quotes Arizona Senator John Kyl as referring to the refusal to conduct selective investigations of Muslim chaplains as the "height of politically correct stupidity."

75. For a discussion comparing political correctness to prescriptivism, see Paul Postal's "Policing the Content of Linguistic Examples," *Language* 79.1 (2003), 182–88.

76. So for example, John Taylor organized his *New York Magazine* article around such headings as "The New Fundamentalism," "Everything is Political," and "Ethnic and Ideological Purity."

77. This is not a new phenomenon, of course. Anti-German sentiment in World War I was reflected in the patriotically correct renaming of such things as *sauerkraut, hamburger, German shepherds, dachshunds,* and *German measles,* none of which were very durable.

78. See Michael Oreskes, "For GOP Arsenal, 133 Words to Fire," *New York Times*, Sept. 9, 1990, sec. 1, 30.

79. George Lakoff, "Framing the Dems," *American Prospect* 14.8 (Sept.1, 2003). Lakoff is one of the founders of the Rockridge Institute, which aims to develop framing language for progressive viewpoints.

80. For examples of critiques along these lines, see James Atlas's *The Book Wars: What It Takes to be Educated in America* (Knoxville: Whittle Communications, 1990) and Jerry Martin's "The Postmodern Argument Considered," *Partisan Review* 4 (1993), 638–54.

81. Robert Hughes, *Culture of Complaint: The Fraying of America* (New York: Oxford University Press, 1993), 20–21.

82. John Baugh's discussion of the term *African-American* is from his *Out of the Mouths of Slaves* (Austin: University of Texas Press, 1999). Baugh suggests that "terminological uncertainty has haunted many liberals in the wake of [Reverend Jesse Jackson's 1988 speech advocating adoption of *African-American*] because they do not want to inadvertently offend members of minority groups" (93).

83. The observation about the Shriners Hospitals is from that organization's press release "Shriners Hospitals Change Name: Seventy-four-year-old Hospital System Eliminates Word '*Crippled*,'" available at www.shrinershq.org/WhatsNewArch/Archives96/namechange7-96.html. The phrase, "for crippled children and adults" was dropped from the Easter Seals organization in 1979.

84. Marilyn Schwartz, *Guidelines for Bias-Free Writing* (Bloomington: Indiana University Press, 1995), 74–75.

5. Bad Citizens

1. Theodore Roosevelt's "Children of the Crucible" speech is reprinted in *Language Loyalties: A Source Book on the Official English Controversy*, ed. James Crawford (Chicago: University of Chicago Press, 1992), 84–85.

2. Daniel J. Boorstin's *The Americans: The Colonial Experience* (New York: Vintage, 1958), chs. 41 and 42, is the source for background on colonial attitudes and for the citation to Franklin's 1760 letter to Hume (278); for Boorstin's views on descriptive linguistics, see *The Americans: The Democratic Experience* (New York: Vintage, 1973), pp. 452–62.

3. The quote from John Pickering's "Essay on the Present State of the English Language in the United States" is excerpted in C. Merton Babcock's *The Ordeal of American English* (Boston: Houghton Mifflin, 1961), 30.

4. David Simpson's *The Politics of American English, 1776–1850* (New York: Oxford University Press, 1988), p. 32, is the source for the citation to Jefferson's 1813 letter. Writers such as John Witherspoon also advocated an American style. Witherspoon saw the issue as a contest between the more cultured nature of British speech and the potential for uniformity that an American language might foster, particularly in light of the mobility of Americans. He saw the common speech in America as less parochial than the common speech of England, but nevertheless cautioned against too common a style, arguing for a language that expressed neither "bombast and empty swelling" nor "low sentiments and vulgar terms." See the excerpts of *The Druid*, no. 5, collected in Babcock's *The Ordeal of American English*, 74.

5. See Adrienne Koch, *The Philosophy of Thomas Jefferson* (Gloucester, MA: Peter Smith, 1957), 109, for the citation to Jefferson's 1920 letter to Adams. As Julie Tetel Andressen notes in her *Linguistics in America, 1769–1924: A Critical History* (London: Routledge, 1990), pp. 57–62, Jefferson also advocated spelling reform and the resurrection of provincial archaisms.

6. Webster is most famous for his spelling reforms, and as a publisher he was sometimes accused of self-interest for these since he would profit from Americanized editions of books. Webster saw spelling reform as a means to reduce the gap between speaking and writing and to foster communication and opportunities for unified political action. Webster's own reforms were largely unsuccessful in his lifetime, and his greatest influence may have been the association of correct language with American values, which ensured the success of his competitors Murray, Brown, and Kirkham.

7. Webster, quoted in Simpson, 65.

8. Simpson, *The Politics of American English, 1776–1850*, 52–72, is the source for the summary of Noah Webster's views. Both Webster and Jefferson were influenced by the revival of interest in Anglo-Saxon as a source of English political and linguistic traditions. Webster, in particular, was influenced by the Saxonist speculations of John Horne Tooke. See Simpson, 81–90.

9. Kenneth Cmiel, *Democratic Eloquence* (New York: William Morrow, 1990), 45.

10. Cmiel, 47.

11. As Shirley Brice Heath notes, antimonarchists in the United States were skeptical of a centralized authority setting cultural norms, so proponents focused the debate on the role of language in education and law. See Shirley Brice Heath, "A National Language Academy? Debate in the New Nation," *Linguistics* 10.189 (1977), 9–43.

12. Simpson (30) is the source for this quote from John Adams.

13. Heath (21) is the source for this quote from Adams and for information generally on the language academy issue.

14. The quote from John Jay is cited in Carol Schmid's *The Politics of Language: Conflict, Identity, and Cultural Pluralism in Comparative Perspective* (New York: Oxford University Press, 2001), 18.

15. The sketch of Native American language policy draws on John Reyhner's "Policies toward American Indian Languages: A Historical Sketch," in *Language Loyalties: A Source Book on the Official English Controversy*, ed. James Crawford (Chicago: University of Chicago Press, 1992), 41–47, and William Leap's "American Indian Languages," in *Language in the USA*, ed. Charles Ferguson and Shirley Brice Heath (Cambridge: Cambridge University Press, 1981), 116–44.

16. The report of the 1868 commission on Indian conditions is cited by Atkins (48).

17. J. D. C. Atkins, Annual Report [of the Federal Commissioner of Indian Affairs] (excerpted as "Barbarous Dialects Should Be Blotted Out" in Crawford, *Language Loyalties*, 50.

18. The Native American Languages Act is Public Law 101–477 (Oct. 30, 1990). For a report on the Native American educational experience, see *Indian Nations at Risk: An Educational Strategy for Action* (Washington, DC: U.S. Department of Education, 1991, ERIC Document Reproduction Service No. ED339587).

19. See Douglas Baynton, *Forbidden Signs: American Culture and the Campaign against Sign Language* (Chicago: University of Chicago Press, 1996), pp. 15–26. Baynton's book was a key source for many of the facts in this sec-

tion: Alexander Graham Bell's views (30–31), Thomas Gallaudet's beliefs (17–20, 113–14), John Tyler's comments (36–38), the influence of evolution (38–44), and teacher statistics (25).

20. Baynton, 29.

21. Baynton, 16. The impetus for assimilation in the post–Civil War period reform mentality was also connected to "widespread fears of unchecked immigration and expanding, multi-ethnic cities."

22. Baynton cites an 1899 keynote address by John Tyler to the American Association to Promote the Teaching of Speech to the Deaf, which characterized sign language as brutish and advocated education based on the characteristics that evolution had promoted, namely speech. Baynton notes also that religious advocates of sign interpreted the origin of language differently, some seeing sign as closer to creation and thus representing a morally superior state.

23. In his 1943 book *Deafness and the Deaf in the United States* (New York: Macmillan, 524), Harry Best notes that opponents of sign continued to stress the social dangers of separatism.

24. Alexander Ewing and Ethel Ewing, *Teaching Deaf Children to Talk* (Manchester: Manchester University Press, 1964), viii.

25. Marc Marschark, *Raising and Educating a Deaf Child* (New York: Oxford University Press, 1997), 54.

26. Herbert Kohl's observations are from his *Language and Education of the Deaf* (New York: Center for Urban Education, 1966), 4–5; for citations to other summaries of the research on sign language and oralism, see Baynton 166, n.11.

27. Baynton (155) suggests that another factor in changing attitudes toward sign was a cultural shift in the 1960s in the way people viewed physicality. He notes that this included "such things as new and more sensuous forms of dance, a greater openness concerning sexuality, and an expanded tolerance for nudity and the celebration of the body, . . . [a] renewed fascination with "body language" generally, . . . more open expressions of passion and personal feelings, . . . [and] the popularity of new psychotherapies."

28. Earlier, the Bilingual Education Act of 1988 had included sign language for the first time.

29. The 1917 Immigration Act, passed over Woodrow Wilson's veto, excluded immigrants over the age of sixteen who were physically capable of reading but could not. Earlier literacy restrictions had been vetoed by Grover Cleveland and William Howard Taft.

30. Jack Rodgers's review of the "The Foreign Language Issue in Nebraska" (*Nebraska History*, 39.1 [1958], 1–22) was a source for the facts of *Meyer v. Nebraska*.

31. The relevant statutes can be found in *Nebraska Laws* 1919, chapter 234 (Nebraska's open meeting law) and chapter 249 (the Siman Law).

32. The 1922 Nebraska Supreme Court ruling can be found at 187 *Northwestern Reporter* 100, 1922.

33. The Supreme Court's *Meyer v. Nebraska* ruling may be found at 262 U.S. 390 (1923) and its *Nebraska District of Evangelical Lutheran Synod v. McKelvie* ruling may be found at 262 U.S. 404 (1923).

34. Dennis Baron's *The English-Only Question: An Official Language for Americans* (64–83) was a valuable source for background on the colonial German questions and on the origins of bilingual education policy, including the objections to Ingersoll's proposal (74–77) and Franklin's comments (66).

35. The quote from Ralph Yarborough's 1967 speech is from Crawford, *Language Loyalties*, 324.

36. The Supreme Court's *Lau v. Nichols* decision may be found at 414 U.S. 56 (1974).

37. Lily Wong Fillmore, "Against Our Best Interest: The Attempt to Sabotage Bilingual Education," in Crawford, *Language Loyalties*, 369.

38. Richard Rodriguez, "Bilingualism Con: Outdated and Unrealistic," *New York Times*, Nov. 10, 1985, sec. 12, 83. See also his *The Hunger of Memory* (Boston: David R. Godine, 1981).

39. Similar efforts passed in Arizona in 2000 and failed in Colorado in 2002.

40. Diane August and Kenji Hakuta, *Educating Language-Minority Children* (Washington, DC: National Academic Press, 1998), 61. The National Academy of Sciences is a private, nonprofit group operating under a congressional charter.

41. Tanton was also associated with the Federation for American Immigration Reform. He resigned from U.S. English in 1988 after the release of a controversial anti-immigration memo. See James Crawford's "What's Behind the Official English Movement," in *Language Loyalties*, 171–77.

42. Geoffrey Nunberg, "Linguistics and the Official Language Movement," *Language* 65.3 (1989), 580–81, was the source of the observations on the range of official English laws and some of their intended consequences. For discussion of English-only workplace rules and legal challenges to these, see Carol Schmid, *The Politics of Language* (New York: Oxford University Press, 2001), 65–68.

43. Judge Paul Rosenblatt's opinion appears as *Yniguez v. Mofford*, 730 F. Supp. 309 (D. Ariz. 1990). Rosenblatt rejected Arizona's position that the amendment was merely intended to be used by the state in its official capacity and that it was not intended as a blanket prohibition on state officials and employees.

44. Geoffrey Nunberg, for example, notes that English-only assumes that "acquisition of English and assimilation to the majority culture are incompatible with retention of the native language and cultural values; that people will not learn a second language as long as the native language is kept available as a 'crutch' and so on" ("Linguistics and the Official Language Movement," 583–84).

45. Reprinted as "In Defense of Our Common Language . . ." in Crawford, *Language Loyalties*, 143–48.

46. Journalist James Crawford also points out that English-only proponents assume that English is best learned by immersion and assume that ethnic leaders who argue for bilingual programs do so out of self-interest (for example, to provide jobs for bilingual educators). See his "What's Behind the Official English Movement," in *Language Loyalties*, 171–77.

47. Schmid, *Politics of Language*, 88–89. Surveys conducted in 1984, 1988, and 1990 found 61 percent, 66 percent and 90 percent of Hispanics agreeing that is was important for citizens to speak and understand English. A 1985 Miami survey found 98 percent of Hispanic parents agreeing that English was essential for children's success.

48. Schmid, *Politics of Language*, 47–48. She also reports on surveys about the relation between education and assimilation. See also Calvin Veltman's *The Future of the Spanish Language in the United States* (Washington, DC: Spanish Policy Development Project, 1988). For a study of African-American attitudes toward English-only, see Geneva Smitherman, *Talkin That Talk* (London: Routledge, 2000), 297–302. Smitherman reports on a survey of 216 African-Americans in five cities in which over half (64.6 percent) said that they would not support English-only laws.

49. Robert King, "Should English Be the Law?" *Atlantic Monthly*, April 1997, 55–64.

50. Schmid, *Politics of Language*, 195–97.

6. Bad Accents

1. On the merger reflected in the Southern pronunciation of *pen* and *pin* (and similar words), see Vivian Brown's 1990 Texas A and M University dissertation *The Social and Linguistic History of a Merger: /i/ and /e/ before Nasals in Southern American English* and her essay "Evolution of the Merger of /i/ and /ɛ/ before Nasals in Tennessee," *American Speech* 66.3 (Fall 1991), 303–15. The area of the most robust merger runs from Southern Virginia westward through Texas, with an irregular northern boundary that includes parts of Indiana. The merger extends into the West, following the resettlement history of Southern speakers. For some discussion of the pronunciation of short

a in *coffee, sausage, chocolate*, and *Florida*, see Allan Forbes Hubbell's *The Pronunciation of English in New York City: Consonants and Vowels* (New York: Octagon Books, 1972), 82–85. Hubbell describes the further variation among some speakers who pronounce many of these words with an additional gliding, so that the words have an AWUH sound to them (*cAWUHfee, sAWUHsage*). The AWUH in New York City speech is most common in words spelled *au, aw, al,* and *ough,* such as *almost, caught, laundry, paw, walnut,* and *Walter.* Before stops, the AWUH is common only in *chocolate, dog,* and *water.* This variation may be characterized as uncultivated, but it still reflects a regular pattern of correspondence among sounds.

2. Daniel J. Boorstin, *The Americans: The Democratic Experience* (New York: Vintage, 1973), 272.

3. Rosina Lippi-Green's 1998 *English with an Accent* (London: Routledge), 122–23). Lippi-Green noted that implementation of the petition would likely have violated Title VII of the Civil Rights Act.

4. See J. K. Chambers, *Sociolinguistic Theory* (Oxford: Blackwell, 1995), 167–69.

5. See Dennis Baron's *The English-Only Question: An Official Language for Americans* (New Haven: Yale University Press, 1990), 162.

6. A March 2003 memo by the Massachusetts commissioner of education outlined English proficiency requirements under the English Language Education in Public Schools law. The text of the memo is available at www.doe.mass.edu/ell/0327profreq.html.

7. The guest opinion "Physics: More English, Less Chinese," by Joshua Robinson, appeared in the February 20, 2004, issue of the *Johns Hopkins Newsletter*, archived at www.jhunewsletter.com.

8. Mark Clayton, "Foreign Teaching Assistants' First Test: The Accent," *Christian Science Monitor*, Sept. 5, 2000 (online: www.csmonitor.com/durable/2000/09/05/fp14s1–csm.shtml).

9. See George Borjas, "Foreign-Born Teaching Assistants and the Academic Performance of Undergraduates," *American Economic Review*, 90.2 (2000), 355–59; Donald L. Rubin, "Nonlanguage Factors Affecting Undergraduates' Judgments of Non-Native English Speaking Teaching Assistants," *Research in Higher Education* 33 (1992), 511–31.

10. U.S. Census Bureau, *The Foreign-Born Population in the United States, March 2002 (2003)*, http://www.census.gov/prod/2003pubs/p20–539.pdf. The report notes that about 21 percent of foreign-born workers were in service occupations and about 23 percent in managerial and professional occupations.

11. Chris Soloman, "Speech Classes Place the Accent on Understanding," *The Record* (Bergen County, NJ), Dec. 12, 2000, A32.

12. From an ad for Accent Services, USA, cited by Barry Newman in his 2002 essay "Accent," in *The American Scholar*, 71.2, 61.

13. The EEOC guidelines, which implement aspects of Title VII of the Civil Rights Act of 1964, say that employers must distinguish between accents that are merely noticeable and ones that actually interfere with someone's ability to perform a job: "Generally, an employer may only base an employment decision on accent if effective oral communication in English is required to perform job duties and the individual's foreign accent materially interferes with his or her ability to communicate orally in English." In other words, the EEOC requires that accents be evaluated objectively in terms of job performance and requirements. The guidelines also note that "Positions for which effective oral communication in English may be required include teaching, customer service, and telemarketing." See http://www.eeoc.gov/policy/docs/national-origin.html#VB1 and for more general information also http://www.eeoc.gov/origin/. Barry Newman reports that from 1996 to 2000 the number of accent bias complaints to the EEOC rose from 77 to 400 ("Accent," 66).

14. Newman (61) suggests that the growth in accent reduction services offered by speech pathologists may be connected to changes in Medicare reimbursement practices in the 1990s. It is difficult to determine the extent of the accent-reduction business, which is spread among private firms, speech pathologists, and university and community college educators. However, the market for such services seems broad in that it appeals to both individuals and corporations and to both domestic and international clients.

15. See Gavin Jones, *Strange Talk: The Politics of Dialect in Gilded Age America* (Berkeley: University of California Press, 1999), 64–71; see also Dennis Baron, *Grammar and Good Taste*, 163, on the "germ theory of language decay." Jones (55–60) notes the ambivalence of Mark Twain's attitude toward Western dialect, which was simultaneously a means of deflating the cultural authority of New England and a form of anarchy.

16. The quote is from Henry James's *The Question of Our Speech* (Boston: Houghton Mifflin, 1906), 41.

17. Jones, *Strange Talk*, 165.

18. The vaudeville tradition remained in the early decades of television comedy with characters like Ricky Ricardo, Bill Dana's *Jose Jimenez*, and Victor Sen Yung's *Hop Sing*, the Chinese cook on the long-running series *Bonanza*. In television advertising it was also possible to find stereotypes like the Frito Bandito and the Funny-Face fruit drink flavor Chinese Cherry (later renamed Choo-Choo Cherry).

19. For some discussion of folk names of dialects, see Laura C. Hartley and Dennis Preston's "The Names of U.S. English," in *Standard English: The*

Widening Debate, ed. Tony Bex and Richard J. Watts (London: Routledge, 1999), 207–38.

20. Other examples in television and film are easy to find and range from the *Beverly Hillbillies* and the *Dukes of Hazzard* to the *Sopranos*, and from *Cold Mountain* to *Barbershop* and *My Cousin Vinnie*. For an in-depth discussion of film stereotypes of the mountain South, see Jerry Wayne Williamson's *Hillbillyland: What the Movies Did to the Mountains and What the Mountains Did to the Movies* (Chapel Hill: University of North Carolina Press, 1995).

21. Steve Mitchell, with art by Sam C. Rawls, *How to Speak Southern* (New York: Bantam, 1976).

22. Louis Alvarez and Andrew Kolker, *American Tongues* (Hohokus, NJ: Center for New American Media, 1986).

23. Kelly Hearn, "Pegged by an Accent," *Christian Science Monitor*, Dec. 18, 2000, 11.

24. Raven McDavid, "Linguistics, Through the Kitchen Door," in *First Person Singular*, ed. Boyd Davis and Raymond O'Cain (Amsterdam: John Benjamins, 1980), 7.

25. Deirdre Fanning, "Just You Wait, 'Enry 'Iggins . . . ," *New York Times*, Sept. 23, 1990, sec. 3, 25. See also Elizabeth Levit Spaid, "Losing That Dixie Drawl," *Christian Science Monitor*, Dec. 9, 1998, 1.

26. See Lippi-Green, *English with an Accent*, 137–38; The quote is from James Bender's 1951 *NBC Handbook of Pronunciation* (New York: T. Y. Crowell, 2nd ed.), ix. The 1984 edition, edited by Eugene Erhlich and Raymond Hand, Jr., reports that it "still adheres to the fundamental principle that guided earlier efforts: to record 'the pronunciations used by educated persons in the greater part of the United States, rather than to insist upon arbitrary standards of pronunciation unrelated to those commonly heard'" (8). The introduction by Edwin Newman states that "Broadly speaking, the pronunciation we recommend is that of General American Speech, that which is acceptable to, and used by, the great mass of competent Americans who use the language well" (17).

27. See *American Tongues* for a discussion of the "voice of directory assistance." The observation on telemarketing is from Eugene Carlson's report "Neutral Accents Help Attract 'Telemarketers' to the Midwest," *Wall Street Journal*, April 8, 1986, sec. 2, 1.

28. Studies on language attitudes include Nancy Niedzielski and Dennis Preston's *Folk Linguistics* (Berlin: Mouton de Gruyter, 1999) and Preston's chapter "A Language Attitude Approach to the Perception of Regional Variety" in vol.1 of the *Handbook of Perceptual Dialectology*, ed. Dennis Preston (Amsterdam: Benjamins, 1999), 359–73.

29. For some discussion of the cultural construction of the region by non-Southerners and Southerners, see Edward L. Ayers, "What We Talk About When We Talk About the South," in *All Over the Map: Rethinking American Regions*, ed. Edward L. Ayers, Patricia Nelson Limerick, Stephen Nissenbaum, and Peter S. Onuf (Baltimore: Johns Hopkins Press, 1996), 62–82.

30 On the impact of in-migration of Northerners to the South, see Daniel Pearl's article "Hush Mah Mouth! Some in South Try to Lose the Drawl— 'Accent Reduction' Becomes a Big Bidness in Atlanta" (*Wall Street Journal*, Dec. 13, 1991, A1). Pearl notes that soon after the 1996 Olympics were awarded to Atlanta, the *Atlanta Business Journal* featured an article encouraging Atlantans to "clean . . . up our speech" and "get the South out of our mouth." Pearl's article also reports on Southerners' attitudes toward their accents, which range from seeing it as a liability, to an asset, to a mark of regional pride.

31. The examples are cited by Lippi-Green, in *English with an Accent*, 211, and are from the April 4, 1995, entry of *The Dave Barry 1995 Calendar* (Kansas City, MO: Andrews McMeel, 1994) and Mike Royko's Oct. 11, 1992, *Chicago Tribune* column "Pithy Questions the Presidential Debate Panel Won't Ask."

32. It also assumes that television and travel would suffice to identify a national Standard English, which is by no means guaranteed.

33. For William Labov's discussion of Martha's Vineyard, see his *Sociolinguistic Patterns* (Philadelphia: University of Pennsylvania Press, 1972) 1–42; for Penelope Eckert's suburban Detroit study, see her *Linguistic Variation as Social Practice* (Oxford: Blackwell, 2000), esp. pp. 211–12.

34. There is good evidence, too, that some urban regional accents are growing stronger and more distinct, with urban areas being the locus of contemporary vowel shifts. For discussion of the shift in urban dialects, see William Labov's *Principles of Linguistic Change. Volume 1: Internal Factors* (Oxford: Blackwell, 1994). Labov identifies three patterns of change in contemporary English, a northern cities shift in vowels that includes the shift of AW to A; a southern cities shift that includes the lengthening of short vowels *i* and *e*; and an east-to-west merger of the vowels of *cot* and *caught*.

35. Creoles are special languages that develop in language contact situations in which the vocabulary of one language, such as English, is manifest in a restricted grammatical structure. On the creolist view, African-American Vernacular is based on a creole that was widely used in the South at one time. The main alternative to the creolist view is known as the Anglicist view, which holds that African-American English can be better traced to the same dialects of British English as other early American English dialects.

36. Gavin Jones's *Strange Talk* (Berkeley: University of California Press, 1999), 101, is the source of the quotes from William Francis Allen's 1867 *Slave*

Songs of the American South (reprinted; New York: Peter Smith, 1951). For a bibliographic survey of dialect in literature, see Eva M. Burkett's *American English Dialects in Literature* (Metuchen, NJ: Scarecrow Press, 1978).

37. James Harrison's 1884 essay "Negro English" is cited in Jones, *Strange Talk*, 104–5.

38. For more discussion of features of African-American Vernacular, see John Russell Rickford and Russell John Rickford's *Spoken Soul* (New York: Wiley, 2000); for a brief summary, see Walt Wolfram and Natalie Schilling-Estes, *American English: Dialects and Variation* (Malden, MA: Blackwell, 1998), 171.

39. The examples are from John Rickford and Russell Rickford, 94–98. The *Amen corner* is the place where the most vocal worshippers sit. *Juneteenth* refers to June 19, 1865, and more generally to the day of celebration of emancipation, and *ashy* refers to dry skin.

40. John Baugh's *Out of the Mouths of Slaves* (101–9) is the source for the discussion of *steady*.

41. Unfortunately, the term African-American English also invites the simplistic view that all African-Americans speak African-American English. But of course some African-American features occur in the speech of non-African-Americans. And African-American English itself also has regional varieties. The African-American speech of the Carolinas is different from that of the Gulf South and the African-American speech of Philadelphia is different from that of Detroit.

42. Gary Simpkins and Charlesetta Simpkins, "Cross-Cultural Approach to Curriculum Development," *Black English and the Education of Black Children and Youth*, ed. Geneva Smitherman (Detroit: Wayne State University Center for Black Studies, 1981), 221–40. For a recent review, see John R. Rickford and Angela E. Rickford, "Dialect Readers Revisited," *Linguistics and Education* 7.2 (1995), 107–28.

43. John McWhorter's observations on bilingual approaches are from *The Word on the Street* (New York: Plenum, 1998), ch. 8, esp. pp. 248–54.

44. The "Students' Right to Their Own Language" was published in a 1974 number of *College Composition and Communication* (25.3 [1974],1–32), along with about 30 pages of explanation and a bibliography of sources. As Stephen Park notes in his *Class Politics: The Movement for the Students' Right to Their Own Language* (Urbana: NCTE, 2000), 199, the National Council of Teachers of English, the parent group of the Conference on College Composition and Communication, passed an affirming resolution version of the resolution but with slightly different language. The NCTE version emphasizes "the responsibility of all teachers to provide opportunities for clear and cogent

expression of ideas in writing, and to provide the opportunity for students to learn the conventions of what has been called written edited American English." Park's book provides an account of the history of the NCTE students' right resolution that places it in the context of 1960s activism. See also some of the essays collected in James Sledd's *Eloquent Dissent* (Portsmouth, NH: Boynton/Cook, 1996).

45. Simon, *Paradigms Lost* (New York: Charles N. Potter, 1980), 160.

46. Arn Tibbetts and Charlene Tibbetts, *What's Happening to American English?* (New York: Scribner's, 1978), 119.

47. Judge Joiner's opinion appears as *Martin Luther King, Jr., Elementary School Children et al. v. Ann Arbor School District*, 473 F. Supp. 1371 (E. D. Mich. 1979).

48. Carl Rowan's comments are from his essay "'Black English' Isn't Foreign," which appeared in the *Philadelphia Bulletin* (July 11, 1979, A15).

49. Editorials and news stories in summer of 1979 included the following: "If Black English Is a Distinct Language, Then What about Cracker Talk?" (Bill Shipp, *Atlanta Constitution*, July 14, 1979, 2B); "What We Think: Black English Must Go" (editorial in the *Michigan Chronicle*, July 14, 1979, 8A); "Black English: Dialect Can Be Dead End" (Donna Britt, *Detroit Free Press*, July 15, 1979, 3A, 8A); "Dis Ain't Right" (*Norfolk Journal and Guide*, July 20, 1979, 10A); "The Menace of 'Black English'" (an editorial in the *Cleveland Call and Post*, July 28, 1979, 9A); "Dialects Stunt People's Growth and Development" (Edwin Roberts, *Detroit News*, July 29, 1979, 19A); "English, Not 'Black English'" (an editorial from the [Baltimore] *Afro-American*, August 4, 1979, 4A); "Black Students Don't Need an Alibi" (Carl Rowan, *Kansas City Star*, Aug. 5, 1979, 2J). Citations are from Richard Bailey's "Press Coverage of the *King* Case," in Smitherman's *Black English and the Education of Black Children and Youth*, 359–89.

50. James Baldwin's "If Black English Isn't a Language, Then Tell Me What Is?" was published in the *New York Times*, July 29, 1979, sec. 4, 19.

51. The 1981 regulation prohibiting federal bilingual education funding for African-American English can be found in the *Federal Register* 1981, 37600.

52. Geoffrey Nunberg's observation on accuracy in reporting is from his article "Double Standards" (*Natural Language and Linguistic Theory* 14.3 [1977], 667–75), 667. For further analysis of press coverage of *African American English* and of Ebonics humor, see Rickford and Rickford's *Spoken Soul*, 181–202 and 203–18).

53. "Linguistic Confusion," *New York Times*, Dec. 24, 1996, A10.

54. See *Spoken Soul*, 5. Other African American opinion leaders, such as Toni Morrison, defended African-American vernacular. The Reverend Jesse Jackson,

while initially denouncing the Oakland resolution, revised his opinion after meeting with school board members.

55. Earl Ofari Hutchison, "The Fallacy of Ebonics," *The Black Scholar* 27.1 (Spring 1997), 36.

56. Citations for press commentary are as follows: "Call It Bad Grammar, Not a Language" (*Milwaukee Journal Sentinel*, Jan. 9, 1997, 15); "Hey Bubba, Whut Chew Think a' Dis Ebonics Nonsense?" (Greg Hamilton, *St. Petersburg Times*, Jan. 5, 1997, 2); "Ebonics: If We Can't Teach 'em, Join 'em?" (James Shaw, *The Sun* [Baltimore], Jan. 5, 1997, 1F); "Hooking Them on Ebonics" (Philip Terzian, *Tampa Tribune*, Jan. 3, 1997, 9); "An Ebonics Plague on Race Relations" (Suzanne Fields, *Tampa Tribune*, Jan. 2, 1997, 9); "Will Appeals to Fund 'Hillbillyonics' Be Next?" (*Columbus Dispatch*, Dec. 31, 1996, 6A); "Black English Is Merely a Form of Bad English" (Garry Wills, *Chicago Sun-Times*, Dec. 30, 1996, 202); "Ebonics Decision a Cynical Ploy" (*Milwaukee Journal Sentinel*, Dec. 27, 1996, 16); "Ebonics Is a Crippling Force" (*Milwaukee Journal Sentinel*, Dec. 27, 1996, 17); "Teaching Down to Our Children" (*St. Petersburg Times*, Dec. 26, 1996, 18A); "Ebonics Is the Latest Educational Sham" (Leonard Greene, *Boston Herald*, Dec. 25, 1996, 4); "'Ebonics' a False Promise of Self-esteem" (editorial by Carl Rowan, *Chicago Sun-Times*, Dec. 25, 1996, 31); "Oakland's Ebonics Farce" (Debra J. Saunders, *San Francisco Chronicle*, Dec. 24, 1996, A15); and "Triumph of Black English Gives New Cred to Street Talk" (Arnold Kemp, *The Observer*, Dec. 22, 1996, 4).

57. See Rickford and Rickford, *Spoken Soul*, 201. Rickford and Rickford note that the ad's tagline "I has a dream" is ironically not an African-American Vernacular usage.

58. The quote from Albert Shanker is from a *New York Times* advertisement of Jan. 5, 1997, E7.

59. The quote from Richard Riley is from *Newsweek* ("Hooked on Ebonics," by John Leland and Nadine Joseph, *Newsweek*, Jan. 13, 1997, 79).

60. The citation of the 1997 California Senate Bill 205 is from Baugh's *Beyond Ebonics*, 125.

61. Ron Emmons, "Ebonics: It Makes English All the Richer," *The Sun* [Baltimore], Jan 5, 1997, 1F.

62. See John Lahr's report "Speaking Across the Divide," which quotes a teenage speaker of African-American English (*New Yorker*, Jan. 27, 1997, 35–41). A 1994 study by Linda Carol Carter titled *African-American Attitudes Concerning African-American English* surveyed 51 African-American speakers in Georgia and California (ERIC, 1994, ED 374 166). Carter found that most of her respondents agreed that African-American English was a valuable part of their heritage but that it had no place in the classroom. Most also

felt that use of African-American English in the wider community would affect economic opportunities.

63. African-American English is not alone, of course. Though it has not received the same degree of national media attention, mixing of English and Spanish known as Spanglish is a topic in parts of the country with large Hispanic populations and is likely to become increasingly politicized nationally as well. As Laureano Corces suggests, criticism of Spanglish will come both from those seeking to preserve English and from Spanish-language purists who see Spanglish as a danger to the language of Cervantes. See his essay "Re-evaluating Spanglish" (*Geolinguistics* 25, 1999, 35–38) and see also Ilan Stavans's *Spanglish: The Making of A New American Language* (New York: Harper Collins, 2003).

7. Images and Engagement

1. For discussion of conceptual blending, see Mark Turner's *Cognitive Dimensions of Social Science* (New York: Oxford University Press, 2001; the discussion of urban blight is from pp. 134–35 and the discussion of the English bulldog is from pp. 70–77). See also his book *The Literary Mind: The Origins of Thought and Language* (New York: Oxford University Press, 1996).

2. John Leo, "Stop Murdering the Language!" *U.S. New and World Report,* April 12, 1993, 23; Harry Warfel, *Who Killed Grammar?* (Gainesville: University of Florida Press, 1952). The metaphor of assault on language and culture is evident as well in rhetoric about "culture wars," in titles like "Destroying Good Words" (a chapter from John Simon's *Paradigm's Lost*), "Protecting English from Assault on the Job" (*New York Times,* Feb. 4, 2001, BU 14), *Who Killed Homer?* and "A War That Never Ends." It arises, too, in the images in comments about "collateral damage in a target-rich environment" and "the wounding of innocent language" (Robert Hughes). And as Julia Penelope points out in her essay "'Users and Abusers': On the Death of English" (in Greenbaum's *The English Language Today,* 80–91), language is sometimes metaphorically a woman.

3. The ecological metaphor is developed in Douglas Bush's "Polluting Our Language," which appeared in the *American Scholar,* June 1972, 238–47.

4. Geoffrey Nunberg, "The Decline of Grammar," 31.

5. The opinions of E. D. Hirsch, Ernest Gellner, Carl Rowan, John Cheke, and Jacques Barzun are all cited in earlier chapters. In addition to the economic metaphor, Barzun also employs the image that new usage "preys on" established vocabulary.

6. The image of the "melting pot" arose from Israel Zangwill's 1908 play of the same name. The play treated America as God's crucible in which

Europeans would be melted, purified, and recast as Americans, shedding old hatreds. The contemporary melting pot metaphor is much attenuated, treating melting pot as a stew (contrasted with a "salad bowl").

7. The slogan "Toward a United America" appears on the US English, Inc website which can be accessed at http://www.us-english.org/inc/news/eng_in_news/#top. The religious imagery of the Tower of Babel is apparent in such titles as Fernando de la Peña's *Democracy or Babel?* (Washington, DC: U.S. English, 1991).

8. George Perkins Marsh, *Lectures on the English Language* (New York: Scribner, 1860), 224–25.

9. In addition, the focus of linguistics on precision and formalism in the analysis of everyday phenomena can defamiliarize grammar, structure, and usage.

10. An early example of efforts to bridge the interests of linguists and language arts teachers is chapter 11 of Fries's *American English Grammar*, which is titled "Some Inferences from This Study for a Workable Program in English Language for the Schools." Another is John Sinclair's "Linguistics and the Teaching of English," in Marckwardt's *Language and Language Learning* (Champaign, IL: NCTE, 1966), pp. 31–41).

11. The questions are as follows: What are the basic units of language? What's regular and what isn't? [and] How do forms relate to each other? How is the lexicon acquired and structured? Are vernacular dialects different from "bad English" and if so, how? What is academic English? Why has the acquisition of English by non-English children not been more universally successful? Why is English spelling so complicated? Why do some children have more trouble than others in developing early reading skills? Why do students have trouble with structuring narrative and expository writing? How should one judge the quality and correctness of a piece of writing? What makes a sentence or text easy or difficult to understand? See Lily Wong Fillmore and Catherine E. Snow's "What Teachers Need to Know About Language," in *What Teachers Need to Know About Language*, ed. Carolyn Temple Adger, Catherine E. Snow, and Donna Christian (Washington, DC: Center for Applied Linguistics, 2002), 7–53.

12. Some of Walt Wolfram's work is discussed in his essay "Dialect Awareness Programs in the School and Community," in *Language Alive in the Classroom* (ed. Rebecca Wheeler [Westport, CT: Praeger, 1999], 47–66), and in the references therein; *Language Alive* also includes other examples of efforts by linguists to make professional connections with schools and communities.

13. The West Virginia Dialect project initiated by Kirk Hazen has a similar focus.

14. Maya Honda's work is reported in her 1994 Harvard University dissertation *Linguistic Inquiry in the Science Classroom: "It Is Science, but It's Not Like a Science Problem in a Book"* (MIT Occasional Papers in Linguistics, no. 6, 1994).

15. The Linguistic Olympics was not affiliated with the U.S. Olympic Committee. The summary and the quote from Thomas Payne are from a report posted on the University of Oregon website (http://darkwing.uoregon.edu/~tpayne/lingolym/LOreport.htm). Puzzles from the 1998 Olympics included ones dealing with Sanskrit, Swahili, Turkish, Hausa, Quechua, Hawaiian, Babylonian cuneiform, Luvian hieroglyphics, the American Indian language Chickasaw, the Endo language of Kenya, and Verlan, a secret language used by French teenagers. For other ways to interest youth, see also Jeannine M. Donna's "Linguistics Iis for Kids" in Wheeler's *Language Alive*, 67–80.

16. The quote regarding Ebonics is from William Raspberry, "To Throw in a Lot of 'Bes' or Not? A Conversation on Ebonics" (*Washington Post*, Dec. 26, 1996, A27); the quote concerning bilingual education is from the 1998 California Voter Information Guide, p. 75, cited by Thomas Scovel in his "The Younger the Better Myth and Bilingual Education," in *Language Ideologies: Critical Perspectives on the Official English Movement*, vol. 1, ed. Roseann Dueñas González, with Ildikó Melis (Urbana, IL: National Council of Teachers of Education and Mahwah, NJ: Lawrence Erlbaum Associates, 2001), 118.

17. Francine Frank and Paula Treichler, *Language, Gender, and Professional Writing* (New York: Modern Language Association, 1989), 153–80. The examples are adapted from Frank and Treichler.

References

Adams, Michael. *Slayer Slang: A* Buffy the Vampire Slayer *Lexicon.* New York: Oxford University Press, 2003.

Adler, Jerry. "Taking Offense." *Newsweek,* Dec. 24, 1990, 48–54.

Agress, Lynne. "If You Think You Speak Good . . ." *Mademoiselle,* March 1983, 66–68.

Alford, Henry. *A Plea for the Queen's English.* New York: Dick and Fitzgerald, 1864.

Allen, Harold. "Attitudes of the National Council of Teachers of English." In *The English Language Today,* edited by Sidney Greenbaum (pp. 136–46). Oxford: Pergamon, 1985.

Allen, William Francis. *Slave Songs of the American South.* 1867. New York: Peter Smith, 1951.

Allport, Gordon. *The Nature of Prejudice.* Reading, MA: Addison-Wesley, 1954.

Alvarez, Louis, and Andrew Kolker. *American Tongues.* Hohokus, NJ: Center for New American Media, 1986.

American Heritage Dictionary. Springfield, MA: Merriam-Webster, 1997.

American Library Association Office for Intellectual Freedom. "Challenged and Banned Books." No date. http://www.ala.org/Content/NavigationMenu/Our_Association/Offices/Intellectual_Freedom3/Banned_Books_Week/Challenged_and_Banned_Books/Challenged_and_Banned_Books.htm#backgroundinformation.

Andressen, Julie Tetel. *Linguistics in America 1769–1924: A Critical History*. London: Routledge, 1990.

Applebee, Arthur. *Tradition and Reform in the Teaching of English*. Urbana, IL: National Council of Teachers of English, 1974.

Ascham, Roger. *The Scholemaster*. Amsterdam: Da Capo Press, 1968.

Atkins, J. D. C. Annual Report [of the Federal Commissioner of Indian Affairs]. Excerpted as "Barbarous Dialects Should be Blotted Out." 1887. In *Language Loyalties: A Source Book on the Official English Controversy*, edited by James Crawford (pp. 47–51). Chicago: University of Chicago Press, 1992.

Atlas, James. *The Book Wars: What It Takes To Be Educated in America*. Knoxville: Whittle Communications, 1990.

Aufderheide, Patricia (editor). *Beyond PC: Toward a Politics of Understanding*. St. Paul: Graywolf, 1992.

August, Diane, and Kenji Hakuta (editors). *Educating Language-Minority Children*. Washington, DC: National Academy Press, 1998.

Ayers, Edward L. "What We Talk About When We Talk About the South." In *All Over the Map: Rethinking American Regions*, edited by Edward L. Ayers, Patricia Nelson Limerick, Stephen Nissenbaum, and Peter S. Onuf (pp. 62–82). Baltimore: Johns Hopkins Press, 1996.

Bailey, Nathaniel. *An Universal Etymological Dictionary*. London, 1721.

Bailey, Richard. *Images of English*. Ann Arbor: University of Michigan Press, 1991.

———. *Nineteenth-Century English*. Ann Arbor: University of Michigan Press, 1996.

———. "Press Coverage of the *King* Case." In *Black English and the Education of Black Children and Youth*, edited by Geneva Smitherman (pp. 359–89). Detroit: Wayne State University Center for Black Studies, 1981.

Baldwin, James. "If Black English Isn't a Language, Then Tell Me What Is?" *New York Times*, July 29, 1979, sec. 4, 19.

Baron, Dennis. *The English-Only Question: An Official Language for Americans*. New Haven: Yale University Press, 1990.

———. *Grammar and Good Taste: Reforming the American Language*. New Haven: Yale University Press, 1982.

Barry, Dave. *The Dave Barry 1995 Calendar.* Kansas City, MO: Andrews McMeel, 1994.

Bartlett, Thomas. "Why Johnny Can't Write, Even Though He Went to Princeton." *Chronicle of Higher Education* 49.17 (Jan. 3, 2003), A39.

Barzun, Jacques. "After Fowler's Generation." 1957. In *A Word or Two Before You Go . . .* , by Jacques Barzun (pp. 105–14). Middleton, CT: Wesleyan University Press, 1986.

———. *From Dawn to Decadence.* New York: Harper Collins, 2000.

———. *The House of Intellect.* New York: Harper and Brothers, 1959.

———. *Simple and Direct: A Rhetoric for Writers.* New York: Harper and Row, 1984.

———. "What Are Mistakes and Why." In *A Word Or Two Before You Go. . . .* (pp. 13–17). Middleton, CT: Wesleyan University Press, 1986.

Basinger, Jeanine. *The World War II Combat Film: Anatomy of a Genre.* New York: Columbia University Press, 1986.

Battistella, Edwin L. "s's." *The SECOL Review* 17.2 (1993), 127–41.

Baugh, Albert, and Thomas Cable. *A History of the English Language.* Englewood Cliffs, NJ: Prentice Hall, 1978.

Baugh, John. *Beyond Ebonics.* New York: Oxford University Press, 1999.

———. *Out of the Mouths of Slaves.* Austin: University of Texas Press, 1999.

Baynton, Douglas. *Forbidden Signs: American Culture and the Campaign against Sign Language.* Chicago: University of Chicago Press, 1996.

Beason, Larry. "Ethos and Error: How Business People React to Errors." *College Composition and Communication,* 53.1 (2001), 33–64.

Bender, James F. *NBC Handbook of Pronunciation.* 2nd edition. New York: T. Y. Crowell, 1951.

Bennett, William. "The Bilingual Education Act: A Failed Path." 1985. In *Language Loyalties,* edited by James Crawford (pp. 358–63). Chicago: University of Chicago Press, 1992.

Berlin, James A. *Writing Instruction in Nineteenth-Century American Colleges.* Carbondale: Southern Illinois University Press, 1984.

Bernstein, Richard. "The Rising Hegemony of the Politically Correct." *New York Times,* Oct. 28, 1990, sec. 4, p. 1.

Best, Harry. *Deafness and the Deaf in the United States.* New York: Macmillan, 1943.

Bloom, Allan. *The Closing of the American Mind.* New York: Simon and Schuster, 1987.

Bloom, Lynn Z., Donald A. Daiker, and Edward M. White (eds.). *Composition in the Twenty-First Century: Crisis and Change.* Carbondale: Southern Illinois University Press, 1996.

Bond, R. Warwick *The Complete Works of John Lyly*, vol. 2. 1902. Reprinted, Oxford: Clarendon, 1967.

Boorstin, Daniel J. *The Americans: The Colonial Experience*. New York: Vintage, 1958.

———. *The Americans: The Democratic Experience*. New York: Vintage, 1973.

Borjas, George. "Foreign-Born Teaching Assistants and the Academic Performance of Undergraduates," *American Economic Review* 90.2 (2000), 355–59.

Boyer, Paul. *Purity in Print: The Vice Society Movement and Book Censorship in America*. New York: Scribner's Sons, 1966.

Braddock, Richard, Richard Lloyd-Jones, and Lowell Schoer. *Research in Written Composition*. Urbana, IL: National Council of Teachers of English, 1963.

Britt, Donna. "Black English: Dialect Can Be Dead End." *Detroit Free Press*, July 15, 1979, 3A, 8A.

Brophy, John, and Eric Partridge. *Songs and Slang of the British Soldier, 1914–1918*. London: Scholartis Press, 1930.

Brown, Goold. *The Institutes of English Grammar*. New York: Gray and Bunce, 1823.

Brown, Vivian. "Evolution of the Merger of /i/ and /ɛ/ before Nasals in Tennessee." *American Speech* 66.3 (Fall 1991), 303–15.

———. *The Social and Linguistic History of a Merger: /i/ and /e/ before Nasals in Southern American English*. Texas A and M University dissertation, 1990.

Burchfeld, Robert. *The New Fowler's Modern English Usage*. 3rd edition. New York: Oxford University Press, 1998.

Burkett, Eva M. *American English Dialects in Literature*. Metuchen, NJ: Scarecrow Press, 1978.

Burnham, John C. *Bad Habits: Drinking, Smoking, Taking Drugs, Gambling, Sexual Misbehavior, and Swearing in American History*. New York: New York University Press, 1993.

Bush, Douglas. "Polluting Our Language." *The American Scholar*, June 1972, 238–47.

Bush, George H. University of Michigan Commencement Address. 1991. Excerpted in *Beyond PC: Toward a Politics of Understanding*, edited by Patricia Aufderheide (pp. 227–28). St. Paul: Graywolf, 1992.

"Call It Bad Grammar, Not a Language." *Milwaukee Journal Sentinel*, Jan. 9, 1997, 15.

Campbell, George. *Philosophy of Rhetoric*. 1776. Edinburgh: Printed for W. Strahan, T. Cadell, and W. Creech. Reprinted, Carbondale: Southern Illinois University Press, 1963.

Carlson, Eugene. "Neutral Accents Help Attract Telemarketers to the Midwest." *Wall Street Journal*, April 8, 1986, sec. 2, p. 1.

Carter, Linda Carol. *African-American Attitudes Concerning African-American English.* San Raphael, CA: Dominican College of San Rafael, 1994. ERIC Document Reproduction Service no. ED 374 166.

Cawdrey, Robert. *A Table Alphabeticall of Hard Usual English Words.* 1604. Reprinted, Gainesville, FL: Scholars' Facsimiles, 1966.

Chambers, J. K. *Sociolinguistic Theory.* Oxford: Blackwell, 1995.

Chaplinsky v. New Hampshire. 315 U.S. 568 (1942).

Choice Dialect and Vaudeville Stage Jokes. Chicago: Frederick J. Drake, 1902.

Claiborne, Robert. *Our Marvelous Native Tongue.* New York: Times Books, 1983.

Clayton, Mark. "Foreign Teaching Assistants' First Test: The Accent." *Christian Science Monitor*, Sept. 5, 2000 (http://www.csmonitor.com/durable/2000/09/05/fp14s1–csm.shtml).

Cmiel, Kenneth. *Democratic Eloquence.* New York: William Morrow, 1990.

Cody, Sherwin. *The Art of Writing and Speaking the English Language.* Chicago: Old Greek Press, 1903.

Cohen v. California. 403 U.S. 15 (1971).

Collier, Jeremy. *A Short View of the Profaneness and Immorality of the English Stage.* 1698. London: for S. Keble, R. Sare, and H. Hindmarsh. Reprinted, New York: Garland, 1972.

Connors, Robert. "The Abolition Debate in Composition: A Short History." In *Composition in the Twenty-First Century: Crisis and Change,* edited by Lynn Z. Bloom, Donald A. Daiker, and Edward M. White (pp. 47–63). Carbondale: Southern Illinois University Press, 1996.

———. "Grammar in American College Composition: A Historical Overview." In *The Territory of Language: Linguistics, Stylistics, and the Teaching of Composition,* edited by Donald A. McQuade (pp. 3–22). Carbondale: Southern Illinois University Press, 1986.

Corces, Laureano. "Re-evaluating Spanglish." *Geolinguistics* 25 (1999), 35–38.

"Court Convicts Cursing Canoeist under Century-old Michigan Law." *St. Louis Post Dispatch*, June 12, 1999, 29.

Crawford, James. "What's Behind the Official English Movement." In *Language Loyalties,* edited by James Crawford, (pp. 171–77). Chicago: University of Chicago Press, 1992.

D'Souza, Dinesh. "The Visigoths in Tweed." 1991. In *Beyond PC: Toward a Politics of Understanding,* edited by Patricia Aufderheide (pp. 11–22). St. Paul: Graywolf, 1992.

De Quincey, Thomas. *Collected Writings.* Ed. David Masson. London: A. and C. Black, 1889–90. 14 vols.

"Dictionary Will Revise Definition of 200 Slurs." *New York Times,* May 3, 1998, 20.

"Dis Ain't Right." *Norfolk Journal and Guide,* July 20, 1979, 10A.

Donna, Jeannine M. "Linguistics Is for Kids." In *Language Alive in the Classroom,* edited by Rebecca Wheeler (pp. 67–80). Westport, CT: Praeger, 1999.

Driscoll, David P. Memo to Superintendents of Schools and Charter School Leaders Outlining English Proficiency Requirements under the English Language Education in Public Schools, March 27, 2003. (http://www.doe.mass.edu/ell/0327profreq.html).

Dumas, Bethany, and Jonathan Lightner. "Is *Slang* a Word for Linguists?" *American Speech* 53.1 (1978), 5–17.

Eble, Connie. *Slang and Sociability: In-group Language Among College Students.* Chapel Hill: University of North Carolina Press, 1996.

"Ebonics Decision a Cynical Ploy." *Milwaukee Journal Sentinel,* Dec. 27, 1998, 16.

"Ebonics Is a Crippling Force." *Milwaukee Journal Sentinel,* Dec. 27, 1996, 17.

Eckert, Penelope. *Linguistic Variation as Social Practice.* Maldon, MA: Blackwell, 2000.

Elbow, Peter. *Writing with Power.* New York: Oxford University Press, 1981.

Elson, Ruth Miller. *The Guardians of Tradition: American Schoolbooks of the Nineteenth Century.* Lincoln: University of Nebraska Press, 1964.

Emmons, Ron. "Ebonics: It Makes English All the Richer." *The Sun* [Baltimore], Jan. 5, 1997, 1F.

Emrick, Richard. "New Dictionary Cheap, Corrupt." *Detroit News,* Feb.10, 1962. Reprinted in *Dictionaries and* That *Dictionary,* edited by James Sledd and Wilma R. Ebbitt (pp. 127–29). Chicago: Scott, Foresman, 1962.

"English, Not 'Black English.'" [Baltimore] *Afro-American,* Aug. 4, 1979, 4A.

Equal Employment Opportunity Commission Guidelines. Code of Federal Regulations, Title 29, Volume 4, Parts 900 to 1899, 29CFR1604.11 (June 27, 2002). (http://www.eeoc.gov/facts/fs-sex.html).

Equal Employment Opportunity Commission. EEOC Directives, Transmittal Number 915.003, Update to EEOC Compliance Manual replacing Section 13 of the New Compliance Manual on "National Origin Discrimination." Dec. 2, 2002. (http://www.eeoc.gov/policy/docs/national-origin.html#VB1).

Erhlich, Eugene, and Raymond Hand, Jr. *NBC Handbook of Pronunciation.* 4th edition. New York: Harper and Row, 1984.

Ewing, Alexander, and Ethel Ewing. *Teaching Deaf Children to Talk.* Manchester: Manchester University Press, 1964.

Faigley, Lester. "What Is Good Writing? Views from the Public." In *The English Language Today*, edited by Sidney Greenbaum (pp. 99–105). Oxford: Pergamon, 1985.

Fanning, Deirdre. "Just You Wait, 'Enry 'Iggins . . ." *New York Times*, Sept. 23, 1990, sec. 3, 25.

Farmer, John, and William Ernest Henley. *A Dictionary of Slang*. New York: Wordsworth, 1987. 2 vols. (originally published as *Slang and Its Analogues*, 1890).

FCC v. Pacifica. 438 US. 726 (1978).

"Female Lawyers See Bias in Their Arrests." *ABA Journal* 81 ABAJ 28, March 1995.

Ferrara, Kathleen, and Barbara Bell. "Sociolinguistic Variation and Discourse Function of Constructed Dialogue Introducers: The Case of Be + Like." *American Speech* 70.3 (1995), 265–90.

Fields, Suzanne. "An Ebonics Plague on Race Relations." *Tampa Tribune*, Jan. 2, 1997, 9.

Fillmore, Lily Wong. "Against Our Best Interest: The Attempt to Sabotage Bilingual Education." In *Language Loyalties*, edited by James Crawford, (pp. 367–76). Chicago: University of Chicago Press, 1992.

Fillmore, Lily Wong, and Catherine E. Snow. "What Teachers Need to Know About Language." In *What Teachers Need to Know About Language*, edited by Carolyn Temple Adger, Catherine E. Snow, and Donna Christian (pp. 7–53). Washington, DC: Center for Applied Linguistics, 2002.

Finegan, Edward. *Attitudes Toward English Usage: The History of a War of Words*. New York: Teachers College Press, 1980.

———. "English Grammar and Usage." In *The Cambridge History of the English Language*, vol. 4, *1776–1997*, edited by Suzanne Romaine, (pp. 536–88). Cambridge: Cambridge University Press, 1999.

———. "Usage." In *The Cambridge History of the English Language*, vol.6, *English in North America*, edited by John Algeo (pp. 358–421). Cambridge: Cambridge University Press, 2001.

"Flawed Question Raised PSAT Scores." Cable News Network. May 15, 2003. http://www.cnn.com/2003/EDUCATION/05/15/psat.question.ap/index.html.

Flesch, Rudolph. *The Art of Readable Writing*. New York: Harper and Row, 1974.

Fowler, H. W. *A Dictionary of Modern English Usage*. Oxford: Clarendon Press, 1926.

Francis, J. H. *From Caxton to Carlyle: A Study of the Development of Language, Composition and Style in English Prose*. Cambridge: Cambridge University Press, 1937.

Francis, W. Nelson. "The Revolution in Grammar." In *Linguistics for Teachers*, edited by Linda Miller Cleary and Michael D. Young (pp. 426–41). New York: McGraw Hill, 1993.

Frank, Francine, and Paula Treichler. *Language, Gender, and Professional Writing*. New York: Modern Language Association, 1989.

Friend, Tad. "You Can't Say That: The Networks Play Word Games." *New Yorker*, Nov. 19, 2001, 44–49.

Fries, Charles Carpenter. *American English Grammar*. New York: Appleton Century Croft, 1940.

"Furor Erupts over Racial Epithet: Activists Seek to Drop or Redefine 'Nigger' in Merriam-Webster Dictionary." *Washington Post*, Oct. 8, 1997, A16.

Garner, Bryan. *Dictionary of Modern American Usage*. New York: Oxford University Press, 1998.

Garner, James Finn. *Politically Correct Bedtime Stories*. New York: Macmillan, 1994.

Gates, Henry Louis, Jr. *Loose Canons: Notes on the Culture Wars*. New York: Oxford University Press, 1992.

Gellner, Ernest. *Nations and Nationalism*. Ithaca: Cornell University Press, 1983.

Gibaldi, Joseph (editor). *The MLA Handbook for Writers of Research Papers*. New York: Modern Language Association, 1984.

Goldstein, Norm (editor). *The AP Stylebook and Libel Manual*. 6th edition. Reading, MA: Addison-Wesley, 1996.

Gomis van Heteren, Annette. *Political Correctness in Context (The PC Controversy in America)*. Almería: Universidad de Almería, 1997.

Gove, Phillip B. (editor). *Webster's Third New International Dictionary of the English Language*. Springfield, MA: G. and C. Merriam, 1961.

Graff, Gerald. *Professing English*. Chicago: University of Chicago Press, 1987.

Greene, H. A. "English—Language, Grammar, and Composition." *Encyclopedia of Educational Research*, edited by Walter S. Monroe (pp. 383–96). New York: Macmillan, 1950.

Greenough, James Bradstreet, and George Lyman Kittredge. *Words and Their Way in English Speech*. New York: Macmillan, 1901.

Hacker, Diana. *A Writer's Reference*. New York: St. Martin's Press, 1999.

Hairston, Maxine. "Not All Errors Are Created Equal: Nonacademic Readers in the Professions Respond to Lapses in Usage." *College English*, 43 (1981), 794–806.

Hake, Rosemary, and Joseph Williams. "Style and Its Consequences: Do as I Do, Not as I Say." *College English* 43 (Sept. 1981), 443–51.

Hall, Linda. "Coolspeak." *Hudson Review* 55 (2002), 411–22.

Hall, Robert A. *Leave Your Language Alone!* Ithaca, NY: Linguistica, 1950.

Halpern, Mark. "The End of Linguistics." *The American Scholar*, Winter 2001, 13–26.

———. "A War That Never Ends." *Atlantic Monthly*, March 1997, 19–22.

Hamilton, Greg. "Hey Bubba, Whut Chew Think a' Dis Ebonics Nonsense?" *St. Petersburg Times*, Jan. 5, 1997, 2.

Hanson, Victor Davis, and John Heath. *Who Killed Homer? The Demise of Classical Education and the Recovery of Greek Wisdom.* New York: Free Press, 1998.

Harris, Sydney J. "Good English Ain't What We Thought." *Chicago Daily News*, Oct. 20, 1961. Reprinted in *Dictionaries and That Dictionary*, edited by James Sledd and Wilma R. Ebbitt (pp. 80–81). Chicago: Scott, Foresman, 1962.

Harrison, James. "Negro English." 1884. In *Perspectives on Black English*, edited by J. L. Dillard (pp. 143–95). The Hague: Mouton, 1975.

Hartley, Laura C., and Dennis Preston. "The Names of U.S. English." In *Standard English: The Widening Debate*, edited by Tony Bex and Richard J. Watts (pp. 207–38). London: Routledge, 1999.

Hartogs, Renatus, and Hans Fantel. *Four-Letter Word Games: The Psychology of Obscenity.* New York: Evans, 1967.

Hawhee, Debra. "Composition History and the *Harbrace College Handbook*." *College Composition and Communication* 50.3 (1999), 504–23.

Hazlitt, William. *Essays.* Ed. Charles H. Gray. New York: MacMillan, 1926.

Hearn, Kelly. "Pegged by an Accent." *Christian Science Monitor*, Dec. 18, 2000, 11.

Heath, Shirley Brice. "A National Language Academy? Debate in the New Nation." *Linguistics* 10:189 (1977), 9–43.

Heilbrunn, Jacob. "Speech Therapy." *New Republic*, Jan. 20, 1997, 17–19.

Henderson, Anita. "What's in a Slur?" *American Speech* 78.1 (2003), 52–74.

Henry, William, III. *In Defense of Elitism.* New York: Doubleday, 1994.

Hirsch, E. D. *Cultural Literacy.* New York: Houghton Mifflin, 1987.

Hodges, John, Mary Whitten, and Suzanne Webb. *The Harbrace College Handbook.* 10th edition. New York: Harcourt Brace, 1986.

Holmes, Oliver Wendell, Sr. "Mechanism in Thought and Morals." In *Pages from an Old Volume of Life* (pp. 260–314). Boston: Houghton Mifflin, 1891.

Honda, Maya. *Linguistic Inquiry in the Science Classroom: "It Is Science, but It's Not Like a Science Problem in a Book."* Cambridge: MIT Occasional Papers in Linguistics, no. 6, 1994 (Harvard University dissertation).

Hubbell, Allan Forbes. *The Pronunciation of English in New York City: Consonants and Vowels.* New York: Octagon Books, 1972.

Hughes, Geoffrey. *Swearing: A Social History of Foul Language, Oaths, and Profanity in English.* London: Blackweil, 1991.

Hughes, Robert. *Culture of Complaint: The Fraying of America.* New York: Oxford University Press, 1993.

Hutchison, Earl Ofari. "The Fallacy of Ebonics." *Black Scholar* 27.1 (1997), 36–37.

Hyde, Stuart. *Television and Radio Announcing.* 8th edition. New York: Houghton Mifflin, 1998.

Indian Nations at Risk Task Force. *Indian Nations At Risk: An Educational Strategy for Action. Final Report.* Washington, DC: U.S. Department of Education, 1991. ERIC Document Reproduction Service, No. ED 339587.

James, Henry. *The Question of Our Speech.* Boston: Houghton Mifflin, 1906.

Jay, Timothy. *Cursing in America.* Amsterdam: Benjamins, 1992.

———. *Why We Curse.* Amsterdam: Benjamins, 2000.

Johnson, Burges. "The Everyday Profanity of Our Best People." *Century Magazine* 92 (1916), 311–14.

———. *The Lost Art of Profanity.* Indianapolis: Bobbs-Merrill, 1948.

Johnson, Samuel. *A Dictionary of the English Language.* London: W. Strahan, 1755.

Jones, Gavin. *Strange Talk: The Politics of Dialect in Gilded Age America.* Berkeley: University of California Press, 1999.

Judy, Stephen. *The ABCs of Literacy.* New York: Oxford University Press, 1980.

Kaisse, Ellen M. "The Syntax of Auxiliary Reduction in English." *Language* 59.1 (1983), 93–122.

Kelman, James. *How Late It Was, How Late.* London: Secker and Warburg, 1994.

Kemp, Arnold. 1996. "Triumph of Black English Gives New Cred to Street Talk." *The Observer,* Dec. 22, 1996, 4.

Kennedy, Randall. *Nigger: The Strange Career of a Troublesome Word.* New York: Pantheon Books, 2002.

Key, Mary Ritchie. *Male/Female Language, with Comprehensive Bibliography.* 2nd edition. Lanham, MD: Scarecrow Press, 1996.

King, Robert. "Should English Be the Law?" *Atlantic Monthly,* April 1997, 55–64.

Kirkham, Samuel. *English Grammar in Familiar Essays.* 2nd edition. Harrisburg, PA: John S. Wiestling, 1824.

Kirkpatrick, David D. "A Black Author Hurls *That* Word as a Challenge." *New York Times,* Dec. 1, 2001, A15–16.

Kittredge, George Lyman, and Frank Edgar Farley. *Advanced English Grammar.* Boston: Ginn, 1913.

Koch, Adrienne. *The Philosophy of Thomas Jefferson*. Gloucester, MA: Peter Smith, 1957.

Kohl, Herbert. *Language and Education of the Deaf*. New York: Center for Urban Education, 1966.

Krapp, George Phillip. *The Knowledge of English*. New York: Holt, 1927.

———. *Modern English: Its Growth and Present Use*. New York: Scribner's, 1909.

Labov, William. *Principles of Linguistic Change. Volume 1: Internal Factors*. Oxford: Blackwell, 1994.

———. *Sociolinguistic Patterns*. Philadelphia: University of Pennsylvania Press, 1972.

———. "The Three Dialects of English." In *New Ways of Analyzing Sound Change*, edited by Penelope Eckert (pp. 1–44). New York: Academic Press, 1991.

Lahr, John. "Speaking Across the Divide." *New Yorker*, Jan. 27, 1997, 35–41.

Lakoff, George. "Framing the Dems." *American Prospect* 14.8 (Sept. 1, 2003), 32–35.

Lakoff, Robin T. *The Language War*. Berkeley: University of California Press, 2000.

Lau v. Nichols. 414 U.S. 56 (1974).

Leap, William. "American Indian Languages." In *Language in the USA*, edited by Charles Ferguson and Shirley Brice Heath (pp. 116–144). Cambridge: Cambridge University Press, 1981.

Ledbetter, James. "Making Booker: James Kelman Fucks With Literature." *Village Voice Literary Supplement*, March 7, 1995, 9.

Leland, John, and Nadine Joseph. "Hooked on Ebonics." *Newsweek*, Jan. 13, 1997, 78–79.

Leo, John. 1993. "Stop Murdering the Language!" *U.S. News and World Report*, April 12, 1993, 23.

———. *Two Steps Ahead of the Thought Police*. New York: Simon and Schuster, 1994.

Leonard, Sterling. *Current English Usage*. Chicago: Inland Press, 1932.

———. *The Doctrine of Correctness in English Usage, 1700–1800*. Madison: University of Wisconsin Press, 1929.

Levine, Lawrence. *The Opening of the American Mind*. Boston: Beacon, 1995.

Lightner, Jonathan. "Slang." In *The Cambridge History of the English Language vol. 6, English in North America*, edited by John Algeo (pp. 219–52). Cambridge: Cambridge University Press, 2001.

"Linguistic Confusion." *New York Times*, Dec. 24, 1996, A10.

Lippi-Green, Rosina. *English With an Accent*. London: Routledge, 1998.

Llewellyn, Karl. "Remarks on the Theory of Appellate Decision and the Rules or Canons about how Statutes Are to be Constructed." *Vanderbilt Law Review* (3 *Vand. L. Rev.* 395, 401–6).

Lowth, Robert. *A Short Introduction to English Grammar.* London: A. Millar and R. and J. Dodsley, 1762.

Lutz, William. *Doublespeak.* New York: Harper and Row, 1989.

Macaulay, Thomas Babington. *Selected Writings.* Ed. John Clive and Thomas Pinney. Chicago: University of Chicago Press, 1972.

Macdonald, Dwight. "The String Untuned." *New Yorker*, March 10, 1962. Reprinted in *Dictionaries and* That *Dictionary*, edited by James Sledd and Wilma R. Ebbitt (pp. 166–88). Chicago: Scott, Foresman, 1962.

Malkin, Michelle. "Racial Profiling: A Matter of Survival." *USA Today*, Aug. 17, 2004, 13A.

Marckwardt, Albert. "Language Standards and Attitudes." In *Language and Language Learning*, edited by Albert Marckwardt (pp. 1–22). Champaign, IL: National Council of Teachers of English, 1968.

Marckwardt, Albert, and Fred Walcott. *Facts about Current English Usage.* New York: Appleton Century, 1938.

Marschark, Marc. *Raising and Educating a Deaf Child.* New York: Oxford University Press, 1997.

Marsh, George Perkins. *Lectures on the English Language.* New York: Scribner, 1860.

Martin Luther King, Jr., Elementary School Children et al. v. Ann Arbor School District. 473 F. Supp. 1371 (E. D. Mich. 1979).

Mathews, William. *Words, Their Use and Abuse.* Chicago: Griggs, 1876.

McDavid, Raven I., Jr. "Linguistics, Through the Kitchen Door." In *First Person Singular*, edited by Boyd Davis and Raymond O'Cain (pp. 3–20). Amsterdam: John Benjamins, 1980.

McDavid, Raven I., Jr. (editor) and Betty Gawthrop, C. Michael Lightner, Doris C. Meyers, and Geraldine Russell. *An Examination of the Attitudes of the NCTE Toward Language.* Urbana: National Council of Teachers of English, 1965.

McWhorter, John. *The Word on the Street: Fact and Fable about American English.* New York: Plenum, 1998.

"The Menace of 'Black English.'" *Cleveland Call and Post*, July 28, 1979, 9A.

Mencken, H. L. *The American Language: An Inquiry into the Development of English in the United States.* New York: Knopf, 1937.

Meriam, Lewis. *The Problem of Indian Administration.* Baltimore: John Hopkins Press, 1928.

Merriam-Webster's Collegiate Dictionary. 11th edition. Springfield, MA: Merriam-Webster, 2003.

Merryweather, L. W. "Hell." *American Speech* 6 (1931), 433–35.

Meyer v. Nebraska. 262 U.S. 390, 1923.

Meyer v. Nebraska (Report of the Nebraska Supreme Court). 187 *Northwestern Reporter* 100, 1922.

Michael, Ian. *The Teaching of English: From the Sixteenth Century to 1870.* Cambridge: Cambridge University Press, 1987.

Miller, Geoffrey P. "Pragmatics and the Maxims of Interpretation." *Wisconsin Law Review* 1990, 1179.

"Minstrel of America: Carl Sandburg." *New York Times,* Feb. 13, 1959, 21.

Mitchell, Steve, with art by Sam C. Rawls. *How to Speak Southern.* New York: Bantam, 1976.

Montagu, Ashley. *The Anatomy of Swearing.* New York: Macmillan, 1967.

Moore, Robert L. "We're Cool. Mom and Dad are Swell: Basic Slang and Generational Shifts in Values. *American Speech* 79.1 (2004), 59–86.

Morris, William, and Mary Morris. *Harper Dictionary of Contemporary Usage.* New York: Harper and Row, 1975.

Morrow, Lance. "The Time of Our Lives." *Time,* March 9, 1998, 84–91 (75th anniversary issue).

Morton, Herbert. *The Story of Webster's Third: Phillip Gove's Controversial Dictionary and Its Critics.* Cambridge: Cambridge University Press, 1994.

Mosley, Walter. *Always Outnumbered, Always Outgunned.* New York: W. W. Norton, 1998.

Murray, James A. H., et al. *A New English Dictionary on Historical Principles.* Oxford: Clarendon Press, 1884–1928.

Murray, Lindley. *English Grammar, Adapted to the Different Classes of Learners.* York, 1795.

Murray, Thomas E. "Positive *Anymore* in the Midwest." In *"Heartland": English: Variation and Transition in the American Midwest,* edited by Timothy C. Frazer (pp. 173–86). Tuscaloosa: University of Alabama Press, 1993.

Myers, B. R. "A Reader's Manifesto." *Atlantic Monthly,* July-Aug, 2001, 104–22.

National Council of Teachers of English. Assembly for the Teaching of English Grammar. 2002. "Some Questions and Answers about Grammar." http://www.ncte.org/positions/grammar.shtml.

National Council of Teachers of English. Commission on the English Curriculum. *The English Language Arts.* New York: Appleton Century Croft, 1952.

Nebraska District of Evangelical Lutheran Synod v. McKelvie. 262 U.S. 404, 1923.

Newman, Barry. "Accent." *The American Scholar* 71.2 (2002), 59–69.

Newman, Edwin. *On Language.* New York: Galahad, 1992.

Niedzielski, Nancy, and Dennis Preston. *Folk Linguistics.* Berlin: Mouton de Gruyter, 1999.

Nunberg, Geoffrey. "The Decline of Grammar." *The Atlantic Monthly.* Dec. 1983, 31–46.

———. "Linguistics and the Official Language Movement." *Language* 65.3 (1989), 579–87.

———. "Double Standards." *Natural Language and Linguistic Theory* 14.3 (1997), 667–675.

Nussbaum, Martha. *Cultivating Humanity.* Cambridge: Harvard University Press, 1997.

Ochs, Adolph. "Business Announcement." *New York Times,* August 19, 1896, 4.

Oreskes, Michael. "For GOP Arsenal, 133 Words to Fire." *New York Times,* Sept. 9, 1990, sec. 1, 30.

Orwell, George. *Nineteen Eighty-four.* 1948. New York: Knopf, 1992.

———. "Politics and the English Language." 1946. In *Shooting an Elephant and Other Essays,* by George Orwell (pp. 84–101). London: Secker and Warburg, 1950.

———. "Propaganda and Demotic Speech." 1944. In *George Orwell* (pp. 636–40). London: Secker and Warburg, 1980.

Paletz, David, and William Harris. "Four-Letter Threats to Authority." *Journal of Politics* 37.4 (1975), 955–79.

Park, Stephen. *Class Politics: The Movement for the Students' Right to the Own Language.* Urbana, IL: National Council of Teachers of English, 2000.

Partridge, Eric. *Shakespeare's Bawdy: A Literary and Psychological Essay and a Comprehensive Glossary.* New York: E. P. Dutton, 1948.

Payne, Thomas. Report on the "Linguistic Olympics" [May 16th, 1998]. Posted on the University of Oregon website (http://darkwing.uoregon.edu/~tpayne/lingolym/LOreport.htm).

Peale, Norman Vincent. Sermon on the Increase of Profanity. *New York Times,* Nov. 9, 1942, 18.

Pearl, Daniel. "Hush Mah Mouth! Some in South Try To Lose the Drawl—'Accent Reduction' Becomes a Big Bidness in Atlanta." *Wall Street Journal,* Dec. 13, 1991, A1.

Peña, Fernando de la. *Democracy or Babel?* Washington, DC: US English, 1991.

Penelope, Julia. "'Users and Abusers': On the Death of English." In *The English Language Today*, edited by Sidney Greenbaum (pp. 80–91). Oxford: Pergamon, 1985.

Perlstein, Linda. "Grammar Glitch Pushes PSAT to Rethink, Rescore." *Washington Post*, May 14, 2003, A1.

Perry, Ruth. "A Short History of the Term *Politically Correct*." In *Beyond PC: Toward a Politics of Understanding*, edited by Patricia Aufderheide (pp. 71–79). St. Paul: Graywolf, 1992.

Pickering, John. "An Essay on the Present State of the English Language in the United States." 1816. Excerpted in *The Ordeal of American English*, edited by C. Merton Babcock (pp. 28–30). Boston: Houghton Mifflin, 1961.

"The Politics of Political Correctness." *Partisan Review* 60.4 (1993) (special issue).

Pooley, Robert. *Teaching English Usage*. New York: Appleton-Century-Crofts, 1946.

Postal, Paul. "Policing the Content of Linguistic Examples." *Language* 79.1 (2003), 182–88.

Preston, Dennis. "A Language Attitude Approach to the Perception of Regional Variety." In *Handbook of Perceptual Dialectology*, edited by Dennis Preston (pp. 359–73). Amsterdam: Benjamins, 1999.

Priestly, Joseph. *Rudiments of English Grammar*. London: Griffiths, 1761. Reprinted, Menston: Yorks, 1969.

"Protecting English from Assault on the Job." *New York Times*, Feb. 4, 2001, BU 14.

R. A. V. v. City of St. Paul, 505 U.S. 377 (1992).

Rachels, James. *The Elements of Moral Philosophy*. New York: Oxford University Press, 1986.

Raspberry, William. "To Throw in a Lot of 'Bes' or Not? A Conversation on Ebonics." *Washington Post*, Dec. 26, 1996, A27.

Ravitch, Diane. *The Language Police: How Pressure Groups Restrict What Students Learn*. New York: Alfred A. Knopf, 2003.

Read, Allen Walker. "An Obscenity Symbol." *American Speech* 9.4 (1934), 264–78.

"The Return of the Storm Troopers." *Wall Street Journal*, April 10, 1991, A22.

"The Reviews Are In." *Time*, March 9, 1998, 193 (75th anniversary issue).

Reyhner, John. "Policies toward American Indian Languages: A Historical Sketch." In *Language Loyalties: A Source Book on the Official English Controversy*, edited by James Crawford (pp. 41–47). Chicago: University of Chicago Press, 1992.

Rickford, John Russell, and Angela E. Rickford. "Dialect Readers Revisited." *Linguistics and Education* 7.2 (1995), 107–28.

Rickford, John Russell, and Russell John Rickford. *Spoken Soul*. New York: John Wiley, 2000.

Roberts, Edwin. "Dialects Stunt People's Growth and Development." *Detroit News*, July 29, 1979, 19–A.

Roberts, Paul Craig. "U.S.S. Cole Torpedoed by Political Correctness." *Capitalism Magazine* [online magazine], Oct. 28, 2000. (www.capmag.com/article.asp?ID=731).

Robinson, Joshua. "Physics: More English, Less Chinese." *Johns Hopkins Newsletter*, February 20, 2004. (Archived at http://www.jhunewsletter.com).

Robinson Paul, "Lost Causes." *New Republic*, Jan. 26, 1980, 25–27.

Rodgers, Jack. "The Foreign Language Issue in Nebraska." *Nebraska History* 39.1 (1958), 1–22.

Rodriguez, Richard. "Bilingualism Con: Outdated and Unrealistic." *New York Times*, Nov. 10, 1985, sec. 12, 83.

———. *The Hunger of Memory*. Boston: David R. Godine, 1981.

Roosevelt, Theodore. "Children of the Crucible." 1917. Speech excerpted in *Language Loyalties: A Source Book on the Official English Controversy*, edited by James Crawford (pp. 84–85). Chicago: University of Chicago Press, 1992.

Rosenthal, Jack. "So Here's What's Happening to Language." *New York Times*, Nov. 14, 2001, K38.

Rowan, Carl. "'Black English' Isn't Foreign." *Philadelphia Bulletin*, July 11, 1979, A15.

———. "Black Students Don't Need an Alibi." *Kansas City Star*, Aug. 5, 1979, 2J.

———. "'Ebonics' a False Promise of Self-esteem." *Chicago Sun-Times*, Dec. 25, 1996, 31.

Royko, Mike. "Pithy Questions the Presidential Debate Panel Won't Ask." *Chicago Tribune*, Oct. 11, 1992.

Rubin, Donald L. "Nonlanguage Factors Affecting Undergraduates' Judgments of Non-Native English Speaking Teaching Assistants," *Research in Higher Education* 33 (1992), 511–31.

Rutenberg, Jim. "Hurt by Cable, Networks Spout Expletives." *New York Times*, Sept. 2, 2001, sec. 1, 19.

Sackheim, Maxwell. *My First Sixty Years in Advertising*. Englewood Cliffs, NJ: Prentice Hall, 1970.

Safire, William. *On Language*. New York: Avon Books, 1981.

Satel, Sally. *P. C., M. D.: How Political Correctness Is Corrupting Medicine*. New York: Basic Books, 2001.

Saunders, Debra J. "Oakland's Ebonics Farce." *San Francisco Chronicle*, Dec. 24, 1996, A15.

Schmid, Carol. *The Politics of Language.* New York: Oxford University Press, 2001.

Schwartz, Marilyn. *Guidelines for Bias-Free Writing.* Bloomington: Indiana University Press, 1995.

Schwesinger, Gladys. "Slang as an Indication of Character." *Journal of Applied Psychology* 10 (1926), 245–63.

Scovel, Thomas. "The Younger the Better Myth and Bilingual Education" In *Language Ideologies: Critical Perspectives on the Official English Movement,* vol. 1, edited by Roseann Dueñas González, with Ildikó Melis (pp. 114–136). Urbana, IL: National Council of Teachers of English and Mahwah, NJ: Lawrence Erlbaum Associates, 2001.

Siegel, Muffy E. A. "*Like*: The Discourse Particle and Semantics." *Journal of Semantics* 19.1 (2002), 35–71.

Senate Special Subcommittee on Indian Education. *Indian Education: A National Tragedy—A National Challenge.* Washington, DC: US Government Printing Office, 1969.

"Sensitivity Fascism." *National Review,* April 27, 1992, 19.

Shanker, Albert. "Where We Stand: Ebonics." *New York Times,* Jan. 5, 1997, E7 [advertisement].

Shaw, James. "Ebonics: If we Can't Teach 'em, Join 'em?" *The Sun* [Baltimore], Jan. 5, 1997, 1F.

Sheils, Merrill. "Why Johnny Can't Write." *Newsweek,* Dec. 8, 1975, 58–65.

Sheridan, Thomas. *General Dictionary of the English Language.* London: printed for J. Dodsley, C. Dilly and J. Wilkie, 1780.

Sherwood, John. "Dr. Kinsey and Professor Fries." *College English* 23 (1962), 275–80.

Shipp, Bill. "If Black English Is a Distinct Language, Then What about Cracker Talk?" *Atlanta Constitution,* July 14, 1979, 2B.

"Shriners Hospitals Change Name: Seventy-four-year-old Hospital System Eliminates Word 'Crippled'." 1996. www.shrinershq.org/Whats NewArch/Archives96/namechange7–96.html. (Last modified March 28, 2003.)

Simon, John. *Paradigms Lost: Reflections on Literacy and Its Decline.* New York: Clarkson N. Potter, 1980.

Simon, Richard Keller. *Trash Culture: Popular Culture and the Great Tradition.* Berkeley: University of California Press, 1999.

Simpkins, Gary A., Grace Holt, and Charlesetta Simpkins. *Bridge: A Cross-Cultural Reading Program.* Boston: Houghton-Mifflin, 1977.

Simpkins, Gary, and Charlesetta Simpkins. "Cross Cultural Approach to

Curriculum Development." In *Black English and the Education of Black Children and Youth*, edited by Geneva Smitherman (pp. 221–40). Detroit: Wayne State University Center for Black Studies, 1981.

Simpson, David. *The Politics of American English, 1776–1850*. New York: Oxford University Press, 1988.

Sinclair, John. "Linguistics and the Teaching of English." In *Language and Language Learning*, edited by Albert Marckwardt (pp. 31–41). Champaign, IL: National Council of Teachers of English, 1966.

Sledd, James. *Eloquent Dissent*. Portsmouth, NH: Boynton/Cook, 1996.

———. "Grammar for Social Awareness in Time of Class Warfare." *English Journal* 85.7 (Nov. 1996), 59–63.

Sledd, James, and Wilma Ebbitt. *Dictionaries and That Dictionary*. Chicago: Scott, Foresman, 1962.

Smith, Erin A. *Hard-Boiled: Working-Class Readers and Pulp Magazines*. Philadelphia: Temple University Press, 2000.

Smitherman, Geneva (editor). *Black English and the Education of Black Children and Youth*. Detroit: Wayne State University Center for Black Studies, 1981.

———. *Talkin That Talk: Language Culture and Education in African America*. London: Routledge, 2000.

Snow, C. P. *The Two Cultures and the Scientific Revolution*. Cambridge: Cambridge University Press, 1959.

Sokal, Alan. "Revelation: A Physicist Experiments with Cultural Studies." *Lingua Franca*, May–June 1996 (reprinted in *The Sokal Hoax*, (pp. 49–53). Lincoln: University of Nebraska Press, 2000).

Solomon, Chris. "Speech Classes Place the Accent on Understanding." *The Record* [Bergen County, NJ]. Dec. 12, 2000, A32.

Southeastern Promotions, Ltd. v. Conrad et al. 420 U.S. 546 (1975).

Spaid, Elizabeth Levit. "Losing That Dixie Drawl." *Christian Science Monitor*, Dec. 9, 1998, 1.

Spellmeyer, Kurt. *Common Ground: Dialogue, Understanding, and the Teaching of Composition*. Englewood Cliffs, NJ: Prentice Hall, 1993.

Stavans, Ilan. *Spanglish: The Making of a New American Language*. New York: Harper Collins, 2003.

Strunk, William, Jr., and E. B. White. *The Elements of Style*. 3rd edition. New York: Macmillan, 1979.

"Students' Right to Their Own Language." *College Composition and Communication* 25.3 (1974), 1–32.

Swift, Jonathan. *A Proposal For Correcting, Improving And Ascertaining The English Tongue*. 1712. Reprinted, London: Scolar Press, 1969.

Taylor, John. "Are You Politically Correct?" *New York Magazine*, Jan. 21, 1991, 32–40.

"Teaching Down to Our Children." *St. Petersburg Times*, Dec. 26, 1996, 18A.

Terzian Philip. "Hooking Them on Ebonics." *Tampa Tribune*, Jan. 3, 1997, 9.

Tibbetts, Arn, and Charlene Tibbetts. *What's Happening to American English?* New York: Charles Scribner's Sons, 1978.

Tiersma, Peter. *Legal Language.* Chicago: University of Chicago Press, 1999.

Turner, Lorenzo Dow. *Africanisms in the Gullah Dialect.* Chicago: University of Chicago Press, 1949.

Turner, Mark. *Cognitive Dimensions of Social Science.* New York: Oxford University Press, 2001.

———. *The Literary Mind: The Origins of Thought and Language.* New York: Oxford University Press, 1996.

United Press International. *The UPI Stylebook.* Lincolnwood, IL: National Textbook Co., 1992.

University of Chicago Press. *The Chicago Manual of Style.* Chicago: University of Chicago Press, 1982.

Updike, John. "Fine Points." *New Yorker*, Dec. 23/Dec. 30, 1996, 142–49.

U.S. Census Bureau. *The Foreign-Born Population in the United States March 2002.* http://www.census.gov/prod/2003pubs/p20–539.pdf.

U.S. English. Fundraising brochure text, 1984, reprinted as "In Defense of Our Common Language . . . " In *Language Loyalties: A Source Book on the Official English Controversy*, edited by James Crawford (pp. 143–148). Chicago: University of Chicago Press, 1992.

Veltman, Calvin. *The Future of the Spanish Language in the United States.* Washington, DC: Spanish Policy Development Project, 1988.

Wachal, Robert S. "Taboo or Not Taboo: That is the Question." *American Speech* 77.2 (2002), 195–206.

Wallace, David Foster. "Tense Present." *Harper's*, April 2001, 39–58.

Warfel, Harry. *Who Killed Grammar?* Gainesville: University of Florida Press, 1952.

Watt, William. *An American Rhetoric.* New York: Holt, 1957.

Webster, Noah. *A Grammatical Institute of the English Language.* Hartford, CT: Hudson and Goodwin, 1783–85.

Wentworth. Harold. *American Dialect Dictionary.* New York: Thomas Y. Crowell, 1944.

Wentworth, Harold, and Stuart Berg Flexner. *Dictionary of American Slang.* New York: Thomas Y. Crowell, 1960.

"What We Think: Black English Must Go." *Michigan Chronicle*, July 14, 1979, 8–A.

Wheeler, Rebecca (editor). *Language Alive in the Classroom*. Westport, CT: Praeger, 1999.

Whipple, Edwin. "The Swearing Habit." *North American Review* 140 (1885), 536–50.

Whitman, Walt. "Slang in America." *North American Review*, 141.348 (November 1885), 431–435.

"Will Appeals to Fund 'Hillbillyonics' be Next?" *Columbus Dispatch*, Dec. 31, 1996, 6A.

Williams, Joseph. "Linguistic Responsibility." *College English* 39.1 (1977), 8–17.

Williamson, Jerry Wayne. *Hillbillyland: What the Movies Did to the Mountains and What the Mountains Did to the Movies.* Chapel Hill: University of North Carolina Press, 1995.

Wills, Garry. "Black English Is Merely a Form of Bad English." *Chicago Sun-Times*, Dec. 30, 1996, 22.

Wilson, John K. *The Myth of Political Correctness.* Durham: Duke University Press, 1996.

Winchester, Simon. "Word Imperfect." *The Atlantic Monthly*, May 2001, 54–86.

Witherspoon, John. "The Druid: Number 5." 1802. Excerpted in *The Ordeal of American English*, edited by C. Merton Babcock (pp. 70–74). Boston: Houghton Mifflin, 1961.

Wolfram, Walt. "Dialect Awareness Programs in the School and Community." In *Language Alive in the Classroom*, edited by Rebecca Wheeler (pp. 47–66). Westport, CT: Praeger, 1999.

———. *A Sociolinguistic Description of Detroit Negro Speech.* Washington, DC: Center for Applied Linguistics, 1969.

Wolfram, Walt, and Natalie Schilling-Estes. *American English: Dialects and Variation.* Malden, MA: Blackwell, 1998.

Yarborough, Ralph. Speech Introducing the Bilingual Education Act.1967. Excerpted in *Language Loyalties: A Source Book on the Official English Controversy*, edited by James Crawford (pp. 322–24). Chicago: University of Chicago Press, 1992.

Yniguez v. Mofford, 730 F. Supp. 309 (D. Ariz. 1990).

Zinsser, William. *On Writing Well.* 5th edition. New York: Harper, 1994.

Index